D1859726

BENGAL DISTRICT GAZETTEERS.

MURSHIDABAD.

BENGAL DISTRICT GAZETTEERS.

MURSHIDABAD.

BY

L. S. S. O'MALLEY,
INDIAN CIVIL SERVICE.

©Reserved

All rights reserved. No part of this work may be reproduced, stored, adapted, or transmitted in any form or by any means, electronic, mechanical, photocopying, micro-filming recording or otherwise, or translated in any language, without the prior written permission of the copyright owner and the publisher. The book is sold subject to the condition that it shall not, by way of trade or otherwise, be lent, resold, hired out, or otherwise circulated without the prior publisher's written consent in any form of binding or cover other than that in which it is published.

The views and opinions expressed in this book are author(s) own and the facts reported by them have been verified to the extent possible, and the publishers are not in any way liable for the same.

ISBN: 978-93-5128-885-5(HB)

First Published in 1914
Indian Reprint in 2017

Published by

Kalpaz Publications
C-30, Satyawati Nagar,
Delhi – 110052
E-mail: kalpaz@hotmail.com
Website: kalpazpublications.com
Ph.: +91-9212142040

Cataloging in Publication Data—DK
Courtesy: D.K. Agencies (P) Ltd. <docinfo@dkagencies.com>

O'Malley, L. S. S. (Lewis Sydney Steward), 1874-1941,
author.
Murshidabad / by L.S.S. O'Malley.
pages cm. — (Bengal district gazetteers)
Reprint. Originally published: Calcutta : The Bengal Secretariat Book Depot, 1914.
Includes index.
ISBN 9789351288855

1. Murshida˜ba˜d (India : District)—Gazetteers. 2. Murshida˜ba˜d (India : District)—Economic conditions. 3. Murshida˜ba˜d (India : District)—History. I. Title. II. Series: Bengal district gazetteers.

DS485.M87O43 2017 DDC 954.14003 23

PREFACE.

I DESIRE to acknowledge, with gratitude, the assistance rendered by Babu Harendra Krishna Mitra, Head Clerk of the Bengal Census office, in reading and checking the proofs. The District Magistrate of Murshidabad has also been so kind as to have each chapter examined in his office.

L. S. S. O'M.

PLAN OF CONTENTS.

TABLE OF CONTENTS.

CHAPTER I.

PHYSICAL ASPECTS.

PAGE

CHAPTER II.

HISTORY.

CHAPTER III.

THE PEOPLE.

CHAPTER IV.

PUBLIC HEALTH.

CHAPTER V.

AGRICULTURE.

CHAPTER VI.

NATURAL CALAMITIES.

CHAPTER VII.

RENTS, WAGES AND PRICES.

CHAPTER VIII.

INDUSTRIES, MANUFACTURES AND TRADE.

CHAPTER IX.

MEANS OF COMMUNICATION.

CHAPTER X.

LAND REVENUE ADMINISTRATION.

CHAPTER XI.

GENERAL ADMINISTRATION.

CHAPTER XII.

LOCAL SELF-GOVERNMENT.

CHAPTER XIII.

EDUCATION.

CHAPTER XIV.

GAZETTEER.

GAZETTEER

OF THE

MURSHIDABAD DISTRICT.

CHAPTER I.

PHYSICAL ASPECTS.

MURSHIDABAD is the north-western district of the Presidency Division or Commissionership, and lies between 23° 43′ and 24° 52′ north latitude and 87° 49′ and 88° 44′ east longitude. It has an area of 2,143 square miles and contains, according to the census of 1911, a population of 1,372,274 persons. It is so called after Murshidābād, a town on the left bank of the Bhāgīrathi, which was the last of the Muhammadan capitals of Bengal. The headquarters, however, are not at Murshidābād, but at Berhampore, six miles further down the river. GENERAL DESCRIPTION.

In shape the district resembles an isosceles triangle with its apex pointing to the north-west. It is bounded along its whole eastern frontier, from the extreme north to the south-eastern extremity, by the Padma or main channel of the Ganges, which separates it from the districts of Mālda and Rājshāhi. On the south it is bounded by the districts of Burdwān and Nadia, the river Jalangi on the south-east forming the boundary between it and Nadia for a considerable distance. To the west lie the districts of Bīrbhūm and the Sonthal Parganas. Boundaries.

The river Bhāgīrathi, flowing from north to south through the district, divides it into two almost equal portions, which, in their geology, their physical characteristics, their agriculture, and even the religion of their inhabitants, form a striking contrast to each other. The tract to the west of the river is locally known as Rārh, and the tract to the east as Bāgri—names which recall the traditional division of Bengal by king Ballāl Sen into four tracts, viz., Rārh to the south of the Ganges and west of the Bhāgīrathi, Bārendra lying, north of the Ganges, between the Mahānanda and Karatoya rivers, Bāgri or South Natural divisions.

Bengal and Banga or Eastern Bengal. East of the Bhāgīrathi the country is low-lying and alluvial, with a humid climate and a fertile soil, which is liable to be flooded by the spill of the Bhāgīrathi and other rivers. On the western side the surface is high and undulating; the soil is a hard clay, on which winter rice alone grows well, and the climate is drier than in the eastern tract. The Bhāgīrathi is more than a mere physical boundary, for west of it Hindus predominate, while on the east Musalmāns are more numerous.

Rārh. The western tract, or Rārh, is substantially a continuation of the sub-Vindhyan region of laterite clay and nodular limestone. The land is, as already stated, high and slightly undulating, but is interspersed with numerous swamps and beds of old rivers. It has the greatest elevation along the western boundary of the district towards Bīrbhūm, but there are places where the eastern limits of this clayey tract are marked by banks or bluffs, fifteen and twenty feet high. The cliff at Rāngāmāti on the Bhāgīrathi, six miles south of Berhampore, is forty or fifty feet above the ordinary level of the river. The soil is greyish or reddish, mixed with lime and oxide of iron; and beds of nodular limestone (*kankar*) are scattered here and there. The rivers in this part, having their sources in hill torrents, are liable to sudden freshets, but they never lay the country under water for any long space of time. The fields, therefore, do not possess the extraordinary fertility of a deltaic country. The chief crop in the central and more elevated portions of the Rārh is the winter rice, which is not dependent upon early rain for a successful harvest, but requires a steady downfall between July and October.

In the Suti and Shamsherganj thanas on the north, however, and in the tract known as the Hijāl to the south, the nature and aspect of the country are entirely different. In the former two thanas, a strip of low-lying country, having an area of about 150 square miles, extends northwards from Mirzāpur until it blends with the basin of the Bānsloi river and other hill streams, which debouch from the western high lands and during the rains form a vast lake, in which the villages appear as islands, the whole of the arable land being submerged. This part of the district is second to none in fertility. The land forming the fringe of the flooded area, where the inundation is shallower, bears two crops, viz., early rice and cold weather crops of wheat and gram with a minor cultivation of oil-seeds, peas, etc. The village sites are well wooded, and in the rains the scenery is highly picturesque. With the Rājmahāl Hills closing in the horizon on the west, it presents a combination of hill, wood and water rarely met with in the plains of Bengal.

The tract called the Hijāl, situated in the south-west of the district near the confluence of the Mor and the Dwārka, and about 50 square miles in area, offers a very different aspect. The country becomes more open, and, in place of rice fields, large stretches of thatching grass cover an almost treeless plain. Village sites are few, and there is a marked absence of forest growth, but round its edges copses of *babul* abound and occasional *pipal* or banyan trees are seen; fruit trees and bamboos are, however, almost entirely absent. On the west the land slopes somewhat abruptly upwards, marking the boundary of the true Rārh, while to the east a narrow line of high country forms the western bank of the Bhāgīrathi and culminates in the cliff of Rāngāmāti. During the rains the Hijāl is widely inundated with water, which varies very much in depth, being in places more than twenty feet, while elsewhere a boat drawing three feet is stranded. The whole of this tract becomes perfectly dry in the cold weather, and a large portion of it, which is yearly increasing in extent, is cultivated with cold weather crops, such as wheat, gram, mustard and linseed. It also affords a considerable area of pasturage, and the thatching grass, which it produces in great quantities, is celebrated for its toughness and durability. Hijāl.

The Bāgri, or eastern tract, differs in no material respects from the ordinary alluvial plains of Bengal. It lies almost entirely between the Ganges, Bhāgīrathi and Jalangi rivers, and is permeated by several other offshoots of the great river. The whole area lies low, and is exposed to annual inundations, which occasionally cause widespread suffering, but usually do no more than deposit over the land a top dressing of almost inexhaustible fertility. In variety of crops, this portion of the district is not surpassed by any part of Bengal. The *aus* or early rice crop is very largely cultivated and forms the bulk of the food supply of the inhabitants; and this harvest is supplemented by the *chaitāli*, a name given to the whole series of cold weather crops from the fact of their being harvested in *Chaitra*, or March. They are cultivated after the *aus* is cut and on the same fields, as well as on the higher lands where rice will not grow. For these two harvests early rains are wanted in April and May, and a few showers in the cold weather. Bāgri.

The twofold division of Murshidābād described above is peculiarly interesting as furnishing a clue to the early formation and development of the western portion of the Gangetic delta. There is no doubt that the present Bhāgīrathi represents the old channel of the Ganges, by which the greater part of the waters of the sacred river were formerly brought down to the sea. The most ancient traditions, the traces of ruined cities, and the indelible record of names, all lead to this conclusion. The geological evidence proves to demonstration that the hard laterite soil formed an insuperable obstacle to the Ganges flowing further to the west than the present course of the Bhāgīrathi, which is thus fixed as the limit of the Bengal alluvium and the ancient means of communication between the Bay of Bengal and the interior.

HILLS. There are no hill ranges in the district. The whole of the portion to the west of the Bhāgīrathi lies at an appreciable elevation, and the land in the extreme west slopes gently upwards towards Bīrbhūm and the Rājmahāl Hills, which rise a few miles beyond the north-western boundary. Here there are some hillocks, of which the best known is called Dhuli Pahāri, covered with small *sāl* and *mahua* trees and surrounded at the base by stony jungle land.

LINES OF DRAINAGE. The general inclination of the district is from north-west to south-east; but, as the channels of the main rivers do not uniformly take this direction, the lines of drainage are somewhat irregular and perplexing.

The western half of the district slopes eastwards toward the Bhāgīrathi; but the greater number of the hill streams do not find their way directly into that river, but are intercepted by *bils* or marshes and for the most part carried off to the south by the Dwārka river. The two chief drainage basins (if such they can be called) in this part of the district are that of the Bānsloi in the north, and that of the Dwārka with its confluents in the south. The large *bils* act as reservoirs to break the violence of the floods of these hill streams, and also serve to drain the surrounding country, discharging their surplus water through the streams which issue out of them.

The eastern half of the district may be described as an isosceles triangle, whose equal sides are formed by the Ganges and the Bhāgīrathi, and whose base is almost closed by the Jalangi. The line of drainage is not along any of these rivers, but may be represented by a line intersecting the base at right angles. The local rainfall in this part of the district does not run off either into the Ganges or the Bhāgīrathi. In the same way the floods of these two great rivers converge towards each other, and ultimately make their way across the country in a south-easterly direction. It may roughly be stated that the greater part of the surplus water ultimately falls into the Jalangi by means of the Gobra Nullah, the Bhairab, and the Siālmāri. These channels are during the rains connected with the different *bils* and creeks (*khāls*), forming a network of water communication. In the hot weather a number of springs may be observed along their banks, caused apparently by the drainage waters percolating through the under-strata of sand and sandy soil.

The river system is composed of the Ganges and its distributaries, of which the most important are the Bhāgīrathi, Jalangi and Bhairab. Formerly large rivers with an active current, they are now merely spill channels of the great river, which during the rains carry off a portion of its flood water, but for the remainder of the year have a very sluggish current. The stream is insufficient to carry off the large quantity of silt they receive, so that shoals form and impede navigation. The rivers in the east of the district are fed to a certain extent during the dry season by infiltration from the Ganges. Where that river is broad, and large islands or *chars* are thrown up, the volume of its discharge is sensibly affected by the portion of the stream which thus passes away through the sand. RIVER SYSTEM.

The Ganges, or Padma, as it is called in this part of its course, first touches Murshidābād at its extreme northern point, and then flows almost due south-east, forming the eastern boundary of the district, and dividing it from Mālda and Rājshāhi. The only tributary of any importance which it receives from the west is the Singa, which effects a junction with it about ten miles from the spot where it first touches the district. The Singa enters the district from the Sonthal Parganas at Adwaitapur, and just below Ankura divides into two branches; one falls into the Ganges near Nayān Sukh, and the other at Dhuliān. The offshoots of the Ganges on its western or right bank comprise the Bhāgīrathi, the Bhairab, the Siālmāri, and the Jalangi. Ganges or Padma.

The fall of the Ganges is about nine inches per mile, but the windings of the river are so great as to reduce this estimate by about one-half. The current varies from about three miles an hour in the cold weather to at least double that rate during the rains. In particular spots, as, for instance, where the stream rushes round some projecting point, this rate of motion is exceeded, and boats and steamers find great difficulty in making their way against the current. The rise of water in the main channel between the middle of May and the middle of August is as much as thirty-two feet.

Every year the Ganges is forming and cutting away land along its course by a constant alternation of alluvion and diluvion. During the rainy season, the current impinges with immense weight upon banks composed of loose soil, which are rapidly undermined. An acre of ground has been known to have been swept away in half an hour. Large islands are continually rising in the channel, some of them many miles in length. In the next year, perhaps, they become covered with grass and tamarisk jungle higher than an elephant. Captain Sherwill states that he has seen such islands "become inhabited, cleared, and cultivated; the population increases, large villages start up; the land revenue is collected for ten or twelve years; and then the whole fabric will disappear within one rainy season."

Owing to their liability to inundation, the people living along its bank are content with temporary structures for their houses. "In the low lands near the Ganges," wrote Colonel Gastrell,* "a light thatch and lighter walls suffice for the wants of the inhabitants, who remove their property, house and all, as soon as the river waters rise high enough to top their *chārpāis* (bedsteads). During an inundation they may often be seen lying on their *chārpāis* with the water well up the legs, either too lazy to move, or trusting to the chance that the water may rise no higher, and save them the trouble of moving at all."

Bhāgīrathi. The Bhāgirathi at present (1913) branches off from the Ganges at Nurpur about 25 miles below Farakka and runs almost parallel to it for about two miles as far as Biswanāthpur (near Suti) with a long narrow strip of *char* land between the two rivers. After leaving Biswanāthpur, its course, which is very winding, is almost due south; and it finally leaves the district below the village of Bidhupāra, just north of the celebrated battle-field of Plassey, part of which it has swept away. As has been already said, it divides the district into two almost equal portions, and on its banks, chiefly on the eastern or left bank, are situated all the historical and wealthy towns of the district. A little above Jangipur it receives from the west the united waters of the Bānsloi and Pāgla rivers; and near Saktipur, the Chora Dekra, a considerable branch of the Dwārka river, flows into it, also from the west.

The banks of the Bhāgīrathi are usually gently sloping on the one side, and abruptly shelving on the other. These changes of slope are due to the varying set of the current, and occur on the same bank by regular alterations from reach to reach. The stream shifts from side to side, sandbanks and other obstructions

* Statistical and Geographical Report of Murshidābād District (1860).

are constantly formed, and the bed has largely silted up. It is a fine river for about four months of the year, when it is full, but for the remaining eight, it has an attenuated stream wandering through a wide expanse of sand. During the rainy season, freshets from the Ganges still come down the Bhāgīrathi; but their permanent influence is obliterated by the large deposit of silt which they bring with them. In addition to this, it is important to recollect that the general line of drainage is not from north to south along the channel of the Bhāgīrathi, but from north-west to south-east. The result is that the main waters of the Ganges display a greater inclination to proceed in their present channel than to turn into the Bhāgīrathi; and that the floods of the Bhāgīrathi have always a tendency to overflow its left or eastern bank, and wander over the country in the old river beds towards the Jalangi river.

The Bhairab is an offshoot of the Ganges, from which it branches off to the south nearly opposite to Rāmpur-Boalia. It empties itself, after a very circuitous course, into the Jalangi at Madhupur. Bhairab.

The name Bhairab means 'the Terrible' and bears witness to the estimation in which this river was once held. It is noticeable that it takes off from the Ganges close to the point where the Mahānanda flows into it, and it has been suggested that it originally formed a continuation of the Mahānanda, which was cut in half by the Ganges as it worked its way eastwards, while lower down it was intersected by the Jalangi. In 1874 its upper channel, which had silted up, was forced open by floods at its intake from the Ganges, and it expanded into an important distributary which poured its waters into the Jalangi 40 miles further south. The result was that the channel of the Jalangi began to close up above the point of junction, and the Bhairab is now the main channel by which the Jalangi obtains its supply from the Ganges. The two are hence commonly treated as a united stream called the Bhairab-Jalangi. The Bhairab bifurcates a little to the north-east of Daulatbazar and joins the Gobra Nullah at Trimohini.

The Jalangi is another important branch of the Ganges, which nowhere intersects the district. It leaves the parent stream a short distance above the village of Jalangi, and flows in a south-westerly direction, with many windings, until it finally leaves the district with an abrupt turn near the village of Bāli. During this part of its course it forms the boundary between Murshidābād and Nadia for about 50 miles. The upper part of its course has silted up for some 36 miles, and it obtains its Jalangi.

supply of water mainly from the Bhairab and the Siālmāri. This river is also known locally as the Kharia.

Siālmāri. The Siālmāri is also an offshoot of the Ganges, which, like the Bhairab, it leaves opposite Rāmpur-Boalia. After a meandering course it empties itself into the Jalangi below Kapila.

Gobra Nullah. The Gobra Nullah is a channel running from the Bhāgīrathi to the Jalangi at Bāli, a distance of about 50 miles. It was probably originally an effluent of the Bhāgīrathi, and it is, in fact, the natural drainage channel for the country east of that river. The action of nature, however, has been interfered with by the construction of a marginal embankment along the left bank of the Bhāgīrathi, called the Lalitākuri or Naltākuri embankment, which extends from Jaiganj to Bhagwāngola *viâ* Kalukhāli and has cut off its connection with that river. Its offtake being closed, it receives only local drainage water south of the embankment. It has silted up in its lower reaches, but still has a good deal of water in the portion lying to the east of the Sadar subdivision; further north, in the Lālbāgh subdivision, it is much narrower and in many places is merely a marshy depression.

Bānsloi. The Bānsloi is the most considerable tributary of the Bhāgīrathi. It enters the district from Bīrbhūm near the village of Husainpur and pursues on the whole an easterly course, until it falls into the Bhāgīrathi a little to the north of the town of Jangipur.

Dwārka or Bābla. The Dwārka or Bābla is a moderate-sized stream, which wanders, under several names and with many tributaries and effluents, throughout the south-western corner of Murshidābād. The channel which is considered the main stream, and which bears the name of Dwārka, enters the district from Bīrbhūm not far from Margrām. At first it flows in an easterly direction, until its waters are augmented by those of the Brāhmini at Rāmchandrapur. It then turns towards the south-east and is joined on its right bank by the Mor and the Kuiya, two rivers which also flow down from Bīrbhūm. Here commence the numerous backwaters and side channels which connect it with the Bhāgīrathi, and cause great confusion by the changes of name which they occasion: the Banka and the Chora Dekra are the two most important of these lines of junction. The main stream forms the eastern boundary of the Kāndi subdivision and quits the district at Raghupur. Like all hill streams it has a rapid current and is liable to sudden floods.

Other rivers. Among minor rivers may be mentioned the Brāhmini, the Mor (or Maurākhi or Kāna) and the Kuiya, which all flow from the west into the Dwārka, and are partially navigable during the rainy season. The beds of all these hill streams are of a yellow clay and pebbly.

Murshidābād, a district standing at the head of the Gangetic delta, affords a striking example of the grand operations of nature produced by fluvial action. There can, as already pointed out, be no doubt that the present channel of the Bhāgīrathi, with its sacred traditions and early settlements, marks the ancient course of the Ganges, while that portion of the district which lies between the Bhāgīrathi and the present channel of the Ganges has been the scene of important river changes both before the dawn of history and within historical times. The whole of this area is scored with the tracks of old river beds, which represent the various channels scooped out by the waters of the great river while they were being gradually diverted to their present course. The whole process and the effect it has had in the formation of the land surface are well described by Dr. Thomas Oldham in an article published in the *Proceedings of the Asiatic Society of Bengal* for 1870:— **CHANGES IN RIVER COURSES.**

"I suppose no one will hesitate to acknowledge that the whole of the country lying between the Hooghly on the west and the Meghna on the east is only the delta caused by the deposition of the debris carried down by the rivers Ganges and Brahmaputra and their tributaries. It is also equally well known that in such flats the streams are constantly altering their courses, eating away on one bank and depositing on the other, until the channel in which they formerly flowed becomes choked up, and the water is compelled to seek another course. It is also certain that, in this peculiar delta, the general course of the main waters of the Ganges has gradually tracked from the west towards the east, until, of late years, the larger body of the waters of the Ganges have united with those of the Brahmaputra, and have together proceeded to the sea as the Meghna. Every stream, whether large or small, flowing through such a flat, tends to raise its own bed or channel by the deposition of the silt and sand it holds suspended in its waters, and by this gradual deposition the channel bed of the stream is raised above the actual level of the adjoining flats. It is impossible to suppose a river continuing to flow along the top of a raised bank, if not compelled to do so by artificial means, and the consequence of this filling in and raising of its bed is that, at the first opportunity, the stream necessarily abandons its original course, and seeks a new channel in the lower ground adjoining, until, after successive changes, it has gradually wandered over the whole flat and raised the entire surface to the same general level. The same process is then repeated, new channels are cut out, and new deposits formed.

"Bearing these admitted principles in mind, look to the delta of the Ganges and Brahmaputra. The Ganges river, emerging from its upper levels round the Rājmahāl Hills, and prevented by their solid rocky barrier from cutting further to the west, sought its channel in the lower ground adjoining, and originally the main body of its waters flowed along the general course now indicated by the Bhāgīrathi and Hooghly. But, gradually filling up this channel, it was again compelled to seek a new course in the lower, because as yet comparatively unfilled-in, ground lying to the east. And the same process being repeated, it wandered successively from the rocky western limit of the delta-flat towards the eastern. If this progress eastwards was allowed to be sufficiently slow to admit of the gradual filling in of the country adjoining, the delta was formed continuously up to the same general level, and the larger streams or channels, passing through this flat to the sea, became unavoidably diminished in size and in the quantity and force of the water they carried, the main body passing around further to the east and having its course in the channels successively formed there."

The Bhāgīrathi formerly afforded a regular means of communication between the upper Gangetic valley and the sea-board, but ever since the British occupation of the country much difficulty has been experienced in keeping it open for navigation throughout the year. The earliest historical mention of its silting up appears to be contained in a letter, dated 6th January 1666, of the French traveller Tavernier, in which he states that Bernier was going overland from a place near Rājmahāl to Cossimbazar because the river route was impracticable. "When the river is low, it is impassable because of a large sand-bank which lies before a town called Suti." Elsewhere Tavernier speaks of the river as a canal, and says it is 15 leagues long. Hedges, again, writing in 1683, said that the river above Nadia was full of shoals, and that, when he arrived at "Maula" (Mohula), he went from thence to Cossimbazar by *pālki*, a distance of 9 or 10 miles. There is ample evidence of the deterioration of the Bhāgīrathi in the next century. Stewart in his *History of Bengal*, which was chiefly compiled from the accounts of Muhammadan chroniclers, states that in 1757, just before the battle of Plassey, Sirāj-ud-daula, "believing that the English ships of war might proceed up the eastern branch of the Ganges to the northern point of the Cossimbazar island* and come down the Bhāgīrathi to Murshidābād, commanded immense piles to be driven in the river at Suti, by which the passage of that river has been rendered merely navigable by boats, and that only during half the year."† In 1781 Rennell wrote that the Cossimbazar river (*i.e.*, the Bhāgīrathi) was almost dry from October to May, and that the Jalangi, although a stream ran through it the whole year, was in some years unnavigable during two or three of the driest months. Captain Colebrook, again, in a memoir on the course of the Ganges (1797) wrote: "The Bhāgīrathi and Jalangi are not navigable throughout during the dry season. There have been instances of all these rivers continuing open in their turn during the dry season. The Jalangi used formerly to be navigable during the whole or greater part of the year. The Bhāgīrathi was navigable in the dry season of 1796. This year (1797), however, I was informed that the passage was no longer practicable for boats proceeding to Calcutta. Experience has shown that none of these rivers are to be depended on."

About the year 1813 the Bhāgīrathi suddenly deserted its old bed near Cossimbazar, and instead of following its former bend to the east of the town took a sweep to the west. Its old channel became a stagnant stretch of water, and the main stream flowed three miles away from its former bed. The cause of this diversion of the channel is not known, but it may perhaps be surmised that it was connected with an attempt to introduce a larger supply of water down the channel by a cut across two bends. That there was some interference with the natural channel is clear from Hamilton's *East India Gazetteer* of 1815, in which it is stated:—"In 1813, a canal was dug between the Bhāgīrathi and great Ganges, partly to ameliorate the unhealthiness of the town (Murshidābād) and adjacent villages by maintaining a permanent stream of wholesome water." There is, moreover, a local tradition that a new channel was actually excavated, as stated by a writer in the *Calcutta Review* of 1873: "All these places (Cossimbazar and the adjacent villages)," he writes, "were originally situated on a curve of the river Bhāgīrathi, but seventy years ago a straight cut was made forming the chord of the curve, thus changing the course of the river. This engineering operation was followed by the breaking out of an epidemic fever, which, in virulence and mortality, is unparalleled

* This was a name given to the triangular tract of country lying between the Ganges, Bhāgīrathi and Jalangi.

† Edition of 1818, pp. 521-2.

by any pestilence save that which destroyed Gaur."* The old channel survives as a *khāl*, which is used by boats in the rains. It is curious that it is called Kātigang as if it were an artificial channel, and there is a tradition that the Sāhebs cut a channel and brought the river out to the north of Farāsdānga.

MAINTENANCE OF NAVIGABLE CHANNELS. It is unnecessary to describe in detail the many changes which have taken place in the entrance of the Bhāgīrathi, the position of which shifts according to the set of the main stream of the Padma or Ganges. Suffice it to say that since 1824 regular measures have been taken by Government to maintain open channels for navigation both in the Bhāgīrathi and Jalangi. In 1888 a separate division of the Public Works Department, called the Nadia Rivers Division, was formed and placed under an Executive Engineer, for the control of the channels in the group of rivers known as the Nadia rivers. These channels had an aggregate length of 509½ miles in 1911, composed as follows:—(1) Farakka channels between the Ganges and Bhāgīrathi, 25 miles, (2) Bhāgīrathi river, 151 miles; (3) Bhairab-Jalangi river, 165½ miles; (4) Mātābhānga river, 136 miles; and (5) Hooghly river, 32 miles. The officers employed in this division are engaged in maintaining channels suitable for boats of small draught, and tolls are levied on boats using the rivers to pay for the work done in training the channels and keeping them navigable; one of the toll stations is at Jangipur in this district, and the other two are at Hānskhāli and Swarupganj in the district of Nadia. The number of boats using the rivers was 17,000 in 1911-12.

The main means employed to keep the channels open are temporary training works, consisting of bamboo and mat spurs or wing dams, called *bandhals*, which are constructed as follows. At the shoals to be operated on a line of bamboo stakes is run out from each bank of the river: they are driven into the bed of the river, supported by struts and fastened at the top by longitudinal ties. These stakes gradually converge, so as to force the current into a narrow channel. Large mat screens (*jhāmps*) are then let down and secured to the stakes. The first result of the current being concentrated in this manner is a great velocity in the channel it is intended to create, and a diminished current on both sides of it. Owing to the increased pressure below, the screens cannot be sunk to the bottom of the river, and through the space left there the water rushes with a rapid circular motion, cutting away the sand and carrying it under the matting and behind the

* *The Kāsimbāzār Rāj, Calcutta Review*, Vol. LVII, 1873.

line of stakes, where, the water being sluggish, constant deposit takes place. At the same time, the force of the current in the centre of the channel cuts away the sand there and bears it downstream, so that by these two processes the depth is increased in the channel, while on each side of it large collections of sand are formed, materially narrowing and deepening the channel. All that is necessary to maintain the works is to drive the bamboo piles further down as the water cuts away the sand and to sink the screens from time to time to suit the fall of the river. It may, of course, happen that the sand swept away by the currents sinks as soon as it gets beyond the *bandhal*, thus forming another shoal which requires the construction of another *bandhal*. These works have met with only moderate success in the Bhāgīrathi and Jalangi, because the volume of water passing down is too small to give much scouring power on the shoals. They have been more successful in the Ganges, where it has been proved that the low water channel can be improved, either by *bandhals* or by dredging, without any great outlay.

For some years past dredging operations have been conducted at the mouth of the Bhāgīrathi, where it opens out from a loop of the Ganges known as the Farakka Channel. This loop commences at Farakka and rejoins the Ganges about four miles below the off-take of the Bhāgīrathi. A shoal known as the Biswanāthpur shoal, about 2½ miles long, with two intermediate deep pools, forms at the entrance of the Bhāgīrathi, and the object in view is to scour this shoal and so admit as large a volume as possible into the Bhāgīrathi. This is done mainly to secure water for drinking, domestic and sanitary purposes, and not only with the object of improving navigation.

It has been urged that the Bhāgīrathi should be made fit not only for country boats, but also for steamer traffic throughout the year, as the water route from Calcutta to up-country would thereby be shortened by 425 miles. To this proposal there are grave objections. It was estimated by the Chief Engineer of Bengal in 1906 that the initial cost of dredging plant sufficient to maintain a navigable entrance would be 126 lakhs, and that the cost of maintenance would be so heavy that it could not possibly be met by any tollage which the steamer companies could afford to pay. Besides this, any increase in the volume of water passed down the Nadia rivers must entail a decrease in the supply of the Ganges lower down and lead to the deterioration of the present channels of that river. Lastly, it is possible that the channels of the Nadia rivers might become so large and deep that they would eventually carry off the main volume of the Ganges, charged with an enormous quantity of silt, which would fill up the deep trough of the Hooghly (at present scoured by tides) sufficiently to prevent the passage of sea-going vessels and so bring about the ruin of the port of Calcutta.

LAKES AND MARSHES.

There are many small lakes or lagoons, commonly called *bils* or *jhils*, most of which are the remnants of old river beds. The best known of these is the Motijhil, or Pearl Lake, a fine horseshoe lake about two miles from the town of Murshidābād, which has been formed by a change in the course of the Bhāgīrathi. Another large lagoon is the Telkar Bil, about three miles long and 2¾ miles broad, which lies two miles to the west of the Bhāgīrathi near the Khāgra Ghāt railway station; it has, however, dried up to a large extent. To the east of Berhampore lie three *bils* known as the Bishtupur, Chaltia and Chanda Bils. The Bishtupur Bil is a crescent-shaped expanse of water stretching from the north-east of Berhampore to about half a mile south-east of the railway station at Cossimbazar. It is connected with the Bhāgīrathi by two sluices, called the Khāgra and Berhampore sluices, which are under the control of the Public Works Department. The Chaltia Bil is another crescent-shaped sheet of water, which starts at the south of Berhampore near the Judge's Court and extends past the villages of Bhakri, Chaltia and Krishnamāti to Kālabaria near Haridāsmāti. The Chanda Bil is a shallow marsh about four miles long and a quarter of a mile broad, which is bounded on the north by Bādurpur, Tārakpur and other villages, and on the south by Mankara. Cuts were made from this *bil* and the Chaltia Bil to the Gobra Nullah in 1872-73, but they were not sufficiently deep for efficient drainage. Another cut has recently been made in the Bishtupur Bil in order to improve its drainage. Other important *bils* in the east of the district are the Goās (8 square miles), Dumkul (6 square miles) and Bhāndārdaha Bils, the last of which requires separate mention.

The Bhāndārdaha Bil is a depression marking the line of an old river, which is nearly 50 miles long and extends from the Bhāgīrathi embankment at Digha and Bhagwāngola on the north to Bāli on the river Jalangi on the south. It is called by a number of different names in different places, viz., (1) Gobra Nullah from the embankment down to Digha village, a distance of three miles. (2) Digha Bil from Digha down to Murādpur, 5 miles. (3) Topkhāna Bil from Murādpur to Gauribāgh bridge; this is a temporary bamboo bridge built for traffic across the *bil*, which is here dammed up. (4) Khāna or Mathurāpur Bil from Gauribāgh bridge to Bhairabpur Ghāt, 6 miles. (5) Bāli Bil from Bhairabpur Ghāt to Akhundbaria Ghāt, 6 miles. (6) Kharia Bil from Akhundbaria Ghāt to Pānchbaria, 7 miles. (7) Bhāndārdaha Bil from Panchbaria to Chāndpur, 8 miles. (8) Suti river or channel from Chāndpur to the junction with the Jalangi river. This *bil* is one of the chief sources of the fish supply of the district. It is connected with the Bhāgīrathi by several sluices, viz., (1) the sluices at Khāgra and Berhampore already mentioned, by which it receives water through the Bishtupur Bil, (2) at Kharia Ghāt through the Public Works Department drainage cut, and (3) sluice at Gora Bazar and Krishnamāti, by which water comes into the *bil* after passing through the Chaltia, Chanda and Boalia Bils by the southern drainage cut. It also receives local drainage and is fed by a number of tributaries, which are called *daras*. There is a continuation of the *bil* beyond the embankment for about five miles towards Lalitākuri. This is called the Bura Thākur Bil, and formed an integral part of the Bhāndārdaha Bil before it was cut off by the embankment. The Boalia Bil above mentioned is a shallow marsh about seven miles from Berhampore. It is four miles long in the rains, but shrinks very much as the flood water subsides, and is used for rice cultivation from April. The north-eastern portion of it, which is connected with the Bhāndārdaha Bil, is called the Putijol Bil.

To the west of the Bhāgīrathi are the Belun, Sakora and Pālan Bils, which lie close together near Khārgrām, about three miles to the south of the junction of the Brāhmini and Dwārka rivers. These appear to be identical with the "Bishnupur swamp," which, according to the manuscript records of the Board of Revenue, was artificially connected with the river, at the expense of Government, in the year 1800. All these *bils* are joined to the rivers by streams and shallow channels, and in the rains form a continuous lake. The Nawāranga, Saulmāri and Sālukuria Bils, together with other small marshes at the union of the Mor and Kuiyā with the Dwārka, also form during the rainy season large sheets of water, about twenty miles square. These large *bils* at the confluences of the hill streams serve during floods as natural drainage basins, into which the river waters pour. On the subsidence of the streams, the waters pent up in the *bils* find their way back again into the rivers gradually and quietly, and are thus drained off. But for these large reservoirs, the southern part of the Rārh would be much injured by floods from the hills.

In the Jangipur subdivision, in the north of the district, there are five large *bils*, viz., the Chacband and Bānsabāti Bils to the west of the Bhāgīrathi, and the Krishnasāil, Porāmāri and Gangni Bils to the east of it. The Krishnasāil Bil is evidently the bed of an old river, and has still some very deep pools, but the greater part of it could be made fit for cultivation. The Bānsabāti Bil extends during the rains almost the whole way from Bālighāt on the Bhāgīrathi to the boundary of the Sonthal Parganas; but during the hot weather the whole of this area is dry except in a few low-lying spots.

In many of the *bils* a process of natural reclamation is going on. Their beds are gradually being elevated by mud washed down by the rivers and streams which pour into them during the rains, and, to a small extent, by the dry soil which is blown over them during the season of the hot winds. Owing to these causes, the margin of tillage is steadily advancing.

There are also some artificial tanks, some of which are large enough to be called lakes. The largest is the Sāgardighi situated near the Sāgardighi railway station, which is about three-quarters of a mile long. Tradition states that it was excavated by one of the kings of the Pāla dynasty. The second largest tank, which is called Sheikhdighi, is near the Mirzāpur police-station about 5 miles north of the Bokhara railway station.

BOTANY. The botanical features of Murshidābād are those characteristic of the deltaic districts of Central Bengal. The swamps afford a foothold for numerous marsh species, while ponds and ditches are filled with submerged and floating water plants. The edges of sluggish creeks are lined with sedges and bulrushes, and the banks of rivers have a hedge-like scrub jungle. Deserted or uncultivated homestead lands are covered with shrubberies of semi-spontaneous species, interspersed with clumps of planted bamboos and groves of *Areca*, *Moringa*, *Mangifera* and *Anona*.

The country is on the whole well wooded with mango groves, bamboo clumps, and banyan, *pipal*, *babul*, jack, *bel*, tamarind, cocoanut and date palm trees. Murshidābād has a reputation for its mango orchards, and the tract lying along the western bank of the Bhāgīrathi in the Jangipur subdivision abounds with *kul* trees, which are cultivated for the propagation of lac.

WILD ANIMALS. A little over fifty years ago Colonel Gastrell remarked in his Statistical and Geographical Report on Murshidābād: "The advance of cultivation is rapidly driving the wild animals away. All are becoming more and more scarce, and but little sport is now to be found in the district." At present, leopards are met with in some parts, more particularly the Jalangi thana (*e.g.*, at Khayramāri) and in the neighbourhood of Murshidābād, where they can find cover in abandoned gardens and ruinous country houses. In the Kāndi and Jangipur subdivisions, where there is scarcely any heavy jungle left, they have practically disappeared, and only a stray leopard is occasionally seen. Wolves, however, are sometimes found in the Kāndi subdivision, where they do some damage to sheep and goats. Jackals are ubiquitous, and have an evil reputation for carrying off and devouring infants, more especially in the Jangipur subdivision. They will even carry them off when sleeping by their parents' side, seizing them by the throat to stifle their cries. Next morning a few bones in the neighbouring jungle are all that is left to tell the tale. Wild pigs are plentiful in the Bāgri and along the *chars* of the Ganges, and also in the Hariharpāra thana. Pig-sticking has long been a favourite form of sport, the country to the east of the Bhāgīrathi lending itself ideally to riding, and excellent bags are made. Monkeys (the black-faced *hanumān* or *langur*) are numerous and destructive in towns, where they do much damage in gardens and orchards and to the mango crop when it is ripening.

GAME BIRDS. The game birds of the district consist of snipe, wild duck, quail, partridge, pigeon, teal and geese. During the cold weather good sport can be obtained with snipe, duck, teal and geese on the *bils*, more especially the Jalangi and Telkar Bils; among ducks the pintail, pochard and gadwall, and among teal the painted, blue-winged and cotton are common. All the usual waders are also met with.

REPTILES. The common varieties of snakes, such as cobras, *karaits*, etc., are found; the mortality from snake-bite is considerable in years of flood, when they are driven to dry ground in the vicinity of villages and homesteads. Crocodiles are fairly common in the rivers and in the swamps or *bils*; they are also met with in tanks in the Jangipur subdivision.

FISH. The more valuable fish caught in the rivers, *bils* and tanks belong to the carp family (*Cyprinidæ*), such as *ruhi, kātla, mirgal*, etc., or are *Siluridæ*, such as *boāil* and *māgur*. Large catches of *hilsa* (*Clupea ilisha*) are made in the Padma or Ganges during the rainy season, when they ascend in shoals. They are also caught in the Bhāgīrathi and in the Khayra Bil, when it is flooded by the Bhāgīrathi, and are exported in considerable quantities. An account of the fisheries of the district will be given in Chapter VIII, and may be so far anticipated by saying that in addition to the rivers, the *bils*, such as the Bishtupur, Chanda, Chaltia, Boalia and Bhāndārdaha Bils, constitute valuable fisheries.

CLIMATE. During the cold weather, from November to January, there is an almost entire absence of cloud and rainfall; the mean rainfall during these three months aggregates only one inch. The mean temperature falls from 73° in November to 66° in December and 65° in January, but humidity remains at a fairly high level; a feature of the cold weather is the occasional occurrence of low-lying morning fogs, which dissipate with the rising sun. In February the temperature begins to rise, the mean for the month being 70°; and as southerly winds become more frequent with the advance of the year, there is a period of transition characterised by occasional thunderstorms, accompanied by rainfall; this, on an average, amounts to an inch in March and 1¾ inch in April. During these latter two months, dry westerly winds of high temperature alternate with southerly sea winds of moderate temperature. The night temperature increases slowly, and the highest monthly mean is 88° in April. In May monsoon weather is occasionally experienced when cyclonic storms form at the head of the Bay of Bengal. When such storms occur, there is heavy rain, and the average rainfall consequently rises to 5 inches in May.

With the commencement of the south-west monsoon (generally in the latter half of June, but in some years not till the beginning of July) humidity increases to 88 per cent. of saturation, heavy cloud is continuous, and rainfall is of almost daily occurrence, the precipitation becoming heavy when there are cyclonic disturbances. The average is 10 inches in June, 11 inches in July, 10½ in August and 9⅓ inches in September. During this period the mean temperature slowly diminishes from 86° in June to 81° in October. During the latter half of September and throughout October cloudy weather alternates with bright sunshine, and the bright periods lengthen till they merge in the continuous fine weather of the cold season.

The following statement gives the salient meteorological statistics for the town of Berhampore:—

Month.	Temperature.					Humidity.	Cloud.	Rainfall.	
	Mean.	Mean maximum.	Mean minimum.	Mean range. Daily.	Mean range. Month.	Mean.	Mean.	Inches.	Days.
January	65	77	53	24	25	87	1·5	0·47	1
February	70	82	57	25	34	80	2·2	0·92	2
March	80	93	66	27	38	71	2·7	1·05	2
April	88	100	75	25	29	76	3·8	1·75	3
May	87	97	77	20	23	82	5·6	4·88	8
June	86	92	79	13	17	88	8·1	9·87	12
July	84	89	79	10	12	92	8·7	10·31	16
August	84	89	79	10	10	92	8·9	10·98	16
September ...	84	89	79	10	11	90	7·2	9·79	12
October	81	88	74	14	20	85	3·6	4·71	5
November ...	73	82	64	18	25	85	1·9	0·40	1
December ...	66	77	55	22	26	85	1·4	0·10	...
Year ...	79	88	70	19	23	84	4·6	55·23	78

CHAPTER II.

HISTORY.

UNTIL the days of Mughal rule there is little distinctive in the history of Murshidābād, which, in fact, was, for the most part, merely the history of Bengal in general. A few isolated facts emerge from the general obscurity in which its early history rests, and there are many lacunæ, which can only be linked together by the thin and uncertain thread of conjecture. It has been suggested by Mr. Beveridge that the present village of Rāngāmāti, six miles south-west of Berhampore, marks the ancient site of Karna Suvarna, the capital of the kingdom of the same name.* According to the Chinese pilgrim, Hiuen Tsiang (or Yuan Chwang), who visited Bengal in the first half of the seventh century A. D., the city, which was 20 *li*, or about 7 miles in circuit, had by it a splendid monastery, called Lo-to-wei-chin, which is his phonetic rendering of Raktavitti or Raktamitti, a name meaning red earth, of which Rāngāmāti is the modern equivalent. This theory is not accepted by other scholars. "The identification," writes Bābu Manmohan Chakravartti, "rests on the similarity of the name Rāngāmāti with Raktamitti, and of an alleged older name of it, Kānsonagar, with Karna Suvarna, on the location of the place in the direction indicated by Yuan Chwang, and on its remains, viz., mounds, images and coins. Unfortunately, the name Rāngāmāti is not uncommon, being derived from the red laterite soil that extends from the foot of the Rājmahāl Hills, through the Bārind, to the Madhupur Jungle in Mymensingh. The name Kānsonagar is not in use now; but, though it might have been in use once before, to judge from the introductory genealogical verse to Rādhakāntadeva's *Sabda-kalpa-druma*,† mere similarity is not sufficient. The village is not named in any Hindu or Musalmān works, and is not found in any map older than Valentyn's, published in 1726 A.D. The pargana Fatehsingh, in which it is situated, was said to have been allotted to an up-country Brāhman by Mān Singh for valour shown in the war; and the remains in the fort might be as well ascribed to him or his descendants."‡

EARLY HISTORY.

* *The Site of Karna Suvarna*, J. A. S. B., 1893, pp. 315-328.

† *Id.*, p. 327.

‡ *Notes on the Geography of Old Bengal*, J. A. S. B., 1908, p. 281.

Whether Rāngāmāti was or was not the capital, there can be no doubt that, at the time of Hiuen Tsiang's visit, the district was included in the limits of Karna Suvarna, which he describes as a moist low-lying land under regular cultivation. It bore flowers and fruits in abundance, and had a temperate climate. The people were wealthy and patrons of learning. There were more than ten Buddhist monasteries with over 2,000 brethren of the Sammatiya school, and three monasteries of Devadatta's school in which milk products were not taken as food. There were 50 Deva temples, and the followers of various religions were very numerous.* This fertile land corresponds to the modern districts of Murshidābād, Burdwān, Bānkura and Hooghly, and was one of the provinces of the empire of Sasānka, a fanatical enemy of Buddhism, whose sway extended from Benares to the Bay of Bengal.

No details of the history of the district are forthcoming for several centuries after this, but the rule of the Pālas is commemorated by the large Sāgardighi tank, which is said to have been excavated by Mahipāla, who ruled in the early part of the eleventh century. His palace is said to have been not far off, at a village called after him Mahipāl, which is situated to the north of the Barela railway station. Tradition also relates that Husain Shāh, King of Bengal from 1493 to 1518, was born at the village of Chāndpāra, south-east of the Mirzāpur police-station and a little to the east of Sheikhdighi on the Jangpur road. It is said that in his early youth he served a Brāhman of the village as a herdsman, and that when he rose to power he granted his old master the estate of Chāndpāra at a quit-rent of one anna. Hence he is known as Rākhal Bādshāh, or the herdsman king, and the village as Ekānā Chāndpāra. Local tradition is so far confirmed that the *Riyazu-s-Salātin* states that he came with his father and brother from Turkestān and settled at Chāndpur in the Rārh country, where he married the daughter of the local Kāzi.†

There is, it may be added, no record of the district having been the theatre of war until 1600, when a decisive battle was fought at Sherpur Atai, in the Kāndi subdivision, in which the imperial army under Mān Singh routed the rebellious Afghāns of Orissa, who had made themselves masters of a considerable portion of Bengal.

EUROPEAN SETTLEMENTS.

In the beginning of the seventeenth century the town of Murshidābād, which then bore the name of Makhsusābād, began to

* S. Beal, *Records of the Western World*, Vol. II, p. 201.

† Blochmann identifies this place with Chāndpur (near Alaipur on the Bhairab) in the Khulna district.

assume importance as a commercial depôt. Its silk attracted the attention of two English agents, Hughes and Parker, who were sent from Agra to Patna to set up a trading station there—so much so that next year they reported that they had invested Rs. 500 in purchasing samples of silk from Makhsusâbâd.*

When, at length, the English established their factories in Bengal, Cossimbazar was one of the first places selected for a station, which was subordinate to the agency at Hooghly.† The East India Company's first representatives there were John Kenn, who was Chief on £40 a year, Daniel Sheldon, second member of Council, on £30, John Priddy on £20 and Job Charnock, fourth member, on £20. Job Charnock was subsequently posted at Patna, but returned as Chief in 1680‡, and stayed there till 1686. During these six years the trade of the Company was seriously hampered by the heavy imposts levied by the Nawâb, Shaista Khān, and the exactions of the local Faujdâr or Governor Bolchând Ray. The disputes between the Company and the Mughal authorities culminated in 1686, when the Company's cargo boats were held up under an embargo and its sale of silver prohibited. Charnock was ordered to pay Rs. 43,000 in settlement of a claim made by some native merchants, and, according to Orme, was scourged by the Nawâb's orders. The Cossimbazar factory was invested by troops to prevent his escape, but in April 1686 he succeeded in getting through the cordon and made his way to Hooghly. After this, the Cossimbazar factory, in common with the other English factories in Bengal, was condemned to confiscation by Shaista Khān.

---

*W. Foster, *The English Factories in India, 1618-21*, pp. 194, 253. In a letter, dated 12th July 1620, they refer to "serbandy silk, the best of Mucksoude and Sideabunde (*i.e.*, Makhsusābād and Saidābād), from whence these sortes are wound of."

† The factory was opened in 1658 or 1659. A letter of the Court of Directors to the Agent at Hooghly, dated 27th February 1758, mentions Hooghly, Balasore, Patna and Cossimbazar as "the four factories which we determine shall be settled in the Bay of Bengal" and sets forth that the four officers above mentioned are to be appointed at Cossimbazar. The use of the future tense makes it uncertain whether the Cossimbazar factory was actually started in this year, and Sir Henry Yule is of opinion that it is doubtful whether it was regularly occupied before 1659.

‡ "In 1678," writes Mr. Beveridge, "a lady with charming ignorance of Anglo-Indian requirements, sends her brother-in-law at Cossimbazar a box containing a cravat and cuffs and ribbon of the newest mode and a border of lace for his night cap. Alas, he was dead before the box left England." *Old Places in the Murshidābād District*, Calcutta Review, Vol. XCIV, 1892, *Cf.* Hedges Diary, Vol. II, p. 242.

The French had also a factory at Cossimbazar at this time,* and the Armenians had made a settlement at Saidābād under the authority of a *pharmān* granted by Aurangzeb in 1665; while the Dutch had a thriving factory at Kālkāpur. The object of all was the silk trade, the importance of which may be gathered from the accounts given by both Bernier and Tavernier. The former says that "the Dutch have sometimes seven or eight hundred natives employed in their factory at Cossimbazar, where, in like manner, the English and other merchants employ a proportionate number." The latter says that Cossimbazar annually exported about 22,000 bales of silk (of 100 lbs. each). "The Dutch generally took, either for Japan or for Holland, 6,000 to 7,000 bales, and they would have liked to get more, but the merchants of Tartary and of the whole Mughal Empire opposed their doing so, for these merchants took as much as the Dutch, and the balance remained for the people of the country for the manufacture of their own stuffs."

REBELLION OF SUBBA SINGH.

The wealth of Murshidābād made it a prize worth winning by the Afghāns who rose in rebellion under Sūbha Singh in 1696. Under his leadership they overran the country on the west of the Ganges from Rājmahāl to Midnapore, and after his death they spread to the east of the river under Rahim Shāh, an Afghān chief, who had been chosen as his successor. In Murshidābād a loyal officer named Neāmat Khān, who resided on his *jāgīr* or royal grant of land, gallantly held out against them. "As the combats in India were, even at that late period, more frequently decided by duels between the chiefs, or champions, of the contending armies than by a general engagement, Tauhar Khān, a nephew of Neāmat's, well mounted and armed, advanced into the plain and challenged any of the Afghāns to meet him. No single warrior daring to advance, a party of Afghāns at once rushed forward, and, before his friends could go to his assistance, cut the youth to pieces."† On hearing of his fate, Neāmat Khān, who was clad only in a muslin coat, seized his sword and, without waiting to put on his helmet and cuirass, sprang on his horse and dashed into the fray. Cutting his way through the Afghāns, he made straight for Rahim Shāh and delivered a blow at his head. His sword shivered on the helmet of tempered steel, whereupon he seized Rahim Shāh round the waist and by sheer strength unhorsed him. Springing to the ground, he drew the

* Streynsham Master, the President of Madras, who visited Bengal in 1676, says in his diary that at Cossimbazar he passed by the plot of ground allotted to the French.

† Stewart's History of Bengal (1813), p. 332.

Afghān's dagger and endeavoured to administer the *coup de grace*. Again he was foiled, for he could not pierce the gorget, and, while he was struggling to do so, the Afghāns rushed up and cut him down. The Afghāns, in admiration of his courage, carried him mortally wounded to one of their tents, and when he signalled for water offered it to him; but "his feelings revolted against taking it from their hands, and thus, with parched lips, he quaffed the goblet of martyrdom."* The rebels then advanced to Makhsusābād, and, after defeating 5,000 of the royal troops, took and plundered the town. The merchants of Cossimbazar having, however, sent a deputation to meet the rebel chief, he spared that place.

In 1697, when the news of the disasters that had befallen the Imperial army reached the Emperor at Delhi, he appointed his own grandson, Prince Azimush-shān, Governor of Bengal, Bihār and Orissa in place of the supine Nawāb Ibrāhim Khān, and placed Zabardast Khān, the latter's son, in command of the Bengal army with orders to advance at once and extirpate the rebels. Zabardast Khān advanced rapidly from Dacca, his army marching up the bank of the Padma attended by a strong flotilla of war boats. Rahim Shāh resolved to give battle and encamped his forces on the river bank near Bhagwāngola. Zabardast Khān drew up his forces behind a stockade formed of bullock waggons, and commenced a cannonade from the boats lying in the river. His guns, which were served by Portuguese artillerymen in the Mughal service, dismounted most of those belonging to the enemy and silenced the redoubts which they had thrown up along their front. A whole day was spent in this fusillade, and next morning a general engagement took place. The Afghāns, who had 12,000 cavalry and 30,000 infantry, were signally defeated and retreated to Makhsusābād, where they were followed by Zabardast Khān, who encamped on an extensive plain to the east of the town and prepared again to give them battle. The Afghāns, however, had not the heart for another bloody conflict and fled to Burdwān. There Rahim Shāh fell in battle against a Mughal army commanded by Azimush-shān, after which his followers were hunted down like wild beasts.

THE DIWANI AND NIZAMAT.

At this time, the provinces of the Mughal Empire were under a dual system of administration, there being two officers in charge of each, who were known as the Nāzim (or Nawāb-Nāzim) and the Dīwān. The Nāzim was the Governor or Viceroy of the

* *Riyazu-s-Salātin*, translation by Abdus Salām, (1904), p. 234.

Province, administered criminal justice, and was in fact the executive and military chief. The Dīwān, who was directly subordinate to the Emperor and independent of the Nāzim, was the Finance Minister; he was responsible for the revenue administration, while he also occasionally administered civil justice. The relations of the two are well explained by Stewart in his *History of Bengal*:—"During the despotic reign of Aurangzeb the offices of Nāzim (military Governor) and Dīwān were kept perfectly distinct: the business of the former was to defend and protect the country from foreign insults or domestic insurrections and to enforce a strict obedience to the laws: to the latter was assigned the collection of the revenues and the disbursement of the requisite expenses. He was, in a certain degree, subject to the orders of the Nāzim, being obliged to comply with all written orders for money from that officer for the service of Government, but the Nāzim was responsible to the exchequer for any improper use of that power: he received his regular salary from the Dīwān and was not entitled to any further emolument from his office. These two officers were, however, commanded to consult with each other upon all important affairs and to act in concert upon every public emergency according to the regulations which from time to time were issued." These regulations were embodied in the *Dastur-ul-Amal*, a Procedure Code containing rules on all revenue and administrative matters, which was issued to each province after being approved by the Emperor. Every year additions or modifications were made in it with the Emperor's sanction, and no Nāzim or Dīwān had authority to deviate from it.

TRANSFER OF THE CAPITAL.

In 1701 Murshid Kuli Khān was appointed Dīwān of Bengal, the Nāzim being Prince Azimush-shān, whose headquarters were at Dacca. Murshid Kuli Khān soon brought about a reorganization of the finances of the province, which, in spite of its richness and fertility, brought comparatively little into the Imperial exchequer. Owing to the evil reputation of Bengal, the higher officers were averse to service in the province, "as they fancied it not only fatal to human life, but an actual haunt of demons."* To induce them to settle in it, large tracts had been made over to them as *jāgirs* or military fief, and the revenue of the *khālsa* or Crown lands was so small that it did not suffice to meet the pay of the Nāzim and the salaries of the military and civil establishment. Money had even to be remitted from other provinces to cover the Bengal deficit. The growing poverty of the Imperial exchequer rendered it necessary that Bengal should pay its proper

* *Riyazu-s-Salātin* (translation by Abdus Salām, 1904), p. 248.

quota, and Murshid Kuli Khān set to work to increase the revenue in no half-hearted fashion. Finding that the receipts were absorbed in improper channels, he appointed his own collectors in the different districts, and soon ascertained that the revenue really amounted to a crore of rupees. His next step was to resume the *jāgirs* in Bengal with the sanction of the Emperor, the *jāgīrdārs* receiving but scant compensation in the shape of *jāgīrs* in Orissa, where the land was far less fertile and valuable. At the same time he effected large retrenchments in the public expenditure and rigorously enforced the payment of revenue by the zamīndārs. "The haughty spirit of the Prince Azimush-shān could ill brook the constant interference in all pecuniary transactions of the Dīwān and his frequent opposition to His Royal Highness's commands. Besides these causes, the Prince was exceedingly jealous of the high favour in which Murshid Kuli stood with the Emperor; and the courtiers and favourites of the Prince, whose extravagance or assumed powers were constantly controlled by the Dīwān, fanned the flame and added fuel to his already exasperated temper." Azimush-shān determined to get rid of the troublesome Dīwān, and sent a party of soldiers to kill him when he was on his way to the palace (at Dacca), but this attempt was foiled by the cool courage of Murshid Kuli Khān, who jumped out of his *pālki* and drawing his sword ordered his attendants to clear the road and drive the assassins away. "After acting in so spirited and independent a manner, Murshid Kuli deemed it unadvisable to remain in the same place with the Prince, and, having consulted with his friends on the most advantageous situation, he resolved to fix his residence at Makhsusābād as being nearly in the centre of the province and equally convenient for collecting the revenue from all parts. Having decided on this measure, he left Dacca without taking leave of the Viceroy, and, carrying with him all the public officers attached to the Dīwāni, proceeded to Makhsusābād." The headquarters of the Diwāni were thus transferred to Murshidābād, the date of the transfer being apparently 1702-03.

When Aurangzeb received Murshid Kuli Khān's report of the attempt on his life, he ordered the Prince to leave Bengal and take up his residence in Bihār. Azimush-shān consequently left Dacca for Patna, appointing his son, Farrukhsiyār, as his representative in Bengal in the capacity of Deputy Nāzim. He does not appear, however, to have had any authority to make such an appointment, and in 1703-04 Murshid Kuli Khān paid a visit to Aurangzeb in his camp in the Deccan and succeeded not only in getting himself confirmed in the post of Dīwān of Bengal, Bihār and Orissa, but also in obtaining the appointment of Deputy Nāzim of Bengal and Orissa—much to the chagrin of the Prince. In the absence of the latter, Murshid Kuli Khān enjoyed all the powers of the Nawāb Nāzim and had thus full executive authority as well as the entire administration of the finances.

His first act on returning to Bengal was to change the name of Makhsusābād to Murshidābād, and, by building a palace and erecting public offices, to make it the capital of the province. The change of name appears to have taken effect from 1705, for the name Makhsusābād appears last on a rupee coined in 1704, and Murshidābād for the first time on a rupee struck at the local mint* next year.

The choice of Murshidābād as the headquarters is sometimes ascribed to the difficulties which Murshid Kuli Khān experienced in carrying on the administration at Dacca owing to the friction with Azimush-shān and his fears of assassination. In the *Riyazu-s-Salātin* it is attributed to the central position of the town—"an excellent site, where news of all four quarters of the Subah could be easily procurable, and which, like the pupil of the eye, was situate in the centre of the important places of the Subah:" a lengthy account of its advantages, from a strategic and commercial point of view, then follows. According to Sir William Hunter, it "seems probable that Murshid Kuli Khān was induced

---

* A rupee of Aurangzeb preserved in the Lahore museum shows that Makhsusābād was a mint-town as early as 1679 A. D. The profits of the Murshidābād mint are stated in the rent-roll of 1728 to amount to Rs. 3,04,103. In 1706 the English at Cossimbazar were induced to pay Rs. 25,000 for the convenience of having bullion, which they imported from Europe, coined into rupees at the Murshidābād mint. One of the chief articles in the petition presented by the English embassy at the Court of Delhi in 1716 was, 'that the officers of the mint at Murshidābād should at all times, when required, allow three days in the week for the coinage of the English Company's money.' It was not till nearly half a century afterwards, in 1757, as one of the results of the battle of Plassey, that the English first struck coins of their own, but still in the name of the Emperor of Hindustān. In 1758, the Council at Calcutta complained, in a letter to the Court, that their mint was of but little use to them, partly because no bullion was arriving from Europe, but more especially because the command of specie possessed by the Seths of Murshidābād was used to force down the exchange value of their *sikkās*. In 1760, on the occasion of the accession of Mīr Kāsim, a *parwanā* was received from the Nawāb, awarding full privileges to the Calcutta mint. From this date the mint of Murshidābād began to decline, and, indeed, was soon abolished. The MS. Records of the Board of Revenue show that in 1785 it was proposed to 're-establish the mint of Murshidābād.' This proposal was apparently carried out, though only for a short time. In 1796 all provincial mints were abolished, but some respite seems to have been granted to that at Murshidābād. It was not till 1799 that 'the Collector of Murshidābād despatched the mint utensils to the Presidency, and disposed of the buildings used as the mint office by public auction.'

to take this step by political considerations. Dacca had lost its importance, for the Maghs and the Portuguese were no longer dangerous; and the banks of the Bhāgīrathi afforded a more central position for the management of the three Provinces of Bengal, Bihār and Orissa. The new city also was situated on the line of trade, along which the treasures of India were now beginning to find their way to the European settlements on the Hooghly; and it commanded the town of Cossimbazar, where all the foreigners had important factories. Moreover, the situation in those days was regarded as very healthy." At the same time, it must be admitted that the choice might have been more fortunate, for the Bhāgīrathi had long been silting up and its passage throughout the year had already become impossible.

MUGHAL VICEROYS.

Murshid Kuli Khān, or, as he is often called in the English records, Jafar Khān,* was the son of a poor Brāhman, who in his infancy was purchased by a Persian merchant. The latter, however, did not condemn him to slavery, but taking him to Ispahān had him circumcised and brought up like one of his own sons under the name of Muhammad Hādi. On the death of the merchant, he proceeded to the Deccan, where he entered the Imperial service. His ability soon brought him to the front, and he was appointed Dīwān of Hyderābād with the title of Kartalab Khān. He was subsequently transferred in the same capacity to Orissa, and in 1701 was appointed Dīwān of Bengal with the new title of Murshid Kuli Khān. As already shown, he had the address to maintain himself in office and obtain further preferment in spite of the hostility of Azimush-shān; and, though he had supplanted Farrukhsiyār, the latter made no attempt to interfere with his government. On the contrary, he also came to Murshidābād in 1707, and, taking up his residence in "the Lālbāgh palace," remained on terms of perfect cordiality with Murshid Kuli Khān until 1712, when he made his way to Patna and there had himself proclaimed Emperor. In the same year Azimush-shān was killed while struggling for the throne of Delhi, and in 1713, when Farrukhsiyār became Emperor, Murshid Kuli Khān was enabled, with the assistance of Jagat Seth, the banker, to purchase the Nizāmat on easy terms for himself. Five years later the government of Bihār, which he had long solicited, was also conferred upon him, and he thus became the Viceroy of Bengal, Bihār and Orissa.

Murshid Kuli Khān, 1704-25.

Murshid Kuli Khān ruled at Murshidābād from 1704 to 1725—a rare continuity of tenure of office in those days, when

* Jafar Khān was one of the titles he received when appointed Nawāb of Bengal.

Emperor followed Emperor in quick succession, from each of whom the Nawāb had to obtain confirmation of his rank and office Nor was he unworthy of his high position, for his administration, though stern and often harsh, was generally just and efficient, and the land had a much needed peace. An able financier, he rigorously cut down the public expenditure, and reduced the strength of the Bengal army to 2,000 cavalry and 4,000 infantry. With this small force, which was not raised primarily for military purposes and scarcely deserved the name of an army, he maintained order and prevented rebellion. Dacoits and robbers were mercilessly hunted down; when a robbery occurred, the Faujdār or zamīndār within whose territory it took place was compelled to arrest the robber or recover the property. The goods, or their equivalent in money, were restored to the person who had been robbed, and the robber, if caught, was impaled alive. By these means, write the Muhammadan chroniclers, travellers journeyed in safety, and every man slept securely in his own house. "Imperial *mansabdārs*, hearing that Bengal had been turned into a fertile garden without a thorn, eagerly sought for offices under him."

His greatest financial reform was the preparation of a new revenue roll based on a survey of the land and a reassessment according to the actual area and produce. The revenue was exacted to the last cowry, and many are the stories of the exquisite devices of cruelty which he employed to extract arrears from defaulting zamīndārs. "They were seized and tormented by every species of cruelty, as by hanging up by the feet, bastinadoing, setting them in the sun in summer, stripping them naked and sprinkling them frequently with water in winter. He ordered a pond to be dug, which was filled with everything disgusting, and the stench of which was so offensive as nearly to suffocate whoever approached it. To this shocking place, in contempt of the Hindus, he gave the name of Baikunth, which in their language means Paradise; and, after the zamīndārs had undergone the usual punishments, if their rent was not forthcoming, he caused them to be drawn, by a rope tied under the arms, through this infernal pond. He is also stated to have compelled them to put on loose trousers, into which were introduced live cats." These drastic methods were effectual in raising the revenue, and he was able to transmit annually to the Imperial treasury at Delhi a crore and fifty lakhs of rupees, besides which enormous sums were retained for his own private fisc and in the coffers of Jagat Seth at Murshidābād. The boxes of treasure were laden upon 200 or more carts drawn by bullocks, and escorted by 300 cavalry and

500 infantry, accompanied by one of the sub-treasurers. Together with the revenue, he sent presents to the Emperor and hi ministers—elephants, horses, antelopes, hawks, shields made of rhinoceros-hide, sword-blades, Sylhet mats, filagree-work of gold and silver, wrought ivory, Dacca muslins and Cossimbazar silks, also a number of European articles procured at the royal port of Hooghly.

At the same time, he was impartial in the administration of justice and rigorously enforced its decrees. He had the *kotwāl* of Hooghly stoned to death for abducting a maiden and is even said to have put his own son to death for an offence against the laws. According to the ideas of political economy then prevalent, he made careful provision against famine and strictly prohibited the exportation of grain. The Faujdār of Hooghly had express orders to see that no ship, whether European or other, carried away more grain than was sufficient for the victualling of the crew during the voyage; neither were any foreign merchants allowed to have stores of grain. The Indian merchants were also prevented from establishing monopolies. If the importation of grain in any area fell short, he sent officers who broke open the *mahājans*' hoards and compelled them to sell their grain in the markets. Rice was then commonly sold in Murshidābād at 4 maunds for a rupee.

The greatest blot upon his administration is the bigoted cruelty with which he treated Hindus, which has led to the saying that he united the administrative ability of a Hindu to the fanaticism of a renegade. He employed Hindus in the collection of the revenue, and, if any was guilty of embezzlement, forced him and his family to embrace Islam. As an outward emblem of indignity, Hindu zamīndārs and other wealthy persons were not permitted to ride in *pālkis*, but had to use the common *duli*. His preparations for his tomb afford an unpleasing example of his conduct in this respect. "The Nawāb," writes Stewart in his *History of Bengal*, "being advanced in years, and finding his health decline very fast, gave orders for building his tomb with a mosque and a *khatra*, or square with shops. The spot selected was in the Khās Tāluk, on the east side of the city. All the Hindu temples in the neighbourhood were pulled down, and their materials used for the new work. The zamīndārs and other Hindus would have preserved their temples at any price, but no entreaties or bribes could prevail; not one was left standing in Murshidābād, or within the distance of four miles' journey from the city. In the remote villages the houses of the Hindus were threatened with destruction, upon pretence of their being dedicated to religious uses, and were only redeemed on payment of large sums of money. The servants of Hindus of all ranks were compelled to work on the new structure, unless their masters paid for their release. By these means the buildings were completed in the course of a year, and a *ganj* (or market-place where dues were collected) was annexed to the *khatra*, in order that out of the dues the whole might be maintained in repair." It is only fair to add, however, that the continued existence of the Hindu shrines at Kiriteswari, 3 miles from the city, throws considerable doubt on this story.

Murshid Kuli Khān chose as his heir and successor in office his grandson, Sarfarāz Khān, and endeavoured to get his choice confirmed by the Emperor; but the succession did not follow his wishes, for his son-in-law Shuja-ud-daula, the father of Sarfarāz Khān, managed by intrigues at the Imperial court to secure the vacant office for himself.

Shuja-ud-daula, 1725-39.

Shuja-ud-daula, or Shuja-ud-dīn Khān as he is also called, came of a Turkoman family from Khorāsān in the east of Persia, and was born in the Deccan. There he formed a friendship with Murshid Kuli Khān, who was at that time Dīwān of Haidarābād and married his only daughter, Jinnatunnissa or Azimunnissa. The Muhammadan chroniclers are profuse in their praises of the government of Shuja-ud-daula. His collection of the revenues was not less exact than that of his predecessor, but he was free from the reproach of cruelty and religious bigotry. He commenced his rule by releasing the unhappy zamīndārs from the rigorous confinement in which they had long been languishing, and permitted them to resume the management of their estates after levying heavy *nazars* from them. By this stroke of policy, he raised the revenue to one crore and fifty lakhs of rupees, which he remitted to Delhi through Jagat Seth, the imperial banker. Convinced that the military establishment kept up by Murshid Kuli Khān was inadequate to the security of the country, he raised the army to 25,000 men, of whom half were cavalry and half infantry armed with matchlocks.

The quiet that endured during his rule, and the accumulated treasures that he inherited from his father-in-law, supplied him with the opportunity and the means to embellish the city of Murshidābād. The buildings erected by Murshid Kuli Khān being too small for his lofty ideas, he dismantled them and built a new palace for himself, with an arsenal, audience hall, reception room, courts and public offices. "His favourite residence was at Dahapāra, on the right bank of the Bhāgīrathi, just opposite Murshidābād. Here he completed a superb mosque, which had been commenced by one of the officers of Murshid Kuli Khān. It stood in the midst of a garden of great beauty, where he retired with his seraglio in the summer. This place to which he gave the name of Farahbāgh, or the Garden of Beauty, had a wide repute for loveliness: "it was a splendid garden, compared with which the pleasances of Kāshmīr paled like gardens withering in autumn." Here he was buried, in a mausoleum erected by himself, after a peaceful rule of fourteen years (1725—1739).

Under his rule the province was divided into four sub-provinces, viz.—(1) Bengal proper, comprising West, Central and part of North Bengal, (2) East Bengal and the remainder of North Bengal, (3) Bihar and (4) Orissa. The first sub-province Shuja-ud-daula kept under his direct administration. The others were placed under Deputy Governors, Alī Vardi Khān being given Bihar, while Sarfarāz Khān was made Dīwān of Bengal. Another administrative innovation was the formation of an Executive Council, which he consulted in all important matters. Until his appointment to Bihar the leading spirit on this Council was Alī Vardi Khān; the other members were the latter's brother Hāji Ahmad, Alam Chand, who had been Dīwān in Orissa and enjoyed the title of Rai Raiān, and Jagat Seth the banker.

Sarfarāz Khān, 1739-40.

During the last few years of his life Shuja-ud-daula, never a vigorous ruler and now enfeebled by age, left the administration to his son, Sarfarāz Khān. The latter succeeded without any opposition, but was so fearful of attempts by rivals that he would not venture out of the fort even to attend the funeral of his father. He ruled only a year and without distinction, for he spent most of his time in the harem, where he is said to have had no less than 1,500 women. "In short, all that could be said in his favour was that he was neither a drunkard nor an oppressor." The administration was left in the hands of the Executive Council consisting of the Rai Raiān Alam Chand, Hāji Ahmad and Jagat Seth, the triumvirate, as they were called. They soon entered into a conspiracy with Alī Vardi Khān to depose Sarfarāz Khān, and sent agents to Delhi to bribe the ministers of the Emperor Muhammad Shāh, and have the appointment of Sarfarāz Khān set aside and Alī Vardi Khān installed in his place. Alī Vardi Khān gathered round him at Patna a large body of Afghān troops, and in the beginning of 1740 felt himself strong enough to unfurl the banner of revolt and march southwards upon Murshidābād. The two armies met at Giria 22 miles north of Murshidābād, the battle beginning with an attack delivered by Alī Vardi Khān before dawn. Sarfarāz Khān, holding the Korān in one hand, mounted an elephant, and was killed by a shot from a musket while fighting bravely. One of his generals named Ghaus Khān, and Pancho, his Portuguese commandant of artillery, gallantly maintained the fight, but the battle ended at nightfall with a complete victory for Alī Vardi Khān. Sarfarāz Khān's faithful *mahaut* brought the body of his master to Murshidābād, where it was buried at dead of night in the grounds of his palace at Naktakhāli.

Alī Vardi Khān, 1740-56.

Murshidābād was sacked by the victorious troops, and, on the third day after his victory, Alī Vardi Khān entered the city and took possession of the *masnad*. Out of the accumulations which he found in the treasury, he sent large presents to the Emperor and his courtiers, and was forthwith confirmed in the government of the three provinces. It appears, however, that he never remitted the revenues to Delhi, for soon after this date the Mughal dynasty lost all semblance of real power. He ruled at Murshidābād for 16 years, during a most troubled period of Bengal history. The commencement of his reign was disturbed by outbreaks in Orissa, and these were no sooner quelled, than the Marāthās began their annual invasions, ravaging the entire country to the west of the Bhāgirathi, and even penetrating to the suburbs of the city of Murshidābād.

Marātha wars.

The first concern of Alī Vardi Khān was to reduce Orissa, where the partizans of the late Nawāb held out under its Governor Murshid Kuli Khān, the son-in-law of Shuja-ud-dīn Khān. This was effected without much difficulty, but this remote province was always a centre of disaffection during his entire reign. In 1741 he was twice called away in person to take the field in Orissa; and on the second occasion, as he was returning in triumph to Murshidābād, he was surprised near Burdwān by the Marāthās. This is the first occasion on which these mounted marauders appeared in Bengal. The invaders consisted of 40,000 cavalry, and were sent by the Marātha chief of Berar to enforce his claim to the *chauth* or one-fourth part of the revenues. The small force that attended the Nawāb was utterly unable to cope with this army. It lost all its baggage, and through want of food was put to the greatest distress. After a three days' running fight, Kātwa was reached, where Alī Vardi Khān was rendered secure from further attack, owing to his command of the water communication. During the rainy season of 1741-42 the Marāthās remained in the neighbourhood, plundering far and wide, but did not dare to cross the Bhāgīrathi in any considerable numbers.

On one occasion, however, instigated by a renegade called Mīr Habīb, who had held high office under former Nawābs, they made an attempt upon the city of Murshidābād. The following account of this raid is given in the *Sair-ul-Mutākharin*. "Mīr Habīb, who had come a simple pedlar from Irān, his country, and was so low-bred as to be unable either to write or read, had now, by dint of merit and services, rendered himself considerable; he had found means to figure as a man fertile in expedients and a general of much resolution. He went so far as to tell the Marātha general that, if money was his object, he would undertake to find a great deal of it for him, and that he requested only the disposal of some thousand cavalry, with which force he would so far avail himself of Alī Vardi Khān's lying at Kātwa as to advance suddenly to Murshidābād, which is a city without walls, and without any defence, where, by plundering only Jagat Seth's* house, he would bring him money enough to satisfy all his wishes. This advice having been supported by a strong reasoning, Mīr Habīb was furnished with some thousand picked horse, and he departed immediately on his expedition. But this could not be done so secretly as that the Viceroy should not have intelligence of it; and as he knew the circumstances of his capital, and did not trust to the talents of either his brother or nephew for the defence of it, he determined to advance himself to its relief; and he set out directly with much expedition. But Mīr Habīb, having already performed the journey in a single day, was beforehand with him, and he had already plundered Jagat Seth's house, from whence he carried full two crores away, and also a quantity of other goods. Some other parts of the city † were also plundered; and Mīr Habīb, having advanced as far as his own lodgings, took away his own brother, Mīr Sharīf, but did not venture farther. For the Viceroy's palace, and also the quarter where lived his nephew, who was Deputy Governor, and likewise the quarter of Ata-ullah Khān, a general officer, were filled with too many troops to be liable to insult; and meanwhile, the enemy, hearing that the Viceroy was at hand, instantly departed from the city. It was about the middle of the day, and in the

* Raymond, the translator of the *Sair-ul-Mutākharin*, adds the following footnote: "This was Jagat Seth Alamchānd, the richest subject of the world. His house, which even now (1786) contains no less than two thousand souls, was plundered of full two crores two millions and a half sterling (and, what is singular, this was all in rupees struck at Arcot); but so amazing a loss which would distress any monarch in Europe affected him so little that he continued to give Government bills of exchange at sight of full one crore at a time; and this fact is too notorious in Bengal to need any proof."

† The *Riyazu-s-Salātin* states that Dahapāra was burnt down.

evening, the Viceroy arrived himself, to the universal joy of his friends, of his whole Court and of all his subjects. . .

"The Viceroy, whose forces had been greatly reduced both by a campaign of twelve months and by labour, sickness and famine, concluded that as the rainy season was at hand it would be too late to think of driving the Marāthās out of his country; and that the only part left for him was to content himself with conserving the city and its territory. He therefore came out and posted himself at some distance from it in a suburb called Amāniganj and Tārakpur. But by this time the rainy weather had set in; and the river of Bhāgīrathi ceasing to be fordable, Kātwa remained on the other side, and the country on the Murshidābād side was become safe from the enemy's incursions. But, then, the same circumstance afforded them a full opportunity of extending their ravages all over Burdwān and Midnapore, pushing their contributions as far as Balasore, and even this port fell in their hands. Nothing remained to Alī Vardi Khān but the city of Murshidābād and the countries on the other side of the Ganges. The peaceful inhabitants of this great capital, who, far from having ever seen such devastations, had not so much as heard of any such things, and whose city had not so much as the cover of a wall, became exceedingly fearful for their properties and families; and they availed themselves of the rainy season to cross over to the countries on the other side of the Ganges, such as Jahāngīrnagar, Mālda and Rāmpur-Boālia, where most of them built themselves houses, and where they passed their lives. Even the Deputy Governor himself, Nawāzish Muhammad Khān, crossed over with his family, furniture and wealth, and lived at Godāgari, which is one day's distance from the city, and where he laid the foundation of an habitation for himself and family. Alī Vardi Khān's furniture and effects were likewise sent over; from whence, however, the Deputy-Governor returned to the city, where he continued to live with his uncle Alī Vardi Khān."*

In October 1742, Alī Vardi Khān crossed the Bhāgīrathi by a bridge of boats, and defeated the Marāthās, who were encamped at Kātwa. Another raid on the district of Murshidābād followed. Bhāskar Pant, the Marātha general, sent a body of armed Bairāgis towards Bihar, and Alī Vardi Khān hastened to follow them. The Bairāgis then doubled back and swooped down on Murshidābād, but Alī Vardi Khān came upon them while they were busy looting Bāluchar and drove them out.†

* *Sair-ul-Mutākharin*, Vol. I, pages 393—396.

† *Rayazu-s-Salātin*, translation by Abdus Salām, p. 347.

From 1742 to 1751, with scarcely a break, Alī Vardi Khān was hard pressed both by the Marāthās and the Afghāns, as well as by the rebellions of his own generals and relatives. Bihar and Orissa were the two most unruly provinces, but it would be tedious to describe the revolts, battles and massacres of which they were the scene. Bengal seems to have remained tranquil and loyal to the Nawāb, and it is recorded that, on one occasion, during the Marātha wars, the zamīndārs advanced to him a crore and a half of rupees. In 1751, Alī Vardi Khān, now an old man, weary of the struggle with the Marāthās, came to terms by which he ceded the province of Orissa, and, in addition, agreed to pay them annually 12 lakhs of rupees as the *chauth* of Bengal. The five years from this date till his death formed the only quiet period of his reign. He died in April 1756 in his eightieth year, and was buried (according to his express wish, at the feet of his mother) in the garden of Khushbāgh, on the right bank of the Bhāgīrathi opposite Motijhil.

Relations with the English.

Stewart, in his *History of Bengal*, quotes a story, from which it would appear that Alī Vardi Khān's attitude to the English was pacific, and that he sought to avoid any conflict with them. Mustapha Khān, his principal general, endeavoured to prevail upon him to expel the English from Calcutta, and seize their wealth. Receiving no reply to his advice, he urged it again through the Nawāb's nephews, Nawāzish Muhammad and Saiyid Ahmad. Alī Vardi Khān still returned no answer, but shortly after said in private to the last named: "My child, Mustaphā Khān is a soldier, and wishes us to be constantly in need of his service; but how come you to join in his request? What have the English done against me that I should use them ill? It is now difficult to extinguish fire on land; but should the sea be in flames, who can put it out? Never listen to such advice as his, for the result would probably be fatal." "In consequence of these sentiments," continues Stewart, "the Europeans were little molested during his government, and were permitted to carry on their commerce according to the tenor of the *farmāns* they had received from the Emperor on making the usual present."

The documents quoted in Mr. Long's *Selections from Unpublished Records* shew, however, that on one occasion at least there was a serious quarrel between the Nawāb and the English. In 1749, an English man-of-war seized some vessels laden with the goods of various Hooghly merchants, Muhammadan and Armenian, and also containing things of value belonging to the Nawāb. Alī Vardi Khān sent a *parwana* to the Governor of Fort William, which concluded with the following menace: "As you are not permitted to commit piracies, therefore I now write you that, on receipt of this, you deliver up all the merchants' goods and effects to them, as also what appertains unto me, otherwise you may be assured a due chastisement in such manner as you least expect." The Council first attempted to pacify the Nawāb by the present of a fine Arab horse, and contemplated measures of retaliation against the Armenian merchants of Calcutta. It soon appeared, however, that Alī Vardi Khān was in earnest. He stopped the boats which were bringing down their goods, and cut off the supply of provisions at Dacca, reducing "the gentlemen" of that place to the greatest straits. He surrounded the factory at Cossimbazar with troops, and finally compelled the English to accept the terms which he dictated. "The English got off after paying to the Nawāb, through the Seths, twelve lakhs of rupees." On another occasion, Alī Vardi Khān demanded the estate of a Musalmān who had died at Calcutta intestate and without relatives. In 1751, after his claim had been paltered with for many years, he again threatened to order an attack on the factory at Cossimbazar. The Council forthwith paid over the value of the estate, and were compelled to add a further sum on account of interest.

Sirāj-ud-daula, 1756-57. Sirāj-ud-daula, or as the name is sometimes spelt Surajah Dowlah, was the grandson and spoilt darling of Alī Vardi Khān. The old Nawāb had nominated him as his successor several years before, and in 1752 or 1753, when Sirāj-ud-daula was only 15 years old, had even placed him on the *masnad*. The first act of Sirāj-ud-daula, when freed from restraint by the death of his grandfather, was to storm the palace at Motijhil, and to wrest from his aunt, Ghasīti Begam, the treasures which it contained. They amounted to 61 lakhs in gold and silver, while the value of the jewels, plate, elephants, etc., was as much more. These treasures had been accumulated by her husband, Nawāzish Khān, Governor at Dacca, who built for himself a stately palace on the Motijhil lake, which he ornamented with pillars of black marble brought from the ruins at Gaur. The young Nawāb next entered on a campaign against the English, whom he was resolved to drive out of the country. The war began in June 1756 with the capture of the residency at Cossimbazar, after which Sirāj-ud-daula marched upon and took Calcutta. It is unnecessary to repeat the oft-told story of the Black Hole, or to tell of the recapture of Calcutta by Clive. Suffice it to say that the war ended in February 1757, when Sirāj-ud-daula signed a treaty by which he restored to the English the goods and villages which he had seized, promised compensation for all that had been damaged or destroyed, recognized all their former privileges, and permitted them to establish a mint and erect fortifications. This treaty having been signed, a defensive alliance was concluded between the English and the Nawāb.

Capture of Cossimbazar.

A fuller description is required of the capture of Cossimbazar, which is an event of no little interest in the local history. Of this there is a full contemporary account in the Hastings MSS. which was first published by Mr. Beveridge in an article entitled *Old Places in Murshidābād*, which appeared in the Calcutta Review in 1892. The paper, which is by an unknown writer, begins with an account of Sirāj-ud-daula's accession, his ill-treatment of his aunt Ghasīti Begam, and his quarrel with the English. It then proceeds as follows—the footnotes are reproduced from Mr. Beveridge's article :—

"On Monday, 24th May 1756, in the afternoon, Omar Beg, a Jamadār, with his forces, about 3,000 horse, came to Cossimbazar by order of the Nawāb. On 25th, 200 horse and some *barkandāzes* reinforced him in the morning, and in the evening he was joined by two elephants and another body of forces, when he endeavoured to force his way in at the factory gate. But he was prevented by the Sergeant of the Guard calling the soldiers to arms, who, fixing their bayonets, kept the gateway. The Jamadār, finding he could not get in by surprise, told them he was not come to fight. The Chief (Mr. Watts) did his utmost to provide a quantity of provisions and water, during which he met with frequent obstructions. Upon more forces advancing, orders were given to load all the great guns with grape and round shot, and to keep a good look-out the whole night.

"*27th May.*—The drums and 8-o'clock gun silenced, and the gate kept shut, which before was always kept open the whole day, and upon the enemy's forces daily increasing, Dr. Forth was sent to the Jamadār to know the Nawāb's intentions, which, he informed them, were to attack the factory unless Mr. Watts went to him and signed such articles as he required. The Munshi, or Persian interpreter, brought Mr. Watts the same intelligence. At this time all provisions and water were entirely stopped, of which there was a great want, particularly of the former, as there were a great number of women, children, slaves and unnecessary persons in the factory, our complement of men consisting of 35 Europeans and as many black soldiers, with a few lascars, Messrs. William Watts, Collet and Batson of Council and Messrs. Sykes, H. Watts and Chambers, writers. Lieutenant Elliot commanded the artillery, as likewise the military, having his son under him as a volunteer.

"As it was apprehended, the Nawāb had no other intent than which the former Nawābs had had, viz., to stop the Company's business till his demands were complied with, by extorting a sum of money, letters were addressed him, written in the most submissive terms, to desire to know in what particulars the English had given him offence. But no other reply was sent than that they must pull down their fortifications, newly built at Perrin's * and the octagon summer house of Mr. Kelsall (which he had also taken for a fortification by a parcel of shells having been proved there from time to time), both places adjoining and within a league of Calcutta. By this time there was near 50,000 men round the factory, and 70 or 80 pieces of cannon planted against it on the opposite side, the river, but not near enough to do any execution.

"*1st June.*—Rādhāballabh † came to speak with Mr. Watts, and brought with him three Jamadārs, who all advised him to go to the Nawāb himself, and that everything might be very easily accommodated. Upon which he was weak enough to inform them, that if the Nawāb would send him a Beetle ‡ as a token for his safety and security, he would very willingly, and with pleasure, wait on him. Whereupon Rādhāballabh took leave and went away, and soon after brought him a Beetle on a silver dish from the Nawāb (at least, as he informed him), and in the evening (of) 2nd June, Mr. Watts and Dr. Forth went to the Nawāb in company with Hākim Beg's son, though the Military for a long time endeavoured to persuade him to the contrary, nay, even refused to let him go out of the factory. Upon Mr. Watts going before the Nawāb with his hands across, and a handkerchief wrapt round his wrists, signifying himself his slave and prisoner (this he was persuaded to do by Hākim Beg, Rādhāballabh and others, who assured him it might be a means of pacifying the Nawāb, his appearing before him in abject submissive manner), he abused him very much and ordered him to be taken out of his sight. But Hākim Beg's son telling the Nawāb he was a good sort of a man and intending, on hearing of his arrival from Rājmahāl, to have come and embraced his footsteps (*hāth bāndh ke sāhib kā qadambos karnā*), he ordered him to Hākim Beg's tent, where he signed a Mochalka and (was) made to send for Messrs. Collet and Batson for the same purpose. But on their arrival they were all three confined.

* The fortification called Perring's Point, and which was situated at what is now the mouth of the Baliaghāta, or Circular Canal, in Chitpur.

† Orme calls him Rai Dulub. He was the Dīwān.

‡ This is not a scarabæus, but a *pān* or *bira* (Piper betel).

The purport of the Mochalka was nearly as follows, viz.,—(1) to destroy the Redoubt, etc., newly built at Perrin's near Calcutta; (2) to deliver up any of his subjects that should fly to us for protection (to evade justice) on his demanding such subject; (3) to give an account of the *dastaks* for several years past, and to pay a sum of money that should be agreed on, for the bad use made of them, to the great prejudice of his revenues; and (4) to put a stop to the Zamīndār's* extensive power, to the great prejudice of his subjects.

"*4th June.*—Mr. Collet was sent back to Cossimbazar to deliver up the factory to the Nawāb, which was punctually put in execution, with all the guns, arms and ammunition, notwithstanding the soldiers were against it, and congratulated his return with the respect due only to a chief by drawing up in two lines for him to pass through.

"*5th June.*—Mr. Batson was sent back to Cossimbazar, and Mr. Collet demanded, when Mr. Watts and he were informed they must get ready to go with the Nawāb to Calcutta. This morning, upon opening the factory gates, the enemy immediately entered in great numbers and demanded the keys of the godowns, both public and private. They no sooner took possession of the arms and ammunition, but they behaved in a most insolent manner, threatening the gentlemen to cut off their ears, slit their noses, *chabuck* them, with other punishments, in order to extort confession and compliance from them. This behaviour of theirs lasted till the 8th, when Lieutenant Elliot, having secreted a pair of pistols, shot himself through the head. The gentlemen's surprise was so great that they instantly sent and informed the Diwān of what had passed, thinking by that means to procure themselves better treatment. He was then searching and examining the soldiers' boxes and chests in order to return to them their clothes and apparel. But on hearing this news, he ordered all the Europeans out of the factory, and put them under a strong guard at Mr. Collet's house, where they all remained that night, except Messrs. Sykes and Batson who happily found means to make their escape and get to the French factory.

"*The 9th.*—All the prisoners were sent to Muxadavad Cutcherry and put in irons, where they remained; except (that), after 15 days' confinement, Messrs. H. Watts and Chambers were permitted to go to either the French or Dutch factories, provided those gentlemen would give a receipt for them, to be responsible for their appearance when demanded by the Nawāb.

* This must mean the Zamīndār of Calcutta, viz., Mr. Holwell.

"*10th July.*—The military were set at liberty. As for the two gentlemen* who were sent to the Aurangs from Cossimbazar, they were also released about the same time but plundered, as those at the factory were, of everything they had."

The MS. account gives the following description of the factory and of the events which led to its capture: "The factory is situated close to the riverside, and consists of four bastions† mounting each ten guns, nine and six pounders, also two eighteen pounders to defend the gateway, and a line of 22 guns, mostly field-pieces, towards the water side. Some time before Cossimbazar was attacked (but preparations only making for it), Mr. Watts acquainted the Governor and Council that he was told from the Darbār, by order of the Nawāb, that he had great reason to be dissatisfied with the late conduct of the English in general. Besides, he had heard they were building new fortifications near Calcutta without ever applying to him or consulting him about it, which he by no means approved of, for he looked upon us only as a Sett of Merchants, and therefore if we chose to reside in his dominions under that denomination we were extremely welcome, but as Prince of the Country he forthwith insisted on the demolition of all those new buildings we had made. The Nawāb at the same time sent, to the President and Council, Fuckeer Tougar‡ with a message much to the same purport, which as they did not intend to comply with, looking upon it as a most unprecedented demand, treated the messenger with a great deal of ignominy and turned him out of their bounds without any answer at all; upon which a second messenger was sent to Mr. Drake to this effect, that unless upon receipt of that order he did not immediately begin and pull down those fortifications, he would come down himself and throw him in the river. This messenger was treated as ridiculously as the other, and an answer sent agreeable thereto, as likewise by a messenger that was sent some time before to demand the delivery up of Kissendasseat. In the meantime we received intelligence that Cossimbazar factory was surrounded with a large body of forces and a great quantity of cannon, but the Council were determined not to submit to the terms proposed, accordingly directed the Chief at Cossimbazar to make the best defence he could, and promised him succour as soon as the season would admit of it."

* Doubtless Hastings was one of them.

† There is a rough plan of the fort in Tieffenthaler, Vol. I, p. 453, plate XXXI.

‡ Fakhar Tajar (properly Fakhr-ul-Tajar), the glory of merchants, a title, I believe, of the Armenian merchant Khwāja Wajid, on account of his salt monopoly.

In the Hastings MSS. there is another paper by Captain Grant, acting Adjutant-General, which gives an account of the defences of Cossimbazar. It runs:—

"The surrender of Cossimbazar on the 4th June by the Chief's being decoyed under many specious pretences to visit the Nawāb in the camp before that place, and on his being made prisoner, induced to deliver it up, you must be informed of ere now, we having despatched Patamars (couriers) as soon as we received the news on the 7th. We may justly impute all our misfortunes to the loss of that place, as it not only supplied our enemies with artillery and ammunition of all kinds, but flushed them with hopes of making as easy a conquest of our chief settlement, not near so defensible in its then circumstances. Cossimbazar is an irregular square with solid bastions, each mounting 10 guns, mostly nine and six lbs., with a saluting battery on the curtain to the riverside of 24 guns, from 2 to 4 lbs., and their carriages, when I left the place in October last in pretty good order. Besides, eight Cohorn mortars, four and five inches, with a store of shells and grenades. Their garrison consisted of 50 military under the command of Lieutenant Elliot, a Sergeant Corporal and 3 Matrossy (*sic.*) of the artillery and 20 good lascars. The ramparts are seen by two houses which lay within 20 yards of the walls; but as each is commanded by 5 guns from the bastions, the enemy could hardly keep possession of them".

In the interval between the capture of Calcutta and its recapture by Clive, Sirāj-ud-daula found time to crush a rival claimant of the Viceroyalty of Bengal. This was his cousin Shaukat Jang, Nawāb of Purnea, whose pretensions had some solid basis, for he had received from the Grand Vizier of the Emperor authority to take over the government of Bengal on condition that he sent the treasures of Sirāj-ud-daula to Delhi and paid three crores of rupees annually as revenue. He had a backing at Murshidābād, where a conspiracy for the overthrow of Sirāj-ud-daula was set on foot by the discontented courtiers, headed by Mir Jafar Khān, who had been dismissed from his post as Bakshi or Paymaster-General. The plot proved abortive, for in a battle fought in the Purnea district on 16th October 1756, Shaukat Jang was killed and his forces dispersed by Sirāj-ud-daula. Sirāj-ud-daula had now no rival to fear: in the words of *Sair-ul-Mutākharin*—"The rash valour of the young Nawāb of Purnea, in delivering Sirāj-ud-daula from the only enemy he had to fear in the country, made it clear to all Bengal that the English were the only power which could bring about the change that everyone was longing for."

Downfall of Sirāj-ud-daula.

Next year a more formidable confederacy was formed, the parties to which were the English Council on the one hand and Mīr Jafar Khan, Jagat Seth, the State banker, and Rādhāballabh (Rai Dulub), the late Dīwān, on the other. They entered into a compact to depose Sirāj-ud-daula and set up in his stead Mīr Jafar, who was to grant the English valuable privileges and distribute large sums of money among them as the price of his elevation. The plot at one time seemed in danger of being exposed by Omichand, one of the intermediaries. This man had advanced a claim of 30 lakhs compensation for the losses he had sustained when Calcutta was taken, and now threatened to inform the Nawāb of the plot unless it was satisfied. Clive closed Omichānd's mouth by means of a machiavellian trick. He had two treaties drawn up, one on white paper and the other on red. The latter guaranteed Omichand's claim and was shown to him. The former, which was the real treaty, contained no such stipulation and was not shown to Omichand. Admiral Watson, who had not the easy political conscience of the other conspirators, refused to sign the sham treaty, and his signature was forged.

On 15th June 1757, Clive advanced against Murshidābād, and ten days later won the battle of Plassey. Sirāj-ud-daula escaped from the battle and fled back to his palace at Murshidābād, and thence to Bhagwāngola, when he embarked. Near Rājmahāl he was recognized by a *fakīr*, whose ears and nose he had had cut off for some real or imaginary offence. This man promptly disclosed the identity of the refugee to the local Governor, who was a brother of Mīr Jafar, and the latter had him arrested and taken back to Murshidābād. There the wretched captive was assassinated in the house of Mīr Jafar by order of his savage son, Mirān. His corpse was placed on an elephant and, after being paraded past his mother's house and through the city, was buried in the cemetery of Alī Vardi Khān at Khushbāgh. Thus miserably perished Sirāj-ud-daula in his twentieth year of his life, when he had been on his throne only 15 months.

Mīr Jafar Khān, 1757-61.

On 29th June 1757, six days after the battle of Plassey, Clive entered the city of Murshidābād, escorted by a guard of 200 Europeans and 300 Sepoys, and took possession of the palace and garden of Murādbāgh, which had been allotted as his residence. On the same day he visited the Nawāb's palace at Mansurganj and in the hall of audience took Mīr Jafar by the hand, led him to the empty *masnad* of Sirāj-ud-daula and seated him thereon. He then presented him with a salver of gold *mohurs*, and congratulated him on his accession to the government of Bengal, Bihār and Orissa.

After this came the division of the spoils of victory. A meeting was held at Jagat Seth's house, at which Omichand was told that the red treaty was a sham and that he was to get nothing. The other conspirators received enormous sums, but, large as they were, they were small in comparison with the amounts demanded as compensation for the losses sustained by the Company and the inhabitants of Calcutta, and as largess for the army and naval squadron. The treasury, which contained 1½ crores, was unequal to the drain upon it, and the English had to be content with the payment of half the stipulated sums and a promise of the remainder in three annual instalments. Mīr Jafar thus commenced his rule with an empty exchequer, and he had not the vigour of character necessary to replenish it. Preferring the pleasures of the zenāna to the cares of government, he merely sought to maintain himself by a policy of subserviency, which earned for him the sobriquet of "Clive's jackass." The ordinary administration and the collection of the revenue remained in a disorganized state. Not only did he fail to pay off the arrears due to the English, but allowed the troops to go unpaid. In 1761 they broke out into mutiny and besieged the Nawāb in his palace at Murshidābād. The English, tired of his incompetency, promptly ordered him to Calcutta and set up his son-in-law, Mīr Kāsim Alī Khān, in his stead.

Mīr Kāsim, 1761-63.

Mīr Kāsim (Meer Cossim), who had won his way to the throne by means of intrigues at Calcutta, distributed 20 lakhs among the members of Council as the price of his elevation, and also assigned the Company the revenues of the districts of Burdwān, Midnapore and Chittagong. One of his first measures was to remove the seat of government from Murshidābād to Monghyr, where he commanded the line of communication with the north-west. "Leaving his uncle, Mīr Turāb Alī Khān, as Deputy Nāzim at Murshidābād, Mīr Kāsim took with him all his effects, his elephants, horses and treasures, comprising cash and jewelleries of the harem, and even the gold and silver decorations of the Imāmbāra, amounting to several lakhs in value, and bade farewell to the country of Bengal." At Monghyr he remodelled his army on European lines and began to intrigue with the Nawāb of Oudh. He also took steps to introduce order and system in the administration, and effected such reforms in the financial department, that within eighteen months he discharged the whole of his pecuniary obligations to the English, and satisfied both his own and his predecessor's troops.

From the first he seems to have resolved to establish his independence, and to reduce the English to the position which they occupied in the days of Alī Vardi Khān. The rupture with the English was not long delayed, but its immediate cause may be distinctly traced to the rapacity of the Company's servants. They laid claim to an absolute freedom from transit duties in all departments of their trade, not only for the operations of the Company, but also for the speculations of each individual. These pretensions could not be resisted, and the state of affairs that resulted is thus described by Mr. Verelst, who was himself in Bengal at the time (*View of Bengal*, pp. 8 and 46) :—"At this time many black merchants found it expedient to purchase the name of any young writer in the Company's service by loans of money, and under this sanction harassed and oppressed the natives. . . . A trade was carried on without payment of duties, in the prosecution of which infinite oppressions were committed. English agents or *gumāshtas*, not content with injuring the people, trampled on the authority of Government, binding and punishing the Nawāb's officers whenever they presumed to interfere. This was the immediate cause of the war with Mīr Kāsim."

Mr. Vansittart was at this time Governor of Fort William, and it should be recorded in his honour that he opposed the system which permitted these abuses. He found, however, only a single supporter in the Council, the great Warren Hastings. The latter was so out-spoken in his protests against the system by which the people were being oppressed, that he was subjected to insult by his brother-councillors. He was charged, together with the Governor, in a minute delivered by Mr. Batson, "with acting the part rather of a retained solicitor of the Nawāb than of a servant of the Company or a British subject." An altercation ensued. Mr. Batson gave him the lie, and struck him in the presence of the Board. Within less than a month, war was declared against the Nawāb by the majority of the Council, while both the Governor and Warren Hastings stood neutral. But the news of the expulsion of the English from Patna arrived at this time, and Warren Hastings recorded his altered views in the following minute :—"It was my resolution, as soon as a war should be declared, to resign the Company's service, being unwilling to join in giving authority to past measures of which I disapproved . . . . But since our late melancholy advices, it is my intention to join my endeavours for the good of the service as long as the war shall last."

The immediate cause of hostilities was as follows. Mīr Kāsim, after much negotiation, had agreed to a convention, which was also accepted by Mr. Vansittart, the Governor, that a duty of only 9 per cent. should be paid by Englishmen, which was much below the rate exacted from other traders. This convention, however, was repudiated by the Council at Calcutta. The Nawāb, in retaliation, resolved to abandon all duties whatever on the transit of goods, and to throw open the trade of the country. This resolution was even more disagreeable to the Company's servants than the convention. A deputation, consisting of Mr. Hay and Mr. Amyatt, was despatched to Monghyr, but the negotiations were infructuous. The Nawāb seized some boats laden with arms for the Patna factory as they were passing up the Ganges under the walls of Monghyr. Mr. Ellis surprised and took the city of Patna; and Mr. Amyatt, who was on his return to Calcutta by river, was attacked by the people of the Nawāb and massacred with all his attendants. The scene of this tragedy was the beautiful reach of the Bhāgīrathi between Murshidābād and Cossimbazar, which also is the *mise-en-scene* of *Chandra Sekhar*, the well-known novel of Bankim Chandra Chatterji.

The war opened favourably for the Nawāb. The English at Patna were attacked while scattered through the town, overpowered, and taken prisoners. The whole of Bengal as far south as the present district of Nadia was occupied by his levies. The Cossimbazar factory was taken by storm, and the survivors sent to Monghyr to join the English prisoners from Patna. The successes of the Nawāb ended as soon as the English could put their forces in the field. A small army under Major Adams recovered possession of Murshidābād, carrying the enemy's lines at Motijhil, and then encountered the main body of the Nawāb's forces at Giria near Suti. Though Major Adams had only 3,000 men under him, and the enemy numbered 20,000 horse and 8,000 foot, drilled and equipped in European fashion, he boldly attacked them and, after an obstinate fight of four hours, completely defeated them. He obtained a second victory at Udhua Nullah, after which the Nawāb retired to Patna, where he had his English prisoners massacred. Patna was taken by the English in November 1763, and Mīr Kāsim took refuge with the Nawāb of Oudh. His hopes of restoration were finally shattered by the battle of Buxar, and he died, in indigence and obscurity, in 1777; the cost of his funeral is said to have been defrayed by the sale of two shawls, which formed his sole property.

The end of Mughal rule.

On the first outbreak of hostilities, the English had resolved to depose Mīr Kāsim, and to place a more complaisant Nawāb on the *masnad*. Negotiations were accordingly opened with

Mīr Jafar, who was residing for the sake of safety at Calcutta. He was willing to consent to every demand made upon him, and was accordingly reinstalled at Murshidābād in July 1763. The price of this new revolution amounted to more than £1,700,000; and, in addition, the Company's servants gained their main object, the exemption of their own goods from all duties and the reimposition of the old charges upon all traders but themselves. Mīr Jafar gained but little by his abject submissiveness, except the transmission of the title to his family. He was already broken by age and disease, and died in January 1765, leaving a legacy of five lakhs to Clive, whom he called the "light of his eyes:" with this sum Clive started a fund for officers and soldiers invalided in the service of the East India Company.

Nāzim-ud-daula, the eldest surviving son of Mīr Jafar, was chosen by the English to succeed his father. He was about 20 years of age at this time, and died within three years; but his short rule witnessed one more of the steps by which the Muhammadan power was gradually superseded. In May 1765, Lord Clive arrived at Calcutta with full power as Commander-in-Chief, President, and Governor in Bengal. Within two months after landing he proceeded to Murshidābād, and there effected a settlement of the relations between the Nawāb and the Company. The Nawāb was required to resign the management of the revenues and the command of his troops—in short, to make over the *subāhdāri* to the Company. An annual sum of *sikka* Rs. 53,86,131 was allowed to him for the expenses of his court and the administration of justice. He was further required to submit to the control of a board of advisers in all his affairs. This board was composed of Rājā Dulabh Rām, Jagat Seth, and Muhammad Reza Khān; and, in addition, an officer of the Company was always to reside at Murshidābād and exercise a general superintendence as Resident at the Darbār. The character of the young prince may be realized from the joy with which he accepted these proposals. "Thank God," he exclaimed, "I shall now have as many dancing girls as I like.*"

Lord Clive next proceeded to the English camp in the north-west, and there, on 12th August 1765, received in person

* The rent-roll, which he abandoned with a light heart, is estimated in Grant's *Analysis of the Finances of Bengal* at Rs. 2,56,24,223. To this total, which was the revenue of Bengal proper alone, there must be added 65 lakhs proceeding from Bihār, and 11 lakhs more as the annual revenue of Midnapore, which was then the only portion of Orissa which recognised Muhammadan authority. The total effective income of Bengal with its dependencies in 1765 was about three crores and 32 lakhs of *sikka* rupees, or nearly 3¼ millions sterling.

from the Emperor, Shāh Alam, the grant of the Dīwāni or financial administration of Bengal, Bihar and Orissa. Thus was instituted the dual system of government by which the English, as Dīwān, received the revenues and undertook to maintain the army, while the Nawāb, as Nāzim, remained vested with the criminal jurisdiction: the actual collection of the revenues, however, still remained for seven more years in the hands of Indian officials.

In the following year Lord Clive took his seat as Dīwān at Motijhil and in concert with the Nawāb, who sat as Nāzim, opened the *punya* or ceremony of commencing the annual collections of revenue, in full Darbār. On 8th May 1766, a few days after this ceremony, Nāzim-ud-daula died suddenly, and was succeeded by Saif-ud-daula, his brother, a youth of sixteen. By the treaty with the Company which placed him on the *masnad*, his annual "stipend" was fixed at *sikka* Rs. 41,86,131. He died of small-pox in 1769, the year of the great famine, and Mubārak-ud-daula, another son of Mīr Jafar, a child of a few years of age, was appointed Nawāb. On his accession, the Governor and Council of Fort William agreed to pay him an annual "stipend" of *sikka* Rs. 31,81,991, but in 1771 the Court of Directors, under the pressure of pecuniary embarrassments, availing themselves of the plea of his childhood, ordered it to be reduced to sixteen lakhs of rupees, at which sum it stood until 1882.

The Court of Directors in England had now resolved on a new policy, to which the infancy of the Nawāb readily lent itself. They determined to "stand forth as Dīwān, and by the agency of the Company's servants to take upon themselves the entire care and management of the revenues." This resolution was formed in 1771, and Warren Hastings, the first Governor-General of Bengal, was to carry it into effect. On 13th April 1772, he arrived in Calcutta, and before that month was out, the great reform had been effected. Muhammad Reza Khān, the Naib Dīwān at Murshidābād, and Rājā Shitāb Rai, who filled the same office at Patna, were both suddenly arrested and brought down as prisoners to Calcutta. Their offices were abolished, and the Council, with Hastings at its head, was constituted a Board of Revenue, assisted by an Indian functionary who was termed Rai Rayān. The exchequer and treasury were removed to Calcutta and also the Nizāmat Sadar Adālat, or Supreme Criminal Court, over which the President and Council assumed control. But it was soon found that this additional duty involved too great a responsibility, and in October 1775 the

Court of Nizāmat Adālat was moved back to Murshidābād, and again placed under the control of Muhammad Reza Khān as Naib Nāzim. There was yet one more step to be taken. Lord Cornwallis, in 1790, announced that he had "resolved to accept the superintendence of the administration of criminal justice throughout the provinces." The Nizāmat Adālat was a second time transferred from Murshidābād to Calcutta, to consist of the Governor-General and members of the Supreme Council assisted by the chief Indian law officers, and (in 1793) four Courts of Circuit, each superintended by a covenanted servant of the Company, were established for the trial of cases not punishable by the Magistrates.

The only function of Government that remained to the Muhammadans was thus transferred directly into English hands. The city of Murshidābād ceased to bear the semblance of a capital; and the Nawāb lost the last shadow of his authority. From this date the words of Lord Macaulay become strictly applicable. "The heir of Mīr Jafar still resides at Murshidābād, the ancient capital of his house, still bears the title of Nawāb, is still accosted by the English as 'Your Highness,' and is still suffered to retain a portion of the regal state which surrounded his ancestors. A pension is annually paid to him by the Government . . . . But he has not the smallest share of political power, and is in fact only a noble and wealthy subject."

Early British Administration.

Revenue Councils.

For some time after the acquisition of the Dīwāni by the East India Company, the direct revenue administration remained in the hands of the Musalmān officials, but a Resident was stationed at Murshidābād to be present at the Darbār of the Nawāb and to control the finances. In 1769 English officers, called Supervisors, were appointed by Mr Verelst with powers of superintending the officers actually engaged in collecting the revenue. The supreme revenue authority was the Select Committee, which corresponded directly with the Supervisors, but in the districts of Bengal proper the Resident at the Darbār, who at this time was Mr. Richard Becher, exercised a good deal of authority over them and appears to have referred little to Calcutta. Towards the end of the year 1770 two new bodies called Comptrolling Councils of Revenue were set up at Murshidābād and Patna with superior authority over the Supervisors. That at Murshidābād consisted of Richard Becher, who was Chief, and three other members, viz., John Reed, James Laurell and John Graham. Muhammad Reza Khān, the Naib Dīwān, also attended the meetings regularly. Becher being ill at Balasore when the Comptrolling Council was constituted, Mr. Reed presided over the first meeting, which was held on 27th September 1770. Becher arrived at Murshidābād on 12th November and three days later presided over the Council for the first time, but retired from the post on 24th December 1770. The Comptrolling Council which was in fact an intermediate revenue authority, continued to exercise power for two years, subject to the control of the Select Committee until April 1771, and then of the Comptrolling Committee of Revenue, which was now appointed with supreme authority in revenue matters. It met for the last time in September 1772. On 10th October 1772 the Comptrolling Committee was superseded by the Revenue Board, which, under the recommendation of the Committee of Circuit at Murshidābād, was to consist of the whole Council at Calcutta.

The Committee of Circuit.

In 1772, soon after Warren Hastings first took his seat as President of Council, it was decided to appoint a committee, of which he was to be President, "to make a settlement in certain districts of the Bengal Soubadary." The Committee of Circuit started in June 1772, as appears from a letter of Warren Hastings (quoted in Gleig's *Memoirs of Warren Hastings*, Volume I, page 260), in which he says: "On the 3rd June I set out with the Committee. We made the first visit to Kissennagor, the capital of Nadia, and formed the settlement of that district, farming it in divisions for five years. We proceeded next to the city, where we arrived till the last of the month." The Committee, which first sat at Krishnagar on the 10th of June, consisted of Warren Hastings as President and Philip Milner Dacres, James Laurell and John Graham. Samuel Middleton, who was one of the members, could not attend, as he was busy in "the city," *i.e.*, Murshidābād, getting together the necessary papers for the settlement of the "Huzoor Zillahs." The district of Nadia having been duly settled, the Committee went on to Cossimbazar, where they were joined by Mr. Middleton. The first meeting of the Committee at Cossimbazar, of which there is a record, was held on 7th July, and the last on 17th September 1772. Warren Hastings left the Committee on the 14th September to proceed to Calcutta, while Samuel Middleton remained behind to take up his new appointments as Resident at the Darbar, Collector of Rājshāhi, and Chief of Cossimbazar; and the circuit was continued by Messrs. Dacres, Laurell and Graham. During the time the Committee sat at Murshidābād it resolved on many important measures, the execution of which changed the system of revenue administration.

The Resident.

Between 1772, when the Comptrolling Council of Revenue at Murshidābād was dissolved, and 1774, when the Provincial

Council of Revenue at Murshidābād was constituted, the Resident at the Darbār (Samuel Middleton) had charge of the collections of the districts which had already been controlled from Murshidābād and occupied a position that was practically that of a Commissioner, as all the Collectors of the districts concerned ("Chunacolly, Luskerpore, Ruckenpore, Rajmahal, Purnea, Dinajpore, Jahangirpore") corresponded through him with headquarters. The Resident continued to exercise these powers till December 1773, and it was not till February 1775, when Edward Baber, the then Resident at the Darbār, became Chief of the Provincial Council of Revenue, that the Resident became solely a Political Agent.

Appointment of Collectors. In 1772 it was decided that the English Supervisors should be designated Collectors, and an Indian officer, with the title of Dīwān, was attached to each for the joint control of the revenues. Next year, it having been resolved that the Collectors should be withdrawn from their districts and replaced by Indian *āmils*, a new system of control was formulated. In Bengal it was decided to establish—(1) A Committee of Revenue at the Presidency, consisting of two members of Council and three other senior officers, for conducting the current business of the collections of the metropolitan districts with the Ray Rayān as Dīwān. (2) Councils of Revenue, consisting of a Chief and four senior officers with an Indian Dīwān, at Burdwān, Murshidābād, Dinājpore and Dacca. The Murshidābād Provincial Council of Revenue was to deal with the following districts: "Radshahy East and West divisions, Rackenpore, Chunacolly, Luskerpore, Jahanguirpore, Khas Talooks, Rajmahal and Boglipore including the annexations lately made to the latter from Monghyr, Carrickpore, Jungletery, and districts under the management of Mr. Brooke."*

The Provincial Councils, which started work in 1774, were abolished in 1781, when their functions were transferred to a new Committee of Revenue at Calcutta, and Collectorships were reinstituted, the President of each of the Provincial Councils officiating as Collector under the Committee's control. The designation of the Committee of Revenue was changed to Board of Revenue in 1786, and at the same time the Collector was vested with the powers of Civil Judge and Magistrate. In the city of Murshidābād, however, separate arrangements were made, there being a District Court, superintended by a Judge and Magistrate, for the administration of justice within its limits.

* I am indebted for the information contained in the above account of early British administration to a report on the Records of Bengal by Mr. A. P. Muddiman, C.I.E.

At this time the zamīndāris of Bīrbhūm and Bishnupur (now in the districts of Bīrbhūm and Bānkura) were included in the jurisdiction of the Collector of Murshidābād. They formed the most difficult part of his charge, for the land had suffered grievously from the great famine of 1770, and distress and destitution drove the people to acts of lawlessness and violence, in which disbanded soldiers lent willing and expert assistance. Armed bands roved through the country, and in May 1785 the Collector was forced to report that the civil authorities were "destitute of any force capable of making head against such an armed multitude." He therefore asked for troops to act against the banditti, who were gathered in bands four hundred strong. Next month their number had risen to "near a thousand people," and they were preparing for an organised raid on the lowlands. The state of affairs was even worse next year, for the marauders had established permanent camps and even intercepted the revenue on its way to the treasury. It was clear that the system under which two such distant tracts as Bīrbhūm and Bishnupur were administered from Murshidābād could continue no longer, and that they required a responsible officer who could deal with them on the spot. Accordingly, in November 1786, Mr. Foley was sent to Bīrbhūm and Mr. Pye to Bishnupur, and in 1787 the two were united in one district, Mr. Pye being "confirmed Collector of Bishenpore in addition to Beerbhoom heretofore superintended by G. R. Foley, Esq."*

The first organized outbreak of the sepoys in the Mutiny of 1857 took place at Berhampore, which at the time was cantoned by the 19th Regiment of Native Infantry, a corps of irregular cavalry, and two 6-pounder guns manned by native gunners. The following account of the outbreak is quoted from Forrest's *History of the Indian Mutiny*:—"The rumours regarding the greased cartridge did not take long in reaching Berhampore. Early in February, a Brāhman pay-havildār, a man of good character, said to Colonel Mitchell, commanding the 19th Regiment Native Infantry: 'What is this story everybody is talking about, that Government intends making the native army use cows' and pigs' fat with the ammunition for their new rifles?' Colonel Mitchell asked him if he believed there was any truth in the report; he replied he could not believe it. On the 24th of February, a small detachment of the 34th Native Infantry reached the station, and they were anxiously questioned by the men of the 19th as to the truth of the story regarding the greased cartridges. What they heard re-awakened their fears. Next

MUTINY OF 1857.

* Hunter's *Annals of Rural Bengal.*

day, when Colonel Mitchell ordered a parade for exercise with blank ammunition for the following morning, the men refused to receive the percussion caps served out to them in the evening, saying 'there was a doubt how the cartridges were prepared.' Upon receipt of this intelligence, Colonel Mitchell went down with the Adjutant to the lines, and called up all the native commissioned officers in front of the quarter-guard, and explained to them that the cartridges about to be served out in the morning were the cartridges made up by the 7th Regiment Native Infantry upwards of a year ago, and that they had better tell the men of their companies that those who refused to obey the orders of their officers were liable to the severest punishment. Two of the native officers afterwards swore that he said that they must take the cartridges, otherwise they would be sent to Burma or China where they would die; but the statement was contradicted by their commanding officer. Colonel Mitchell, after ordering a morning parade of all the troops, returned home. About ten or eleven at night, as he was falling asleep, he heard the sound of drums and shouts proceeding from the lines. 'I dressed immediately, went over to my Adjutant's quarters, and directed him to assemble all the officers at my quarters quietly. I then went to Captain Alexander, and directed him to bring his cavalry as soon as possible into cantonments, and to be ready at some distance on the right of our lines. I then went to the artillery lines and got the detachment of artillery, guns and ammunition ready for immediate action. I must explain that by the time I got to the Adjutant's quarters, the drill-havildār of the regiment was making his way to the Adjutant's quarters. I asked what was the disturbance in the lines; he said the regiment had broken open the bells-of-arms, and had forcibly taken possession of their arms and ammunition, and that they had loaded their muskets. As soon as I got the cavalry and artillery ready, I marched down with the officers of the regiments to the lines. I found the men in undress formed in line and shouting. Some voices among them called on 'Do not come on, the men will fire.'

"Colonel Mitchell then loaded the guns with grape, and, leaving them in range, dismounted some of the troopers, and marched down on the men. He sounded the officers' call, on which a number of native officers and sepoys surrounded him. He demanded the meaning of the disturbance. The native officers made all kinds of excuses, begging that he would not be violent with the men. He then addressed them, and pointed out the absurdity of their fears and the gravity of their offence.

'I told the officers they must immediately call upon the men to lay down their arms; the native officers told me the men would not do so in the presence of the guns and cavalry, but if I would withdraw them, they would go quietly to their lines. This was about three in the morning. I ordered a parade at sunrise, and retired, sending the cavalry to their lines and the guns to the magazine.' The next morning the regiment fell in for parade without a symptom of insubordination. After inspection, Colonel Mitchell had the Articles of War read to the men, saluted the colours, and dismissed them.

"The action of Colonel Mitchell was severely criticised at the time. It has been urged that he should have made no concession to the demand of sepoys with arms in their hands and in open mutiny. Colonel Mitchell, however, in his defence before the court of inquiry held to investigate his conduct, maintained that he made no compromise with the men, and that before he ordered the guns and cavalry off, the native officers declared to him that some of the companies had lodged their arms, and that the rest were doing so. The Governor-General, in his minute referring to the proceedings of the court, remarked: 'It is no doubt true that there was no arranged bargain between Lieutenant-Colonel Mitchell and his men; but whereas it was his duty to listen to no proposals, and to accept no assurances, until he had satisfied himself, through his European officers, that every musket in the ranks was laid down, he did yield to representations made on behalf of a regiment in mutiny, with arms in its hands, and he did so in order to obtain from them that which he ought to have exacted as an act of obedience. It is impossible not to view the mode in which Lieutenant-Colonel Mitchell withdrew the coercing force as a triumph to the mutinous sepoys." It must, however, be borne in mind that Colonel Mitchell had only 200 men to coerce 800 sepoys, and, as he told the court of inquiry, he was uncertain 'whether, if it came to a fight, we were able to coerce the men of the 19th Native Infantry, and that I was in consequence exceedingly desirous of avoiding a collision.' The subsequent career of the native cavalry and artillery renders it probable that had Colonel Mitchell resorted to force, the men would have joined the revolted regiment, and therefore the course he adopted may be regarded as prudent. But the Indian Empire was won by rash and daring deeds."

After this brief *emeute*, the sepoys remained quiet and continued to discharge their duties without any insubordination. So far indeed from attempting to break out again, they submitted a petition to the Governor-General offering to proceed to China or to serve anywhere on land or sea, if they were pardoned. Their previous insubordination could not, however, be overlooked, and, as a punishment, they were marched down to Barrackpore and there disbanded on 31st March. No further trouble was experienced in the cantonment or in the town of Murshidābād, though some seditious placards were posted up in the latter, until 23rd June, when a panic broke out owing to a rumour that the 63rd Native Infantry and the 11th Irregular Cavalry, which were cantoned there, had mutinied. Quiet was soon restored, and further confidence was given to the people by the despatch to Berhampore of detachments of two European regiments (Her Majesty's 84th and 25th), of whom part were sent by steamer to Alātoli (Bhagwāngola) on the right bank of the Ganges, and thence conveyed by elephants and carriages rapidly and secretly to their destination. The remainder were sent up in brake-vans with four horses each, and, notwithstanding the difficulty of rapid travelling during the rainy season, arrived speedily and unexpectedly at Berhampore. At the end of December there was again some suspicion of the loyalty of the sepoys at Berhampore, and a body of 100 European sailors was therefore sent up as a precautionary measure; but these fears proved groundless. In his final minute on the Mutiny the Lieutenant-Governor, Sir F. J. Halliday, summarized the position as follows:—"Berhampore, garrisoned by native troops, both cavalry and infantry, was rescued from threatened danger, first by the rapid despatch of European troops by land and by steamer, and secondly by the prompt and well-conceived measures for disarming the native garrison."

FORMATION OF THE DISTRICT. It has already been mentioned that the zamīndāris of B hūm and Bishnupur, which now form a large part of the present districts of Bīrbhūm and Bānkura, were included in Murshidābād, but were formed into an independent district in 1787. Other considerable changes appear to have taken place at the same time. In 1786, Mr. Dawson, then Chief of Murs idābād, declared that his jurisdiction was become "so changed from what it formerly was, that had I all the plans that at various times have been made thereof before me, it would be difficult to point out with any degree of accuracy my mutilated Chiefship, so intersected it is and interspersed." The former pre-eminence of Murshidābād came to be so far forgotten, that in 1806 it seems to have been proposed to do away with it altogether as a separate Collectorate. The office of Judge and Magistrate of the district of Murshidābād was for the time abolished, but in the end "it was deemed inadvisable to transfer the collections of Murshidābād to the charge of the Collector of Bīrbhūm." The result of these many changes was to cause discrepancies between the areas comprised under the revenue and the criminal jurisdiction. The revenue area depended upon the old *parganas* or fiscal divisions, which continued to pay their revenue into the treasury of the district to which they were attached, however subdivided and scattered they might have become. The area of the criminal jurisdiction was determined simply by motives of administrative convenience and the necessity of more effectually suppressing of crime in remote parts of the district.

The difficulties caused by these anomalies of jurisdiction long continued, chiefly on the southern and western frontiers of the district. The Revenue Surveyor in 1857 stated that he had found in Murshidābād lands belonging to estates that paid revenue to the Collectorates of Dacca and the 24-Parganas. In 1870 it was reported:—"The boundary line to the west is most confused, lands belonging to one district being frequently found within the boundary of another. In fact, boundary-line on this side there is none. The question whether a particular village belongs to Murshidābād or to Bīrbhūm has often to be decided by a reference to the survey records." At the same period, there were no less than 18 *parganas* which were altogether beyond the civil and magisterial jurisdiction of Murshidābād, but in which most of the villages were subject to the fiscal authority of its revenue officials.

In the year 1872 important rectifications of the boundary were effected between Murshidābād and Bīrbhūm, and the old sources of perplexity were in large part removed. By a notification of Government, dated 11th February 1875, and published in the *Calcutta Gazette* of the 24th of that month, the north-eastern, eastern, and south-eastern boundaries were fixed by the flowing streams of the Ganges or Padma and the Jalangi; and such villages of the district of Mālda as lay to the right bank of the former river were transferred to Murshidābād. The boundaries on the south were also simplified. A very extensive change was also effected on the west, where thirty-nine villages were transferred to Murshidābād from Bīrbhūm, and seven villages from the Sonthal Parganas. Later in the same year, by a notification dated 30th October, which was published in the *Calcutta Gazette* of 10th November, further changes were made on the western frontier, no less than 170 villages being transferred from Murshidābād to Bīrbhūm. The last extensive change of jurisdiction took place in 1879, when thana Barwān, with an area of 108 square miles, was transferred to Murshidābād from Bīrbhūm, while thānas Rāmpur Hāt and Nalhāti (including the present thana of Murarai), which formed part of the Lālbāgh subdivision of Murshidābād, were added to Bīrbhūm.

THE LATER NAWABS. This chapter may be concluded by a brief account of the Nawābs subsequent to Mubārak-ud-daula, to which will be added a sketch of the history of the Seths of Murshidābād, who played an important part in the history of that city.

Mubārak-ud-daula was succeeded in 1793 by his eldest son, Bābar Jang, who died in 1802. Viscount Valentia, who visited Murshidābād in 1802 and had an interview with Mani Begam, the widow of Mīr Jafar, as well as with the Nawāb, has left an interesting account of the latter in his *Voyages and Travels by the Ganges.* He describes the palanquin of the Nawāb as being all of cloth of gold, with panels of glass, and doors of the same material, and states that the magnificent jewels which the Nawāb was wearing at the time of his visit had been taken out of pawn for the occasion, and that the creditors were waiting downstairs to get them back again on his departure. There is little of interest to record regarding the next three Nawābs, viz., Ali Jāh (1810—21), Wāla Jāh (1821—24) and Humāyun Jāh (1824—38). The present palace at Murshidābād was built during the time of Humāyun Jāh, who purchased from the East India Company the old court houses at Fendalbagh and converted the grounds into a garden.

The last of the family who enjoyed the title of Nawāb Nāzim of Bengal was Feredun Jāh (or Saiyid Mansur Alī Khān), who succeeded his father Humāyun Jāh in 1838, when he was nine years of age. At that time the Nawāb's stipend stood at the old figure of 16 lakhs, of which 7½ lakhs were allotted for his personal expenditure: from the remainder were paid the stipends of collateral branches of the family, and the balance constituted a deposit fund. This stipend was subsequently reduced, and certain privileges enjoyed by former Nawābs were abrogated. He was refused control over the Nizāmat deposit fund, and his exemption from personal appearance in the civil courts was cancelled. His salute of 19 guns was moreover reduced to 13 guns, but was restored to the old number after the Mutiny in recognition of the services which he rendered by throwing the weight of his influence into the scales on the side of place and order. "I must," wrote Sir Frederick Halliday, Lieutenant-Governor of Bengal, in his final minute on the Mutiny, "do the Nawāb the justice to say that he has throughout conducted himself with the utmost loyalty, giving all the assistance in his power, and always showing himself ready to anticipate any requisition on the part of Government."

In 1869 the Nawāb went to England to represent his grievances to the House of Commons, which in 1871 rejected his appeal by a majority of 57 votes. He continued to reside in England, and in the meantime his affairs became so heavily involved that a Commission had to be appointed to arrange with his creditors. By a formal deed executed on the 1st November 1880 he resigned his position and title, and renounced all right of interference with the affairs of the Nizāmat in consideration of an annual stipend of £10,000, the payment to him of 10 lakhs of rupees in settlement of various miscellaneous claims, and a suitable provision for his children born in England. The title of Nawāb of Murshidābād was conferred on Saiyid Hasan Alī Khān, his eldest son, and the title of Nawāb Nāzim became extinct. The Nizāmat deposit fund ceased to exist, the office of Agent to the Governor-General was abolished, and the allowances to the various members of the Nizāmat family were in future to be paid to them direct by the Collector of Murshidābād. Feredun Jāh (Mansur Alī Khān) returned to India in 1881 and died of cholera at Murshidābād on the 5th November 1884. He was buried in the family cemetery at Jāfarganj in the only available space left in the line of tombs of Nawāb Nāzims, but the remains were subsequently re-interred at Karbela in accordance with his will. His eldest son, Saiyid Hasan Alī, was given the hereditary title of Nawāb Bahādur of Murshidābād in February 1882, and that of Amir-ul-Omrāh in July 1887, with the rank of the Premier Noble of Bengal. Subsequently provision was made, by Act XV of 1891, and an indenture attached to the Act, for the support and maintenance of the Nawāb Bahādur and of the honour and dignity of his station. He was succeeded by his eldest son, Wāsif Ali Mirza Bahādur (born on the 7th January 1875), the present Nawāb Bahādur of Murshidābād, who was made K.C.S.I. in 1909 and K.C.V.O. in 1912. His full title is Itishām-ul-mulk, Rais-ud-Daula, Amir-ul-Omrāh, Nawāb Sir Asif Qadr Saiyid Wāsif Alī Mirza Khān Bahādur, Mahābat Jang, Nawāb Bahādur of Murshidābād, K.C.V.O., K.C.S.I.

THE SETHS OF MURSHIDABAD.

The history of the Seths of Murshidābād is connected with some of the most critical revolutions in Bengal during the 18th century. They owed their influence to their position as bankers and financiers. They were, in fact, predominant in the sphere of Indian finance: Burke said of them that "their transactions were as extensive as those of the Bank of England," and they have been not unworthily styled "the Rothschilds of India." The designation by which they are commonly known, viz., Jagat Seth, is, it may be explained, not a personal name but a title, meaning 'Banker of the World," which was conferred by the Mughal Emperor.

They belonged to the well-known tribe of Mārwāris, the Jews of India, as they have been called, whose hereditary enterprise carries them as traders to every part of the country. The original home of the family is said to have been at Nagar, a town in the Rājput State of Jodhpur. Towards the close of the seventeenth century, Hirānand Sāho, whom the Seths regard as the founder of their family, migrated from his native city and settled at Patna, which was one of the greatest trade centres in the lower valley of the Ganges. To Hirānand Sāho were born seven sons, who seem to have all followed their father's profession, and established banking firms in different parts of India. The eldest of the seven, Mānik Chand; betook himself to Dacca, which was as that time the seat of the Muhammadan Government, and the natural centre of attraction to an enterprising man. When Murshid Kulī Khān transferred the capital to Murshidābād, the banker followed his patron, and became the most influential personage at the new court.

It would seem that Mānik Chand was the right-hand man of the Nawāb in his financial reforms, and also in his private affairs. The establishment of the mint at Murshidābād, by which the city was conspicuously marked as the new capital of Bengal, was rendered easy by the command of specie possessed by the banker. The same qualification perhaps suggested, as it certainly facilitated, the fundamental change introduced by Murshid Kuli Khān, in accordance with which the zamīndārs, or other collectors of revenue, paid the land tax by monthly instalments at Murshidābād. These payments passed through the hands of Mānik Chand, and it was through him also that the annual revenue of one crore and fifty lakhs of rupees was annually remitted to the Mughal Emperor; whether in specie, as stated in Muhammadan accounts of the rule of Murshid Kulī Khān or in drafts and orders, drawn by Mānik Chand on the corresponding firm of his brother in Delhi, as is suggested in the family history and as certainly appears to have been the case after the death of Murshid Kulī Khān.* The coffers of Mānik Chand were, moreover, the depositary of the private hoards of Murshid Kulī Khān; and on the death of the latter it is

* According to the *Riyazu-s-Salātin* the revenue was sent in a convoy of 200 waggons escorted by 600 horse and 500 foot during the rule of Murshid Kulī Khān, but under his successor was "remitted to the Imperial treasury through the banking agency of Jagat Seth Fathi Chand."

said that five crores of rupees remained still unpaid. Under these circumstances, it is easy to believe that the influence of the banker became almost as great as that of the Governor. On the one hand, Murshid Kulī Khān is said to have obtained for Mānik Chand the title of "Seth" or banker from the Emperor Farrukhsiyyar, in 1715. On the other hand, it is asserted in the family history that Mānik Chand had previously helped Murshid Kulī to purchase the continuance of his office as Nawāb of Bengal after the death of Aurangzeb. It is at least certain that from this time the banker and his descendants were recognised as members of the Nawāb's Council, that their influence was of chief importance in deciding the result of every dynastic revolution, and that they were in constant communication with the ministers of the Delhi Court.

Mānik Chand, having no children, adopted his nephew Fathi Chand, the head of the firm at Delhi, who had also received the title of Seth. The latter was in high favour with the Emperor Farrukhsiyyar, who was under heavy pecuniary obligations to the firm. Mānik Chand died, full of wealth and honours, in 1722; and his adopted son at once took his position as the richest banker in India and the most influential man in matters of finance. In 1724, on the occasion of his first visit to Delhi, the Emperor Muhammad Shāh conferred on him the title of "Jagat Seth," or "the banker of the world." According to another account, this title was granted by Farrukhsiyyar; but it is admitted by all that Fathi Chand was the first of the family to bear the name of Jagat Seth, which has since become so well known in history. On the death of Murshid Kulī Khān, in 1725, the new Nawāb, Shuja-ud-daula, appointed Fathi Chand to be one of his four Councillors of State, and seems to have submitted to his advice during the fourteen years of his peaceful rule.

On the accession of Sarfarāz Khān in 1739, the banker retained his position in the Council; but the voluptuous passions of the Nawāb led to a rupture, which is thus described in Orme's *History of British India*:—"There was a family of Gentoo merchants at Muxadavad, whose head, Juggut-Seat, had raised himself from no considerable origin to be the wealthiest banker in the empire, in most parts of which he had agents supplied with money for remittances, from whom he constantly received good intelligence of what was transacting in the governments in which they were settled. In Bengal his influence was equal to that of any officer of the administration; for, by answering to the treasury as security for most of the renters farming the lands of the province, he knew, better than any one, all the details of the revenues; while the great circulation of wealth which he commanded rendered his assistance necessary in every emergency of expense. His eldest son was married to a woman of exquisite beauty, the report alone of which inflamed the curiosity of the Nawāb so much, that he insisted on seeing her, although he knew the disgrace which would be fixed on the family by showing a wife unveiled to a stranger. Neither the remonstrances of the father, nor his power to avenge the indignity, availed to divert the Nawāb from this insolent and futile resolution. The young woman was sent to the palace in the evening, and, after staying there a short space, returned, unviolated indeed, but dishonoured, to her husband." Such is the cause commonly assigned to account for the fact that Jagat Seth fell away from the Nawāb Sarfarāz Khān, the last heir of the great Murshid Kulī Khān, the patron of his family, and allied himself with Alī Vardi Khān. The Seth family give another explanation, which they regard as more honourable to their ancestor. They say that Murshid Kulī Khān had, in the course of business, deposited with Mānik Chand a sum of seven crores of rupees, which had never been repaid. When Sarfarāz Khān, on his accession, pressed for payment, Fathi Chand begged for a reasonable period for its liquidation, and, in the meanwhile, leagued himself with Alī Vardi Khān, who was already preparing for revolt in Bihār. The successful issue of this revolution has already been described.

Fathi Chand died in the year 1744, and was succeeded in his title of Jagat Seth by his grandson, Mahtāb Rāi. His two sons had died in his lifetime, but each had left a son; and the two cousins, Mahtāb Rāi, the son of the elder brother, and Swārup Chand, the son of the younger, who received the title of Mahārājā, were joint heirs of his wealth. They are said to have possessed a capital of ten crores of rupees, or ten millions sterling, and tradition estimates their wealth by saying that they could have, if they chose, blocked up with rupees the head of the Bhāgirāthi at Suti. That the stories of their riches are not idle is clear from the account given in the *Sair-ul Mutākharin* :—

"Mahtāb Rai and Rāja Swarūp Chand were both grandsons to Jagat Seth Fathi Chand by two brothers, who died both in the time of Shuja Khān, Viceroy of Bengal; so that his fortune, which was literally immense, and past all belief, passed to those his grandsons, who, in Alī Vardi Khān's time, lived in Bengal with so much credit and authority as is hardly credible at such a distance of time. Their riches were so great that no such bankers were ever seen in Hindustān or the Deccan, nor was there any banker or merchant that could stand a comparison with them all over India. It is even certain that all the bankers of their time in Bengal were either their factors, or some of their family. Their wealth may be guessed by this fact. In the first invasion of the Marāthas, and when Murshidābād was not yet surrounded by walls, Mīr Habīb, with a party of their best horse, having found means to fall upon that city, before Alī Vardi Khān could come up, carried from Jagat Seth's house two crores of rupees, in Arcot coin only,* and this prodigious sum did not affect the two brothers, more than if it had been two trusses of straw. They continued to give afterwards to Government, as they had done before, bills of exchange called *darsanis* of one crore at a time, by which words is meant a draft, which the acceptor is to pay at sight without any sort of excuse. In short, their wealth was such that there is no mentioning it, without seeming to exaggerate, and to deal in extravagant fables.†

Among the modes by which their profits were gained may be mentioned the receipt of the revenue of Bengal and its transmission to Delhi, the exchange on depreciated currency, and transactions with European merchants. There were in those days no treasuries scattered over the country in the several districts. The zamīndārs collected the revenue, and remitted it to the viceregal treasury at Murshidābād. Every year, at the time of Punyā, or annual settlement of the revenue (a custom introduced by Murshid Kuli Khān) the zamīndārs assembled at the bank of the Seths, in order to settle their accounts, adjust the difference of *battā* or discount, and negotiate for a fresh supply of funds. From a report on this subject by Mr. Batson in 1760, in Long's *Selections from Unpublished Records*, it appears that Jagat Seth had the privilege of having his money stamped at the Murshidābād mint, on paying a duty of ½ per cent. 'By which privilege, and by his great wealth and influence, in the country, he reaps the great benefit arising from the above-mentioned practice (*bāttā*); and the Nawāb finds it convenient to indulge him therein, in recompense for the loans and exactions to which he obliges him."

With regard to the dealings of the firm with European merchants, an element of confusion is introduced by the circumstance that the term 'Seth' means merely banker, so that when dealings with the Seths are mentioned, it does not follow that

* Arcot coin signifies rupees struck at Madras or at Pondicherry.

† *Sair-ul-Mutākharin*, Vol. II., pp. 457, 458.

these were the Seths of Murshidābād. There is, however, a passage in Orme's *History of Hindustān* which shows the magnitude of their transactions with the French. In connection with Clive's attack on Chandernagore, it is stated that 'the French had many friends at the court of the Nāwāb; amongst others the Seths, Mootabray and Roopchand (Māhtāb Rai and Swarūp Chand), to whom the Government of Chandernagore was indebted for a million and-a-half of rupees.' It may also be mentioned, in illustration of this point, that it is believed to this day by the people of Bengal that the Seths advanced large sums of money to the English, prior to the battle of Plassey; and that 'the rupees of the Hindu banker, equally with the sword of the English colonel, contributed to the overthrow of the Muhammadan power in Bengal.'

The *Selections from Unpublished Records of Government* by Mr. Long contain a few allusions to the Seths during the rule of Alī Vardi Khān. In 1749, when the Nawāb blockaded the factory of Cossimbazar, the English got off by paying him Rs. 12,00,000 through the Seths, of which sum they appear to have retained a certain proportion. In 1753, in answer to the Court of Directors, who were pressing the Council to obtain the establishment of a mint in Calcutta, the President wrote, 'It would be impracticable to effect it with the Nawāb, as an attempt of that kind would be immediately overset by Jagat Seth, even at the expense of a much larger sum than we could afford; he being the sole purchaser of all the bullion that is imported into this province, by which he is annually a very considerable gainer.' The President, however, suggested that an effort might be made to obtain permission direct from the court of Delhi. This would require at least Rs. 20,0,000, 'and the affair must be carried on with the greatest secrecy, that Jagat Seth's house might not have the least intimation of it.' In 1758, the year after the establishment of the Calcutta mint, we find Mr. Douglas, a large creditor of the Company, absolutely refusing to take payment in Calcutta *sikka* rupees, on the ground that "his fortune would be daily exposed to being curtailed from 5 to 10 per cent. at the pleasure of Jagat Seth, who has the sole management of the current money of the country, and can always make it fluctuate in such a manner as he sees convenient for his purpose."

After the death of Alī Vardi Khān in 1756, the Seths were brought into much closer intercourse with the English. The negotiations with Sirāj-ud-daula after the capture of Calcutta were to a large extent carried on through the agency of the Seths.

Unlike some of the other negotiators, the bankers would seem never to have played, or to have threatened to play, the part of traitors, nor to have stipulated for any excessive share in the enormous sum of money which concluded the bargain. We first hear of the Seths as in communication with the English at the time when the fugitive Bengal Council met on board a schooner off Faltā. Calcutta was taken on 22nd June; and on August 22nd the Council resolved to write a complimentary letter to Jagat Seth, amongst others, that he might intercede for them with the Nawāb. In the consultations dated 5th September 1756, there is a good deal of curious information. Umā Charan (Omichand), for reasons of his own, had refused to forward the letter to Jagat Seth. Mr. Bisdom, the Dutch Governor of Cossimbazar, and Warren Hastings, who was still permitted his liberty at the same place, sent important news from Murshidābād. The Nawāb of Purnea, supported by a faction at Delhi, had declared against Sirāj-ud-daula; and a quarrel had broken out between Sirāj-ud-daula and Jagat Seth. The Nawāb had reproached the banker for not obtaining for him the imperial ratification of his office, and had ordered him to raise from the merchants three crores of rupees. Jagat Seth pleaded the hardships of the already oppressed people, but received a blow in the face, and was confined. Mīr Jāfar insisted upon his being set at liberty, but in vain. On 23rd November, the Council, who were still at Faltā, instructed Major Kilpatrick to write again to Jagat Seth, "to let him know that their dependence was upon him, and upon him alone, for the hopes they had of resettling in an amicable manner."

After the arrival of Clive, and the recapture of Calcutta, the Seths are not heard of until fresh negotiations were opened with the Nawāb, in order to lead to the isolation of Chandernagore. "Owing to the exasperation of the Nawāb, the Seths," says Orme, "were afraid to appear openly as friends to the English; but they deputed their ablest agent, Ranjit Rai, to attend the Nawāb and ordered him to correspond with Colonel Clive." The treaty of February 1757, by which Sirāj-ud-daula granted the demands of the English, was effected by this person. After the capture of Chandernagore by Clive, when a quarrel with the Nawāb again became imminent, the first overture for the overthrow of Sirāj-ud-daula came from the Seths. On 23rd April, the day before the same proposals were made on behalf of Mīr Jafar, a Muhammadan officer, named Yar Latif Khān, asked for a secret conference with Mr. Watts, the Resident at Cossimbazar. This man commanded 2,000 horse in the Nawāb's service, but received a stipend from the Seths to defend them on any occasion of danger, even against the Nawāb himself. He brought a proposal for betraying Murshidābād to the English with the help of the Seths, which ultimately ripened into the plot by which Mīr Jafar was raised to the *masnad.* It was in their house at Murshidābād that on 30th June 1757, seven days after the battle of Plassey, the arrangements for carrying out the pecuniary bargain were concluded, and the trick of the red treaty was disclosed. The position, which the family continued to occupy under the new order of things, may be estimated from the following circumstances. In September 1759, when the Nawāb Mīr Jafar paid a visit to Calcutta, he was accompanied by Jagat Seth, and they were both lavishly entertained for four days at the expense of the Company. The charges for the Nawāb on this occasion amounted to nearly Rs. 80,000; and Arcot rupees 17,374 were expended on the entertainment of Jagat Seth.

It is from about this time that the misfortunes of the Seths began. They had assisted in raising Mīr Jafar to the *masnad,* but they were unable to satisfy his continuous demands for money. One of their quarrels with the Nawāb is thus narrated and commented on by Malcolm, in his *Life of Lord Clive*:—" Jagat Seth and his brother [cousin (?)] had obtained leave to proceed on a pilgrimage to Parasnāth, and had commenced their journey, when information was received that they were in correspondence with the Shāhzāda (who was at that time threatening to invade Bihār), and had actually furnished him with the means of paying his new levies. The Nawāb, giving credit to this report, sent to stop them; but they refused compliance with his order, and proceeded under the guard of 2,000 men, who had been furnished for their escort. These troops, on receiving a promise of the liquidation of their arrears, readily transferred their allegiance from the prince to the bankers. The Nawāb, even if he had had the disposition, would probably have found himself without the means of coercing these wealthy subjects into submission. The principal bankers of India command, through the influence of their extensive credit, the respect of sovereigns and the support of their principal ministers and generals. Their property, though often immense, is seldom in a tangible form. Their great profits enable them to bear moderate exactions; and the prince, who has recourse to violence towards one of this class, is not only likely to fail in his immediate object of plunder, but is certain to destroy his future resources, and to excite an impression of his character that must greatly facilitate those attempts against his life and power to which it is the lot of despots to be continually exposed."

In 1763, one of the first things Mīr Kāsim did when war broke out between him and the English was to seize the two cousins who were at the head of the firm, Mahtāb Rai Jagat Seth and Mahārājā Swarūp Chand, whose attachment to the English made them objects of suspicion. The English immediately remonstrated against this act, which was, no doubt, intended to prevent intrigues between them and the Seths. The following is the protest from the Governor to the Nawāb, dated 24th April 1763 :—" I am just informed by a letter from Mr. Amyatt that Muhammad Taki Khān went on the 21st instant at night to the house of Jagat Seth and Swarup Chand, and carried them to Hirājhil, where he keeps them under a guard. This affair surprises me greatly. When your Excellency took the government upon yourself, you and I and the Seths being assembled together, it was agreed that, as they are men of high rank in the country, you shall make use of their assistance in managing your affairs and never consent that they should be injured ; and when I had the pleasure of seeing you at Monghyr, I then likewise spoke to you about them, and you set my heart at ease by assuring me that you would on no account do them any injury. The taking of men of their rank in such an injurious manner out of their home is extremely improper, and is disgracing them in the highest degree. It is, moreover, a violation of our agreement and therefore reflects dishonour upon you and me, and will be the means of acquiring us an ill name from everybody. The abovementioned gentlemen were never thus disgraced in the time of any former Nāzims." As is well known, this remonstrance was unavailing.

After the defeat of Udhua Nullah, Mīr Kāsim's wrath was turned against his prisoners, and the two Seths, whom he dragged with him in his flight, were cruelly put to death. Tradition states that they were flung into the Ganges from one of the towers of the fort of Monghyr, and that a faithful old servant, named Chuni, begged that he might share their fate and was thereupon thrown into the river after them. This picturesque story does not appear to be warranted by fact, for not only does the *Sair-ul-Mutākharin* state that they were hacked to pieces by Kāsim Alī's orders at Bārh in the Patna district, but Major Grant, who was an officer in Major Adams' army, states that he found their bodies buried in one of the rooms of a house there. The tradition, however, seems to have sprung up soon after their death, for the translator of the *Sair-ul-Mutākharin* (Raymond *alias* Hāji Mustapha), writing about 1786, says—"Out of 10,000 boatmen who pass every year by a certain tower of the castle of Monghyr, there is not a man but will point out the spot where the two Jagat Seths were drowned, nor is there an old woman at Monghyr, but would repeat the speech of the heroical Chuni to his master's executioners."

The two cousins were succeeded by their two sons, Seth Khushāl Chand, the eldest son of Mahtāb Rai, who was confirmed in the title of Jagat Seth by the Emperor Shāh Alam in 1766, and Seth Udwat Chand, the eldest son of Swarūp Chand, who was permitted to inherit his father's title of Mahārājā. It would appear that the two new heads of the firm were as united in their dealings as their fathers had been; and that, like them, they were commonly regarded as brothers. In a letter to Lord Clive in May 1765, they represented in piteous language their distressed situation, and especially complained of the hardships suffered by their younger brothers, Seth Golāb Chand and Bābu Mahir Chand. So far as can be ascertained, these brothers were really second cousins, being younger sons of the two Seths who had been murdered by Mīr Kāsim. They had been carried off with their fathers, and had been finally handed over to the tender mercies of the Emperor of Delhi and the Wazir of Oudh. We find that Mīr Jafar, the reinstated Nawāb of Bengal, had been induced to intercede for them with the Wazir; but they were not delivered back to their brethren at Murshidābād until a heavy ransom had been paid. The Seths represented their impoverishment on this account to Lord Clive, but he replied to them in the following stern letter, dated November 1765:—"You are not ignorant what attention and support I always showed to your father, and how cordially I have continued it to you and the remainder of the family. It cannot, therefore, but be matter of great concern to me to learn that you do not seriously consider what part you ought to act, to establish your own credit and the public interest. Instead of keeping up to the original intention and necessity of having the treasury under three separate keys, I find all the money has been lodged with your family in your own house, and that you have been consenting at least to the farming of the Bengal province under the rents I am assured it will bear. I am informed also that you have been pressing the zamīndārs to discharge their debts to your fathers, at the time when they are five months in arrear to the Government. This is a step I can by no means approve of or allow. You are still a very rich house; but I greatly fear that tendency you seem to have to avarice will not only turn greatly to your disadvantage, but at the same time destroy that opinion I had of your inclination and disposition to promote the public good."

In the following year the Seths laid a claim before the English for between 50 and 60 lakhs of rupees, of which 21 lakhs had been advanced to Mīr Jafar for the support of his own and the English army. For this latter sum Lord Clive accepted liability, and suggested that it should be repaid in equal moieties by the Company and the Nawāb. In the same year it is incidentally recorded that the Council had been under the necessity of applying to the Seths for a loan of 1½ lakhs of rupees. When Lord Clive received from the Emperor, Shāh Alam, the grant of the Dīwāni on behalf of the Company in 1765, he immediately appointed Khushāl Chand Jagat Seth, who was then only eighteen years old, to be the Company's *sarraf* or "shroff"; and in the treaties of 1766 and 1770, which confirm the appointments of two successive Nawābs, Jagat Seth is mentioned as one of the three ministers who were entrusted with the supreme management of affairs.

Tradition dates the decline of the Seths from the time of Khushāl Chand. It is said that he refused an annual stipend of 3 lakhs of rupees which was offered to him by Clive, and that his own expenses were at the rate of one lakh per month. He died at the early age of thirty-nine; but during his short lifetime, he was the most lavish benefactor of all his family to the sacred Jain hill of Parasnāth. The prodigal expenditure of the Seths, as indicated by their religious donations, may have contributed to drain the inherited resources of the family, but the real cause of their ruin must be sought in the change which was now taking place in the Government of Bengal. The great famine of 1770, which revolutionized the financial condition of the country, first impaired their position; and, finally in 1772, when Warren Hastings transferred to Calcutta the *Khālsa* or Government Treasury, they ceased to be any longer the bankers of the English. Instead of accounting for their downfall by these adequate causes, the Seths themselves explain it by the following story. The vast treasures of the family, they say, had been buried under ground by Khushāl Chand, and death came upon him suddenly before he was able to disclose the secret. In spite of their reduced circumstances, the Seths appear to have lived in Oriental state, for Raymond, the translator of the *Sair-ul-Mutākharin*, says:—"Even so late as the year 1780 there were 1,200 women in the seraglios of the two remaining brothers and about 4,000 persons of all sorts in their palaces."

Like many other members of the family, Khushāl Chand was childless. He adopted his nephew, Harakh Chand, upon whom the title of Jagat Seth was conferred by the English without any reference to Delhi. It is said that he was in pecuniary difficulties until he inherited the fortune of a second uncle, Gulāb Chand. Harakh Chand Jagat Seth was the first of the family who abandoned the faith of his ancestors, and embraced the creed of Vishnu. Having no son, and being very anxious to have an heir born of his own body, he had recourse to the various observances enjoined in such a case by the Jain religion, but all to no purpose. At last he followed the advice of a Bairāgi and propitiated Vishnu. He then obtained his desire, and became a Vaishnava. Harakh Chand left two sons, Indra Chand and Vishnu Chand, who inherited his property in equal shares. Indra Chand, the elder, on whom the title of Jagat Seth was conferred, was succeeded by his son, Gobind Chand, who is said to have dissipated the remaining wealth of his ancestors. He lived for some time on the sums he obtained by selling the family jewels, and finally became dependent on a pension of Rs. 12,000 a year, which was allowed him by the East India Company in consideration of the services rendered by his ancestors. He was not otherwise recognized by the Government, and the title of Jagat Seth became extinct, being last held by his father. On the death of Gobind Chand, the headship of the family, together with the pension (reduced to Rs. 8,000 a year) passed to Krishna Chand, the son of Vishnu Chand.

CHAPTER III.

THE PEOPLE.

GROWTH OF POPULATION.

DURING the thirty-nine years which have elapsed since 1872, when the first census was taken, the population of Murshidābād has increased by 158,170, or 13 per cent.: the figures of each census are given in the margin.

Year of census.	Population.	Increase per cent.
1872 ...	1,214,104	......
1881 ...	1,226,790	+1·0
1891 ...	1,250,946	+2·0
1901 ..	1,333,184	+6·6
1911 ...	1,372,274	+2·9

The growth of population between 1872 and 1891 was very small, being barely 3 pero ent.; the slow rate of progress is attributed to the ravages of Burdwān fever which spread to the district shortly before 1881 and caused heavy mortality. In the next decade, however, there was a marked recovery, the increase recorded in 1901 representing 6·6 per cent. The growth of the people, however, was far from uniform, for in the low-lying tracts to the east it amounted to only 3 per cent., whereas in the higher country to the west it averaged 13 per cent., and even rose as high as 26 per cent. in thanas Sāgardighi and Nabagrām, two sparsely populated thanas which attract immigrants from Bīrbhūm and the Sonthal Parganas.

The decade 1901—1910 was one of chequered prosperity. In 1904 there were severe floods by which a considerable area was submerged. Next year there was an epidemic of cholera, which caused over 8,000 deaths, and this was followed by an epidemic of small-pox in 1907. In that year too the

THANA, ETC.	Population, 1911.	PERCENTAGE OF VARIATION. 1901—1911.	Density per square mile.
DISTRICT TOTAL ...	1,372,274	+ 2·93	640
SADAR SUBDIVISION ...	517,723	− 0·65	621
Gorābazar (Sujaganj)	35,074	− 13·41	523
Berhampore	26,143	+ 7·16	2,905
Beldānga	118,938	+ 13·85	743
Noāda	50,779	− 2·00	577
Hariharpāra	53,351	− 6·70	544
Daulatbazar	35,543	− 4·82	564
Kāninagar	85,553	− 3·81	545
Damkal	112,342	− 3·54	585
LALBAGH SUBDIVISION	195,128	+ 2·73	535
Bhagwāngola	59,254	+ 5·64	589
Shāhānagar	21,902	− 13·43	913
Mānullabazar	11,169	− 8·65	1,241
Asānpur	12,546	− 3·80	738
Sāgardighi	40,424	− 9·02	470
Nabagrām	49,833	+ 7·84	419

THANA, ETC.	Population, 1911.	PERCENTAGE OF VARIATION. 1901–1911.	Density per square mile.
JANGIPUR SUBDIVISION	357,930	+ 7·10	703
Lalgola	66,517	+ 7·91	700
Raghunāthganj ...	73,559	+ 0·07	1,036
Mirzapur	47,597	+ 4·01	476
Suti	67,292	+ 4·44	491
Shamsherganj	102,965	+ 15·89	971
KANDI SUBDIVISION ...	301,493	+ 9·75	589
Bharatpur	96,821	+ 0·63	745
Khargaon	68,549	+ 7·49	562
Kāndi	34,798	+ 9·00	1,087
Barwān	74,378	+ 6·55	703
Gokaran	26,947	+ 2·80	586

Lalitākuri embankment in the Lālbāgh subdivision gave way, and there was a partial failure of the winter rice crop. Taking the average of the whole decade, however, crops were almost normal, and a demand for labour was created by the construction of three new railway lines, viz., the Rānāghāt-Murshidābād branch of the Eastern Bengal State Railway and the Barharwa-Azīmganj-Kātwa and Ondāl-Sainthia branches of the East Indian Railway.

An inquiry regarding the relative healthiness and unhealthiness of different parts of the districts was made by the Bengal Drainage Committee in 1906-07, and the conclusions at which it arrived were that:—"(1) The most malarious thanas are Bhagwāngola, Mānullābazar, Shāhānagar, Daulatbazar, Sujāganj, Hariharpāra, Asānpur and perhaps Jalangi; and (2) the least malarious areas are comprised in the whole of the Kāndi subdivision and the thanas of Shamsherganj, Suti, Raghunāthganj, Mirzāpur and Sāgardighi." These conclusions are confirmed by the results of the census of 1911. The Kāndi subdivision has developed at the rate of 9·75 per cent., and all the other thanas mentioned as least malarious have an increase, except Raghunāthganj where the population is stationary. Shamsherganj, which made the greatest progress between 1872 and 1901, is still growing rapidly and has added another 16 per cent. to its population. Of the eight thanas mentioned as most malarious, six are distinctly decadent.

DENSITY. The east and west of the district are clearly differentiated by their physical configuration. The portion lying to the west of the Bhāgīrathi is a continuation of the Chota Nāgpur plateau: its general level is higher than that of the rest of the district, the surface is undulating and the climate is comparatively dry. The eastern portion is a deltaic tract in which the land is still being gradually raised by the deposition of silt from the rivers which traverse it, though the action of nature has been interfered with to some extent by the marginal embankment along the left bank of the Bhāgīrathi, which prevents the inundation which would otherwise occur.

These conditions affect the density of population, which is considerably greater in the alluvial country to the east of the Bhāgīrathi than in the less fertile country to the west. In the latter tract the mean density is reduced by the figures for the central thanas, which, though now growing rapidly, are still sparsely inhabited. The most populous thanas lie along the Bhāgīrathi, four of them having a density of over 1,000 per square mile, while in four thanas to the west there are under 500 persons to the square mile.

MIGRATION.

The scale of migration both to and from the district is comparatively small, for the immigrants represent only 5·5 per cent. and the emigrants 7·8 per cent. of the population: the actual figures recorded at the census of 1911 are given in the margin.

DETAILS.	Male.	Female.	Total.
Actual population ...	678,292	693,982	1,372,274
Immigrants	39,002	36,569	75,571
Emigrants	51,958	55,325	107,283
Natural population ...	691,248	712,738	1,403,986

The volume of emigration is growing, the number of persons born in the district but enumerated outside it being nearly 29,000 more than in 1901. The result of this increase is that the balance of migration is decidedly against the district, which loses nearly 25,000 more by emigration than it gains by immigration.

The north of the district suffers from diluvion, a good deal of land on its southern bank being washed away by the Ganges and thrown up on the opposite side in Mālda and Rājshāhi. There is consequently a movement of cultivators and others to the new alluvial formations, which causes the emigrants to Mālda to exceed the immigrants from that district by 20,000, while the loss to Rājshāhi amounts to nearly 16,000. The exodus to Mālda appears to have been stimulated by the opening of the Kātihar-Godāgari railway line. The number of persons born in Murshidābād who were enumerated in Mālda has risen from 12,000 to 27,000, and the movement has not stopped there, but has extended to Purnea, which in 1901 contained under 1,000 natives of Murshidābād but now has 5,000. There is a fair amount of immigration from Bihār and Orissa and the United Provinces, but with the exception of the Sonthal Parganas, which contributes 15,000 immigrants, comparatively little of this is permanent, for though the immigrants stay for some years, *e.g.*, in the service of zamīndars, they form their matrimonial connections in their own country and ultimately return thither.

TOWNS. Altogether 94 per cent. of the people live in villages, and the urban population amounts to only 83,483 persons. There are six towns, as shown in the margin, their average population being 13,914. The most progressive town is Berhampore, the district headquarters, the inhabitants of which have increased by 7 per cent. since 1901; the subdivisional headquarters of Kāndi and Jangipur have also registered increases. Murshidābād and Azīmganj, a municipality in its suburbs, are both decadent, sustaining a continuous and steady decline of population since 1872. In both towns the earthquake of 1897 overthrew a great number of buildings, which the people have not been able to replace, and the untouched ruins give to the visitor an uncomfortable impression of poverty and decay.

Town.	Population.
Berhampore	26,143
Murshidābād ...	12,669
Kāndi	12,638
Azīmganj	12,327
Jangipur	11,408
Dhuliān	8,298

VILLAGES. The census village corresponds to the *mauza* or survey unit of area, and not to the residential village, *i.e.*, a continuous collection of houses, bearing a common name, with its dependent hamlets. The two may, of course, correspond, *e.g.*, where the *mauza* contained only one village at the time of the survey, and no other village has since been built; but in other cases a *mauza* may contain several residential villages, which have sprung up since the survey was made. Altogether 1,879 inhabited villages (in the census connotation of the term), with an average population of 686, were returned in 1911. Of the rural population, 20 per cent. reside in villages with under 500 inhabitants, 53 per cent. in villages with a population of 500 to 2,000, 23 per cent. in villages with a population of 2,000 to 5,000 and 4 per cent. in villages containing 5,000 or more people.

The following account of the villages is quoted from Colonel Gastrell's Report on Murshidābād (1860). Though more than 50 years have passed since it was written, conditions have not changed. "Nearly every one of the permanent villages is buried in a thick jungle of bamboos, trees, underwood, and long rank weeds and creepers. If, on raising a new village, the people do not find trees available to build under, they plant them of all kinds to afford themselves shade, and to their frail tenements protection from storms and the strong north-westers which precede the rains. The humidity of the atmosphere and rich soil soon supply a flourishing crop of brushwood, grass and gigantic weeds of all kinds. Holes are dug in all directions for earth to raise the houses. These, filled with water by the first rains, supply each man with water at his door if he wishes it. Then, in course of time, when the jungle is full-grown, the wind totally excluded, and the pools of stagnant water are coated over with thick green *confervæ*, the Bengali may be seen enjoying himself, and keeping out the mosquitoes by filling the inside of the house with smoke. Easily contented, lazy, and not over-burdened with wealth, the peasants choose the evils they consider the least, and habit accustoms them to look on their village as perfection.

"They offer a strong contrast in their choice of sites to the Santāls, their neighbours, some of whom are domiciled in the north-west of the district. These latter invariably select the highest and driest spot for their villages, and carefully cut and keep down every particle of jungle in and about them, growing only a few useful trees in the long central road, either for shade, fruit or oil-seeds. Each Santāl's house is a complete little farm enclosure, holding the owner's dwelling house, granary, cow and pigeon-houses and pig-sty. Their villages extend in one long line, with houses built on each side of the road; the head-man's or *mānjhi's* house being generally in the centre.

The huts of the poorer classes, in the north-west portion of Murshidābād, are built with mud walls and thatched with rice straw. In other parts of the district a framework house of bamboo is usually made first. The floor is then raised of mud, well rammed to the necessary height to afford protection from inundation. In some places the walls are made of mud, enclosing the uprights; in others plaited grass or matting or slips of bamboo are used instead of mud, and are sometimes covered again with a coating of clay and cow-dung. Sometimes the gable ends are left open at the top for ventilation, but the generality are closed up. In the low lands near the Ganges the houses are temporary constructions. A light thatch and lighter walls suffice for the wants of the inhabitants, who remove their property, as soon as the river waters rise high enough to endanger their huts.

RELIGIONS. The Muhammadans number 713,152 or 52 per cent. of the population, and the Hindus 643,291 or 47 per cent. There are 14,419 Animists, while the Christian community has only 413 representatives. In addition to these, there are 999 members of minor religions, including 975 Jains, 15 Brāhmos, 5 Buddhists, 2 Jews, 1 Parsi and 1 Sikh.

Hindus and Musalmāns. The Musalmāns predominate in the Sadar subdivision, where there are three of them to every two Hindus, and also in the

Jangipur subdivision, where there are four followers of the Prophet to every three Hindus. The two religions are in equal strength in the Lālbāgh subdivision, and the most distinctively Hindu subdivision is Kāndi, where there are nearly double as many Hindus as Musalmāns. The growth of the Musalmān population is more rapid than that of the Hindu, for since 1881 the former has increased from 48 per cent. to 52 per cent. of the district population, whereas the latter has fallen from 52 to 47 per cent.

Primâ facie, it appears natural that the Muhammadan capital of Murshidābād should have attracted a large number of Musalmāns to the district, but it is noteworthy that in Murshidābād itself and in the immediate suburbs Hindus predominate. The fact is that the creation of this capital was of a comparatively late date, and until the time of Murshid Kuli Khān the climate of Bengal was regarded as so unhealthy that service in it was regarded by the Mughal nobles as a sentence of banishment. Murshid Kuli Khān himself sought to proselytize by force, one of his regulations being that any zamīndār who failed to pay his revenue or make up the arrears due should be compelled to embrace Islām with his wife and family. This order cannot, however, have affected the bulk of the population or any but a limited class. The strength of the Musalmān population must be due to other causes, and it may certainly be connected with the general geographical distribution of their co-religionists in Bengal. It is in the alluvial river basins of the Ganges and Brahmaputra that the Musalmāns are found in greatest numerical strength. They outnumber the Hindus in every district of the Presidency Division except the 24-Parganas; in North Bengal they constitute two-thirds of the population, and in East Bengal they are more than twice as numerous as the Hindus. On the other hand, Hinduism prevails in the districts to the west of the Ganges and Bhāgīrathi. In Murshidābād district their distribution follows the same general rule, for they are most numerous in the flat alluvial tract to the east of the Bhāgīrathi.

The numbers, therefore, of the Muhammadans in Murshidābād cannot be attributed to the planting of the last Musalmān capital on the banks of the Bhāgīrathi. The court of the Nawāb has been equally destitute of effect in determining the sect or other characteristics of the general Muhammadan population. The Nawāb Bahādur himself is a Shiāh, and there is no other Musalmān family in the district which can compare either in position or wealth with the leading Hindu *zamīndārs*. The great majority of the Muhammadan population, however, are not Shiāhs, but Sunnis of the Hânafi sect, though some of the poorer cultivators have embraced the doctrines of the Farâzi sect.

Of the Animists, 10,847 are Santāls, mostly immigrants from the Sonthal Parganas who have settled in the Sāgardighi, Nabagrām and Asānpur thanas of the Lālbāgh subdivision and in the Mirzapur thana of the Jangipur subdivision. There are also 1,619 Oraons, 371 Mundas and 105 Koras, whose religion was returned as Animistic. In addition to these, there are 3,546 Santāls, 988 Oraons, 939 Koras and 194 Mundas, who claim to be Hindus, but of whom it may safely be predicated that their Hinduism is not far removed from the Animism of their brethren. The Oraons are also commonly known as Dhāngars, a name meaning merely a contract labourer, or as Bunas, a generic designation for the aboriginal tribes of Chota Nāgpur. Both these latter names date back to the time when they were employed as labourers by the indigo factories. Animists.

The figures for Christians include 83 Europeans, 25 Anglo-Indians, 3 Armenians and 302 Indian converts. Various Christian missions have from time to time established stations in the district, but have not met with much success. The only mission now at work is a branch of the London Missionary Society, which began work in 1824 and has 202 adherents according to the census figures. It maintains a high school at Khāgra near Berhampore. Christians.

The Jains, though not numerous, are an influential section of the community owing to their importance as bankers and land-holders. The wealthy up-country merchants, commonly called Kayahs, who are settled at Azīmganj, belong almost exclusively to this sect; the number enumerated in that town is 795. They have almost monopolized the trade of the district, and are indeed among the wealthiest merchants in Bengal. As stated in the last chapter, the great banking family of the Jagat Seths were originally Jains, but Harakh Seth became a Vaishnava. Other Jain families migrated to Murshidābād from Bikanir in the eighteenth century. Their temples are conspicuous on the banks of the Bhāgīrathi, and three of the temples at Parsanāth have been constructed at the expense of the Murshidābād Jains, who continue to fulfil their duties as founders through their *panchāyat* or committee. The great majority also of the Jain images at Parasnāth bear Sanskrit inscriptions, showing that they were dedicated by various members of the family of Jagath Seth, between 1765 and 1816 A. D. The Jains domiciled in the district are mostly Oswāls by caste. Jains.

CASTES AND TRIBES.

The marginal statement shows the Hindu castes, and in the case of the Musalmāns the social groups, numbering over 25,000. More than nine-tenths of the Musalmāns are Sheikh, this being now a common designation for practically all who cannot claim to be Saiyads, Pathāns or Mughals, or who do not belong to some well recognized functional group, such as Jolāhas or Kulus. The only other Muhammadan groups with any considerable numerical strength are the Pathāns (10,662), Jolāhas (10,908) and Saiyads (7,427).

Name.	Number.
Sheikh	661,637
Chāsi Kaibartta or Māhishya	89,021
Sadgop	43,875
Bāgdi	40,543
Chain	37,654
Brāhman	34,274
Goāla	32,466

The chief Hindu castes are those characteristic of Central and West Bengal, with the exception of the Chains. The latter have a limited geographical distribution, the only other places where they are numerous being Mālda, which contains 44,000 of them, and Bihār, where they aggregate 32,000. They are a low caste, whose occupations are mainly cultivation and labour. Two other castes which are more or less peculiar to this district are the Pundāris and Chāsātis. The Pundāris or Puros, who are also found in Bīrbhūm and Mālda, are agriculturists, vegetable-growers and silk-worm rearers by occupation. They are thought by some to be an offshoot of the Pod caste, the cause of separation being the adoption of an occupation not followed by the main body of the caste. Both the Pods of the 24-Parganas and the Puros of Murshidābād are said to "exhibit in physical appearance an approach to the aboriginal type*." They themselves disclaim connection with the Pods, and as a proof of respectable origin are anxious to be known by the grandiloquent designation of Pundra Kshattriya. They forbid widow marriage, and follow the ordinary observances of middle-class Hindus. The Chāsātis, who are found in Mālda as well as in Murshidābād, are also cultivators and silk-worm rearers. The name Chāsāti is not confined to them, but is also assumed in this district by the Chāsādhobas, who number 14,272, out of a total of 57,626 for the whole of Bengal. They are a cultivating caste who are anxious to disclaim any previous connection with the Dhoba caste, and therefore are beginning to adopt the name of Satchāsi in the place of their old name, which they are afraid may be taken to imply that they were orginally Dhobas who took to cultivation.

*Hunter's Statistical Account of Bengal, Volume IX, page 54.

Among the lower castes the old system of self-government still has considerable vitality. The members of the caste themselves adjudicate upon matters affecting the purity or solidarity of the caste, and inflict punishments upon fellow members who are proved guilty of offences against the caste laws. The sentence is passed either by a *majlis*, *i.e.*, a general meeting of the caste men, or is the decree of a committee of elders; its ultimate sanction is expulsion from the community, which naturally depends on the unanimous consent of all belonging to it. As a rule, the caste councils deal with individual offences already committed, and do not prescribe rules for future conduct. They are tribunals rather than legislative assemblies. There are however exceptions to this rule, such as the general ordinance passed a few years ago by the Muchis of a number of villages in this district (Māniknagar, Kālitala, Beldānga, Audiran, Chumrigācha, Dayānagar and other villages). A report which appeared in the *Statesman* of 16th February 1909 states :—" The Muchis convened a meeting for the purpose of considering what steps should be taken to save themselves from the unenviable notoriety they had gained by some of them being cattle-poisoners. More than two hundred cobblers assembled with their priests at Beldānga. Their first business was to try those of their caste men who had been guilty of poisoning cattle. It was at first proposed that the guilty persons should be ostracized altogether. But this proposal was negatived, and the guilty members were severely warned against recurrence of the crime. They were also fined and ordered to roll on the ground in the presence of the gathering and shake their heads as a sign of penance. Finally a document was signed by all present holding themselves liable to a fine of Rs. 101, if they poisoned any cattle or aided and abetted any one else doing the same." CASTE GOVERNMENT.

The authority of the caste councils in this district appears to be weaker than it is in other parts of the country, such as Bihar, and their verdicts are not treated with the same unquestioning respect. On this point the District Census Officer writes :—"The caste Panchāyats are daily losing influence. The members, in the majority of cases, do not mete out justice as fairly as they used to. The Panchāyats have become amenable to external influences, and in the discharge of their duties distinguish between the rich and the poor. Ostracism has lost its old terrors. A man who cannot get admission into the society of his own village can leave it and enjoy equal privileges in other places. A spirit of individual independence has been born, and men who used silently to bow to the decisions of the caste Panchāyat are now ready to defy it. For crimes such as adultery, etc., for which there is a remedy in law, no one, unless he is very poor, cares to refer his case to a caste Panchāyat. In some places, where education has spread, the caste Panchāyats have been replaced by caste Samitis (*e.g.*, the Māhishya Samiti, the Sadgop Samiti, etc.), in which the formalities of meetings are observed ending with the drawing up of resolutions." At present the Panchāyats deal mainly with such matters as the breach of caste rules regarding eating, drinking and marriage, or the adoption of some occupation which is looked upon as degrading. They also uphold discipline in the caste, punishing such offences as abusing a Mandal and even mutual abuse among relatives, and cases are reported of their effecting family partitions. The following sketch of the system as still in force among a few of the castes of this district sufficiently explains the general organization and methods of procedure.

Bāgdis. The Bāgdis regulate their affairs by means of caste councils (Panchāyats), which may exercise jurisdiction over one village or over several villages, according to the strength of the caste in any locality. Sometimes also, when a village is split up between two antagonistic parties, each has its own Panchāyat. There is a headman in each village called the Mandal, who holds his office by hereditary right. When a Mandal dies, his heir succeeds even if a minor; in such a contingency, however, he is assisted in the discharge of his duties by some close relative. If the heir is disqualified for the post by absence from the village, incompetence, etc., the assembled villagers elect another man. When an offence against caste laws has been committed, the local headman is informed. In places where the Panchāyat has authority over several villages, there is one man in supreme authority, who is called the Parganait Mandal or Pradhān. There are also sometimes two subordinate officials called the Bārik, who carries out the orders of the Mandal, and the Gorait, who summons the members to meetings. When an offence has been committed, the village Mandal is informed, and he in his turn informs the Parganait Mandal if there is a union of villages. The Parganait Mandal tries the case with the help of the Mandal and two or three other Bāgdis of the village in which the accused man resides. If, however, the Panchāyat governs only one village, the Mandal decides the case with two to five other leading villagers: in his capacity as President he is called the Pradhān. When important cases affecting the whole Bāgdi community have to be discussed, there is a larger meeting composed of the Panchāyats of all the neighbouring villages. This is called a Bāisi, meaning literally a Panchāyat of 22 villages. When a Bāisi Panchāyat is convened, the Mandal of the village in which the accused resides puts the case before the meeting.

When a Panchāyat has met, the culprit is called on to explain his conduct. If he pleads guilty, it only remains to decide on the nature of the punishment. Otherwise evidence is taken, and the whole case is thrashed out. The proceedings are not regulated in any strict way, and the trial is frequently noisy, not to say uproarious. The usual punishments are fines and outcasting, which may be either temporary or permanent. A woman found guilty of grave immorality (*e.g.*, a liaison with a man of another caste) is outcasted, and her husband shares her sentence if he takes her side. If he does not attempt to screen her, he has to perform *prāyaschitta* before being re-admitted to caste fellowship. The fines are expended in providing a feast for the members or in toddy for them to drink. If a delinquent is contumacious, *e.g.*, does not pay up or refuses to undergo his punishment, he is outcasted till he comes to his senses and make full submission.

Chains. The functionaries of the Chains are the Pradhān or local headman and a subordinate called Bārik or Parāmānik, who executes the orders of the Pradhān and summons members of the caste to Panchāyat meetings. Each Panchāyat has jurisdiction over a village or a *dihi*, *i.e.*, a group of villages. Appeals from the verdicts of these Panchāyats lie to the Bāisi Panchāyat. Sometimes too all the *Dihi* Panchāyats meet at a Chaurāsi Panchāyat, literally a meeting of 84 villages. At the Bāisi and Chaurāsi Panchāyats the tribunal consists of a President (Pradhān) and four village Pradhāns, two being supposed to be representatives of the accused's side and two of the other side. The accused himself stands with folded hands wearing a cloth round his neck while they discuss the case. In addition to inflicting fines or decreeing excommunication (temporary or permanent), the Panchāyats sentence delinquents to corporal punishment or to perform some humiliating task, *e.g.*, the Parāmānik holds his ear and makes him run round the assembled meeting.

Sheikhs. The Sheikhs have no permanent officials or regular organization like that in force among the lower Hindu castes. They merely hold Panchāyats when the conduct of any member of the community renders it necessary that he should be subjected to punishment. Such Panchāyats are generally held on the Jama day, and are composed of men whose age, position, education or influence qualify them for the exercise of judicial powers. If a man is adjudged guilty, but proves contumacious, he is not only outcasted but beaten by his relatives.

In addition to acknowledging the authority of these occasional tribunals, the Sheikhs obey the fiats of spiritual rulers. Over each group of villages there is a *maulvi*, enjoying the title of Pīr, who acts as an arbiter in religious questions. He imposes fines on the villagers who are his disciples, of which he keeps part for himself, while the remainder is distributed among *fakīrs*. Should he strain the obedience of his followers to breaking point, they have a right to supersede him and call in a neighbouring Pīr.

FAIRS AND RELIGIOUS GATHERINGS.

The most important fairs and religious gatherings are as follows:—(1) The Tulsī-Bihār *Mela*, which is held at Jangipur in May, and also at Nāshipur in the Lālbāgh subdivision. That at Jangipur lasts a month and is attended by about 10,000 people. (2) The Keshabpur *Mela* in the Kāndi subdivision, which lasts seven days and is attended by about 12,000 people. (3) The Gangāsnan *Mela* at Manganpāra in the Sadar subdivision, which is held on the first day of Māgh, when some 10,000 visit the place to bathe in the sacred river. (4) The Purānhāt and Kālītala *Melas* in the Kāndi subdivision. The latter lasts only a day and attracts about 14,000 people. (5) The Kiriteswari *Mela* held on every Tuesday during Māgh at the temple of Kiriteswari, 5 miles west of Lālbāgh. (6) *Melas* at Baneswar in Mirzapur thana during the Sivarātri and Chaitra Sānkrānti festivals: they last two days and attract about 7,000 people. (7) A *mela* held at Lālgola during the Rathjātra festival, which is attended by about 10,000 people. Minor religious gatherings are:—(1) The Chaltiamaltia *Mela*, in honour of Rāma, is held at a spot about a mile south of Berhampore, commencing on the 9th day of the month of Chaitra (March-April) and lasts for about thirty days. (2) Sharveswar *Mela* is held at Dhuliān in April, in honour of the god Siva, and lasts for eight days. (3) Jayadeva Thākur's *Mela* is held at Sāgardighi in January. (4) Kāpileswar *Mela* is held in May at Saktipur, in honour of Kapileswar, one of the many names of Siva. Other fairs of less note are Ananta Baruāh's *Mela* at Mangalpur in December and Rāmnabami *Mela* at Mirzāpur in March.

CHAPTER IV.

PUBLIC HEALTH.

THERE is little detailed information regarding the general healthiness of the district till half a century ago, but the somewhat scanty references to its climate which are found in existing records, though mainly concerned with the towns of Murshidābād and Berhampore and their neighbourhood, are sufficient to show that for the last 100 years it has had a somewhat evil reputation. "There are," it was observed in Hunter's *Statistical Account* (1876), "certain spots in the district which have been desolated by fever within the present century, and which still remain deserted. Of these the most conspicuous is Cossimbazar, where the old stagnant channel of the Bhāgīrathi still attests the cause of the pestilence which overthrew this once flourishing city. It is said that the place was depopulated by a malarious fever in 1814, the year which immediately followed the change of course of the river. There are still a few miserable inhabitants, who haunt the banks of the Cossimbazar lake, as the stagnant pool is yet called; but their sickly condition can never be ameliorated until either that lake be drained, or a current of fresh water be diverted into it. Bīrnagar, the residence of the celebrated Rāni Bhawāni, is said to have been destroyed in the beginning of this century by a similar catastrophe. The village of Mirzāpur, in the thana of the same name, has also been ruined by fever; though in this case the cause of the malaria was not equally manifest. Prior to 1862, Mirzāpur was considered a very healthy place, and had a large population, chiefly composed of silk manufacturers and weavers. But in that year a virulent outbreak of malarious fever took place; and it is said that in a few months half the inhabitants either died or left their homes. Medical relief was at length sent, and the mortality greatly diminished; but at the present time the village cannot boast of a single healthy person. A neighbouring village called Belghāta has met with the same fate. Both these two villages have dirty holes and old ponds, with innumerable clumps of bamboos and other trees on the sides." GENERAL CONDITIONS.

Further evidence of the unhealthiness of the district is given in Colonel Gastrell's *Geographical and Statistical Account of the Murshidābād District* (1860):—"The district of Murshidābād cannot be called healthy. The western side of the Bhāgīrathi has more claims to the title than the eastern, but on neither bank do the inhabitants appear robust and strong; they are all weakly-looking and short in stature. Fever and cholera are the great scourges of the district, more especially in the towns and villages on the Bhāgīrathi, and above all in the city of Murshidābād and its environs. In fact, in the large bazars cases are to be found all the year round. As a general rule, the months of March, April and May, preceding the rainy weather, and October, November and half of December, which follow the cessation of the rains, are the most unhealthy months. No sooner does the Bhāgīrathi fall sufficiently low to allow the *jhil* waters to drain off into it, than sickness commences all along the river banks. It is to this influx of *jhil* water that the natives themselves attribute the sickness so prevalent before the cold season has fairly set in. When to this is added the numerous half-burned bodies that are daily thrown into the river, which is then almost a chain of stagnant pools, there is little cause to wonder at the sickness of those who habitually use this water for drinking and cooking purposes."

SPECIAL INQUIRIES. A special inquiry into the state of the district was made by the Bengal Drainage Committee in 1906-07, in connection with which an investigation into the prevalence and distribution of malaria was carried out (in January and February 1907) by Captain G. E. Stewart, I.M.S., and Lieutenant A. H. Proctor, I.M.S. The areas visited by these two officers were (1) a strip of land on each side of the river Bhāgīrathi from Gorābazar on the south to the retired line of the Bhāgīrathi embankment on the north, (2) that part of the Bhagwāngola thana which lies outside the retired line of the embankment, (3) the Hariharpāra thana and (4) the Lālgola thana. The prevalence of malaria was ascertained by taking the spleen rates of children under 12 years of age. Altogether, 4,744 children were examined in 70 villages, and 1,952 were found to have enlarged spleens, giving a spleen rate of 41 per cent.: this, it may be remarked incidentally, was a lower rate than that observed in either Nadia or Jessore.

The actual mortality due to malaria was estimated by inquiries into the real cause of the illnesses of 242 persons who had been returned as dying of "fever." The result was to show that malaria, either acute or chronic, was the cause of one-third of the deaths, 21·6 per cent. being due to acute and 13·6 per cent. to chronic malaria. Dysentery and diarrhœa were responsible for 15·3 per cent. of the so-called "fever" deaths, and 1·6 per cent. were attributed to the Leishman-Donovan infection. Regarding the latter the investigators remarked:—"This disease is extremely difficult to separate from chronic malaria by the method of questioning the relatives of deceased persons, but it appears to be present only in small amount in this district."

Other causes of death were bronchitis (10·7 per cent.), pneumonia (4·1), phthisis (5·4) and typhoid (2·5). Nearly half of the deaths that were due to acute malaria occurred among children under five years of age, and about half of the deaths caused by malaria among children under 10. The latter accounted for no less than two-fifths of all the deaths inquired into.

The marginal statement shows the spleen rates recorded in the different villages according to their situation. The high rate of villages on dry land which is not flooded annually was associated with thick jungle, collections of casual water and dirty tanks in the villages. The rate for *bil* villages was reduced by the inexplicably low figure returned for three villages on the Telkar *Bil*; and it was remarked that the average (80) for the other villages "probably represents the usual prevalence of malaria in the *bil* villages, at any rate on the east side of the Bhāgīrathi river, more accurately than the average of 49 for the whole class." The explanation of the low rate for villages that are flooded annually was that "probably the majority of such villages are inundated annually by the overflow of the Bhāgīrathi, which thoroughly washes out the village and its surroundings, and sinks rapidly with the fall of the river, and also that a large proportion of these villages are very free from jungle."

Situated on—	Average spleen rate.
Dry land not flooded annually.	57
Dead rivers ...	51·6
Bils	49
Dry land flooded annually.	39
Live rivers ...	38·6

The general conclusion arrived at by the officers who conducted the investigation was as follows :—

"Malaria appears to be prevalent, and there is a large mortality directly due to malaria over the whole area visited but particularly in the area lying south of the retired line of the embankment between the Bhāgīrathi river and the Gobra Nullah, and in the Hariharpāra thana. The area lying north of the retired line of the embankment appears to be more healthy. Average spleen rates have been shown to be highest in villages with the most jungle, and also in villages and areas where the sinking of the subsoil water since the rains has been least. It is probable that it is to the combination of these two factors that the large amount of malaria is due, and not to either of them by itself."

With reference to the report submitted by the investigating officers, and also to the facts disclosed by the census of 1901 and by the thana statistics of vital occurrences, the Drainage Committee came to the following conclusions:—

"Taking the average annual district death-rate from fever (1901—1905) as 29·7 per mille, it may be concluded that the thanas which exhibit a rate of 25 and under are fairly healthy, and those in excess of 40 noticeably the reverse. The healthy thanas of Khargāon, Kāndi, Barwān, Gokaran and Bharatpur (constituting the Kāndi subdivision) occupy a compact block in the south-west corner, while Raghunāthganj and Mirzāpur, along with Shamsherganj, Suti and Sāgardighi (the rates for which are only slightly higher) lie to the north-west—all (except Raghunāthganj) to the west of the Bhāgīrathi. The only other thanas on that side of the river are Nabagrām, which is neither specially healthy nor the reverse, and Asānpur, which falls within the area of high rates. The feverish thanas group themselves in a well-defined tract, running north to south along the east bank of the Bhāgīrathi from Bhagwāngola, through Manullābazar, Shāhānagar, Daulatbazar, Asānpur (west of the Bhāgīrathi), Sujāganj and Gorābazar. The average annual mortality from fever (1901—1905) in these thanas runs higher than any rates in either Jessore or Nadia, with the one exception of the Gāngni thana in the latter, which exceeds the rate of Bhagwāngola only. Hariharpāra adjoining to the east is only slightly less unhealthy. The eastern portion of the district, Gowās, Jalangi and Noāda, stands midway in point of health between the two areas above defined.

"The variations in the total population recorded in the three censuses, especially during the decade 1891—1901 (the figures for the earlier ten years were affected by epidemic fever), corroborate these conclusions in a marked manner. The district as a whole showed a fair increase in population at the last census (+6·6 per cent.), but all the noticeably unhealthy thanas, with the exception of Bhagwāngola and Hariharpāra, and Gorābazar and Asānpur, which were practically stationary, showed a falling off, although it is to be remarked that the declining prosperity of the trade which used to centre around Murshidābād and Cossimbazar has also contributed to this result. The only other decrease in Suti, which is a healthy area, was due to emigration, not illness.

"Turning to the totals of births and deaths during the five years 1901—05, we get further evidence to the same effect. All

area of greatest intensity being between the Bhāgirathi and Gobra Nullah. It was unusual, however, to find more than two houses in a village infected, and he never saw more than four typical cases in any village. Further, he was of opinion that the disease was gradually dying out in the district, that it was no longer epidemic, but had assumed an endemic character, and in many cases ran a chronic course; and he was inclined to believe that there was a comparatively high recovery rate resulting in adult immunity. Briefly, his conclusions may be summarized as follows :—

The feature of the vital statistics of the district is a steadily rising mortality, which is principally due to the causes of splenomegaly. For practical purposes, the causes of splenomegaly in this district are malaria and *Kāla Azār*. The question is—Which of them is the cause of the rising mortality? While admitting that there is a good deal of malaria of the very worst type (malignant tertian) in the district, he held that the steady rise in mortality was due to *Kāla Azār* spreading slowly from one part to another.

A few subsidiary points in Major Forster's report, which are of some interest, may be mentioned here:—

(1) "Phthisis is not common in the villages. Roughly it may be said that the larger the village, the greater the probability of cases of phthisis being present. In municipal towns, however, a different state of affairs prevails, and cases of this disease are very common indeed. An interesting clinical point in connection with this disease is the very rapid course it runs as compared with cases under similar conditions in Europe.

(2) "The only type of fever at all prevalent was that associated with enlargement of the spleen.

(3) "It was ascertained that in 1907, in addition to fever with enlarged spleen, there had been a great outbreak of small-pox, particularly in the Bhagwāngola thana. It appeared that the chaukīdārs were in the habit of returning deaths from this disease under the head of fever to avoid the inconvenience of making daily reports, which are required in cases of epidemic disease.

(4) "Whilst it appears from observations on the endemic index that the district of Murshidābād is not strikingly malarious, it must be remembered that the season 1908-09, during which these observations were made, was a remarkably healthy year in the whole of the Presidency Division. On the other hand, the previous season was one of the worst on record, and if the total mortality of that season had been largely due to the ravages of malaria, one would have expected to find more marked traces of

the malaria epidemic than were brought to light in the course of this inquiry. During a malaria epidemic, and for some time after, one commonly finds that infected children have all three varieties of parasites, whereas in this district mixed infection was the exception. With regard to the varieties of malaria parasites in the district, it will be noted that, as in the case of the Jessore district, malignant tertian is the commonest variety."

Major Forster's views as to the prevalence of *Kāla Azār* are not accepted by Major A. B. Fry, I.M.S., Special Deputy Sanitary Commissioner for Malaria Reserch, Bengal, who criticizes them as follows in his *First Report on Malaria in Bengal* (1912):—

"Major Forster bases his belief that a large amount of the splenomegaly is due to *Kāla Azār* on the fact that he found a low endemic index, which in his opinion did not accord with the then existing spleen rates. Major Forster records that 186 blood films from *patients with fever* gave an endemic index of 34·9 per cent., and that 1,000 blood films collected from *selected fever* cases by Sub-Assistant Surgeons and examined in Calcutta by two Assistant Surgeons gave an endemic index of only 18 per cent. My figures are very different. The films collected from selected fever cases during November gave an index of 79 and 82 per cent. Even the blood films taken fairly at random and at odd seasons, as a sample of the child population, give rates considerably higher than Major Forster's. I therefore criticize his method. In the first place his films were collected by Sub-Assistant Surgeons. I tried this; 1,000 blood films were collected for me by 24 Sub-Assistant Surgeons, each of whom was provided with specially cleaned slides, and each one was individually practised by me in the art of taking films. Out of these 1,000, only 418 were usable, and they were very bad, being much hæmolysed. Now in Major Forster's report there is no remark that all bad films were scrapped, but 1,547 were examined with an infection rate of 9·49 per cent. I think it possible that a large number of slides too bad to be of any use were classed as negative by the microscopists in Calcutta. A second possible explanation is the fact that the year 1908, when Major Forster was at work, was the least malarious of any year for 20 years, which is quite enough to account for the high spleen rate (residual) and very low endemic index. I think that Major Forster's argument based on low endemic index therefore fails.

"Touring from village to village, it is impossible to make splenic punctures. I have seen many chronic *Kāla Azār* cases in Patna and Purnea districts, and find nothing approaching the number in this Division. If *Kāla Azār* is at all rife as a fatal disease, a fair number of advanced wasted cases must be seen. They are extremely rare in Lower Bengal. In my preliminary report I wrote that two places in Murshidābād district, viz., Tārakpur and Choa*, were hot beds of *Kāla Azār*. I judged on the ground of an enormous proportion of large spleens and extremely low endemic index. I have had these places under observation for 1½ years and find that no deaths have occurred, and all the children are recovering and their spleens are much smaller though endemic index is very low. They appear to be residual spleens from an earlier outbreak of malaria. I am of opinion, therefore, that splenomegaly is chiefly due to malaria, and that the small error due to *Kāla Azār* may safely be neglected."

As regards the distribution of malaria, Major Fry finds that the disease is hyper-endemic in the southern portion of the district, and also in a smaller area which has its centre in and around Berhampore, and which spreads to the south-east, where it merges in the larger area. His classification of malarial intensity in the different thanas, as evidenced by the mortality returns, is shown in the marginal statement; the thanas are classified according to the prevalance of the disease, Class 1 showing the areas in which epidemics are most frequent and Class 5 those which have the greatest immunity.

Class 1.

Noāda.

Class 2.

Asāupur.
Bhagwāngola.
Lālgola.
Manullābazar.

Class 3.

Hariharpāra.
Rāninagar.
Sāgardighi.
Shāhānagar.

Class 4.

Daulatbazar.
Gokaran.
Raghunāthganj.
Shamserganj.
Suti.

Class 5.

Barwān.
Beldānga.
Bharatpur.
Kāndi.
Khargāon.
Mirzāpur.
Nabagrām.
Sujāganj.

The following note on the types of fever prevailing in the district was written in 1906 by the then Civil Surgeon :—

TYPES OF FEVER.

"A reference to the death rates of the various thanas will indicate the portions of the district in which the higher mortalities from fever are met with, but in more general terms it may be stated that the half of the district lying to the east of the river Bhāgīrathi has a much higher death rate than the half to the west, and that, on both sides of that river, the thanas lying to the south of the district return lower death rates than those on the same side of the river to the north: the subdivision of Kāndi, extending in the south of the district from the Bhāgīrathi to the borders of Bīrbhūm, is, in this respect, much the most healthy part of the district. It will be noted that this portion of the district comprises most of the country known as the Rārh, which is much more undulating and better drained than the part lying

* In Hariharpāra thana.

between the rivers Bhāgīrathi, Ganges and Jalangi. The highest death rates from fever are met with in the four thanas of Shāhānagar, Manullābazar, Daulatbazar and Bhagwāngola, which are situated between the Bhāgīrathi to the west and the Ganges (Padma) to the north and east.

"There is no reasonable doubt that throughout the district the majority of the deaths recorded from fever are really due either to malarial fever (including its complications and sequelæ), or to the yet as imperfectly understood fever which has been provisionally named cachectic fever, *i.e.*, the fever which is distinguished by the presence of Leishman-Donovan bodies in the blood, and is, according to our present knowledge, identical with the *Kāla Azār* of Assam. This will be referred to later, after noticing the evidence of the presence of other specific fevers, which, if not of importance in considering the death rate, are of considerable clinical import. It seems hardly necessary to remark that a percentage of deaths are returned under the head of fever which have been due to systematic disease, of which a rise of temperature is one of the most apparent symptoms. These include tuberculosis, which certainly in the towns is very prevalent, pneumonia, influenza, and even infantile contagious diseases, such as measles.

"The specific fevers which are met with, excluding malarial and cachectic (Leishman-Donovan) fevers, are enteric fever, filarial fever and, more doubtfully, a continued fever, neither enteric nor malarial, which corresponds to the urban type of fever described by Crombie, and which is as yet the subject of much discussion; the microscopical pathologists mostly deny its existence, and the clinicians feel, on the other hand, that there is a disease having a fever of a continued type, which is seldom fatal, but of which the pathology has not yet been worked out, some believing it the justly called paratyphoid.

"*Enteric fever.*—It is impossible to give any opinion whether this disease is at all common in the villages amongst the ordinary agricultural population, and whether the theory is a true one that the majority of native children suffer from typhoid fever in a mild form in early life and then become immune. There is no evidence whatever of such being the case, but it is impossible to deny that such may be the case, and that it has as yet escaped detection. As regards the towns, and especially as regards Berhampore, its presence both amongst the European and native population has been definitely ascertained. As regards Europeans, the record is not a very bad one. The European troops were moved finally from the cantonments before the days of accurate diagnosis of fever had arrived, but tradition points to their having suffered more from dysentery and chronic forms of fever than from enteric. But within the last ten years reliable information from European sources points to some ten cases of enteric having been diagnosed definitely by the Civil Surgeon of the time, and of these one or two were fatal. During the last 2½ years that the writer has seen practically every case of continued fever among Europeans, there has only been one case of which there has been any reasonable suspicion that it was enteric.

"Amongst natives, the jail records show one death in 1903 verified by *post-mortem*. The writer's own observations do not point to it being frequent amongst the better class of native residents. He has, however, ventured to diagnose definitely a few cases in consultation, and one or two cases amongst police constables. There have been no cases in the jail hospital and very few in the charitable dispensary which gave rise to any suspicion. The hot weather months, March to June, have been the time when the cases diagnosed as enteric, and those giving rise to a doubtful diagnosis, have mostly occurred. As regards Europeans, it may be noted that the population of late years has been much reduced, and very few of those remaining are of the most susceptible age. The water-supply, on the whole, during the last five or six years has been good.

"*Fevers of filarial origin.*—Two varieties are noticed, and, although no doubt both varieties are pathologically identical, yet they present well-marked and easily recognized differences—

'(1) A disease which is characterized by a high fever of a continued type lasting generally three or four days and recurring at irregular and often lengthy intervals. In this type there is a distinct initial vigour, and it has a superficial resemblance to a pernicious form of malarial fever, but a moderate enlargement of the inguinal or femoral glands is always detectable, and, on examination of the blood, filarial embryos are almost always found. This type of fever is not associated with elephantoid enlargement of the lower extremities, or enlargement of the genital organs. It may be that in a later stage such may develop, but observations and inquiries from patients who have such enlargements point to it being uncommon to have such a preliminary stage, and doubtless the blocking of lymphatics is not a necessary result of the presence of adult filaria. The filarial embryos that have been found are usually the Filaria Nocturna, but varieties corresponding to Filaria Ozzardii have been detected.

'(2) The regularly recurring attacks of fever associated with enlargement of the lower extremities or genital organs. This is the type which is popularly believed to recur at the same phase of the moon. That there is some truth in this is believed by most medical practitioners who have had considerable acquaintance with the disease.'

"There is a belief amongst medical practitioners that filarial diseases are largely confined to people living within five or six miles of the river Bhāgīrathi, but I myself have been unable to entirely corroborate this view.

"*Malarial fevers.*—In the town of Berhampore the type is most commonly malignant tertian, the temperature curve being of a remittent type. All clinical varieties are met with in the town from mild cases lasting for three or four days to the severest malignant type; thus, comatose, algide and hyperpyrexial forms are frequently met with. Typical intermittent types are rare in the town, and it must be said that it is rather the exception than the rule to find malarial organisms in the peripheral blood, though from the clinical symptoms there is no doubt of the malarial character of the fever. In the mufassal villages, on the other hand, typical intermittent types are quite common; quotidian, tertian and quartan fevers are all met with. In a considerable number of villages within easy reach of Berhampore quartan fever is quite common: this is rather against the usual experience in Lower Bengal. Out-patients come to the dispensary, and, without prompting, accurately prognosticate the day of the onset, and volunteer that they are free from fever for two days. These quartan cases are met with at all times of the year; they attract particular notice in the earlier months of the year when other forms of malarial fever are uncommon.

"Both simple tertians and well-marked double tertians are moderately common in villagers coming to the Berhampore dispensary, though well-marked simple tertian is less so than non-typal varieties. All these types of intermittent are very amenable to treatment by quinine. The spleen is commonly enlarged, but of a different character to the enlarged spleen of cachectic fever. The following are villages in the vicinity of Berhampore from which well-marked cases of quartan fever habitually present themselves:—Nawāda, Sailadānga, Bohāra, Pulinda, Mehdipur, Bāsudebpur, Haidarpur, Gajādharpur, Pānchātia, Sialmāra, Mājda, Uttarpāra, Rukanpur, Karigāsi, Kaya and Palāspukur.

"*Chronic Cachectic fever.*—A large number of cases of the type of disease which was formerly called malarial cachexia attend the hospital and can be met with on the roads; and no doubt in the more unhealthy villages to the east of the Bhāgīrathi a considerable proportion of the inhabitants are affected. In Berhampore itself few, if any, such cases occur The symptoms are marked cachexia with pigmentation of the skin, great anæmia, great enlargement of the spleen with much induration, and a long continued fever of an irregular character and generally very low degree. The cases are very protracted, but generally end in death, œdema of the extremities and diarrhœa being the terminal symptoms. There is no doubt that these cases are identical with the disease called cachectic fever, and on examination no doubt the Leishman-Donovan bodies would be found. Choa and Daulatābād send some of the most severe and typical cases to the Berhampore Dispensary."

INFIRMITIES.

The record of infirmities which was made during the census of 1911 shows that the district contains 1,023 insane persons (including inmates of the lunatic asylum), 885 deaf-mutes, 1,527 blind persons and 780 lepers. The marginal statement shows the ratio of the afflicted of each sex per 100,000 of the population: in working out the proportion for insane persons, all inmates of the lunatic asylum who were born outside the district have been excluded, so as to obtain only the incidence for the district-born population. Blindness is more common than in any other district of Bengal, while the incidence of leprosy is the highest outside the leper-centres of Burdwān, Bīrbhūm and Bānkura. The proportional figures for insanity and deaf-mutism, however, are below the provincial average. In the decade 1901-10 altogether 1,717 successful operations for cataract were performed in the dispensaries; this was the largest number performed in any district in Bengal.

Infirmity.	Male.	Female.
Insane ...	37	18
Deaf-mutes ...	70	59
Blind ...	114	109
Lepers ...	90	24

MEDICAL INSTITUTIONS.

There are five charitable dispensaries under Government supervision as shown in the statement below, which gives the salient statistics for the year 1911:—

PLACE.	Number of beds.	Income.	Expenditure.	TOTAL NUMBER OF PATIENTS.		DAILY AVERAGE OF PATIENTS.	
				In-door.	Out-door.	In-door.	Out-door.
1	2	3	4	5	6	7	8
		Rs.	Rs.				
Berhampore	73	1,06,078	1,13,038	1,594	38,598	59·80	181·91
Murshidābād (Lālbāgh)	18	5,209	5,517	242	9,309	8·49	61·07
Jangipur	12	6,294	5,671	183	10,126	4·79	52·86
Azimganj	16	4,149	2,755	189	12,675	4·93	85·27
Kāndi	25	6,395	6,025	392	20,352	14·32	121·77

NOTE.—The total income shown in column 3 excludes the balance of the previous year.

The Berhampore Dispensary, which was started in 1855, has been greatly improved, during the present century, by the addition of a female ward for in-patients, the construction of a cottage ward and the addition of a separate out-door dispensary from a donation of Rs. 6,000 given by Rājā Jogendra Nārāyan Ray Bahādur of Lālgolā for the purpose. With the help of a further gift of Rs. 5,000 from the same gentleman, a new operation room has been built, which is well equipped in every detail. Further, an eye hospital has been constructed; the Rājā Bahādur has given Rs. 20,000 for the building and Rs. 64,000 for the maintenance of 16 beds in it. In addition to these munificent donations, he has given a lakh of rupees for the upkeep of the female portion of the hospital. New buildings have also been erected to provide quarters for the Assistant Surgeon, the nursing sisters, the lady doctor and some of the hospital servants. The hospital has been fortunate in securing the services of three Italian nursing sisters to look after the patients, and has thereby largely enhanced its popularity. It is a third class dispensary. Its income in 1911 was derived from the following sources:—Municipal grant Rs. 2,550, District Board grant Rs. 5,000, Government grant Rs. 3,976, private subscriptions Rs. 86,678 and other sources Rs. 7,874.

The Murshidābād (Lālbāgh) Dispensary has also been greatly improved of late years as regards accommodation, equipment and general working. Quarters have been built for the staff. It has attached to it a lady doctor, for whom quarters have been built, and it appears to be gaining both in attendance and popularity. It is a third class dispensary. Its income in 1911 was made up as follows:—Municipal grant Rs. 2,367, District Board grant Rs. 180, Government grant Rs. 1,295, private subscriptions Rs. 1,186 and other sources Rs. 181.

The Jangipur Dispensary was first founded in 1864, and re-organized in 1873. Up to the latter date it had been merely a small and not very efficient establishment in connection with the subdivisional lock-up. But at the commencement of 1873 a meeting was held of the inhabitants, who guaranteed a local subscription of Rs. 500 per annum, and forwarded a request to Government for a separate dispensary under a special doctor. It is a third class dispensary. Its income in 1911 was obtained from the following sources:—Municipal grant Rs 2,100, District Board grant Rs. 1,500, Government grant Rs. 579, private subscriptions Rs. 997 and other sources Rs. 1,118.

The Azīmganj Dispensary was founded in 1866 by Rai Dhanpat Singh Bahādur, and was transferred to a new building in 1909. This building was erected from a donation of Rs. 15,000 given by Rai Dhanpat Singh Naulākha Bahādur, who made a further gift of Rs. 2,000 for out-houses, besides giving Rs. 1,300 for levelling the site and Rs. 1,000 for the equipment of the dispensary. It is a third class dispensary. Its income in 1911 was as follows:—Municipal grant Rs. 2,247, District Board grant Rs. 120, Government grant Rs. 138, private subscriptions Rs. 1,641 and other sources Rs. 3.

The Kāndi Dispensary, the full title of which is the Kāndi Girish Chandra Hospital, owes its establishment to the generosity of the late Kumār Girish Chandra Sinha of Paikpāra, who bequeathed the sum of Rs. 1,25,000 for its construction and maintenance. It was built at a cost of Rs. 19,000 and was opened in 1888. It is maintained from the interest of the endowment, which amounts to Rs. 1,60,400 invested in Government promissory notes, supplemented by an annual grant of Rs 600 from the local municipality. In 1908 a new out-door block for male patients was erected, and a tank for the use of the hospital was re-excavated.

LUNATIC ASYLUM. There is a central lunatic asylum at Berhampore, which is accommodated in part of the old barracks. It was opened in 1874 (prior to which the asylum was in an old unhealthy building at Maidāpur, three miles from the civil station) and was enlarged in 1905 at a cost of three lakhs. It has accommodation for 583 male and 127 female lunatics, but, in spite of this, it is overcrowded and has for some years past been condemned as below the standard of modern requirements.

VACCINATION. Inoculation for small-pox appears formerly to have been a common practice in Murshidābād. Forty years ago the Civil Surgeon wrote:—"There is a large number of Hindus and some Musalmāns from Bihar and the North-West residing in the district, who absolutely refuse to have themselves and their children vaccinated. These people therefore suffer most; and when small-pox gets among them, it continues for a long time. They do not isolate the attacked to prevent contagion; they buy and sell, and wash and go into the infected houses, utterly regardless of the result. One woman told me lately: 'If Kālī takes my child, she will. It is not our custom to offend her by vaccination.' Stopping inoculation has had one good effect; the inoculators are now taking to vaccination as a means of living."

The practice has not yet died out, for even 10 years ago it was reported:—"Vaccination is compulsory only in the towns, and the people in the villages (as is generally the practice with the people of Bengal) are inoculated from the virus of small-pox taken from human patients. The operation is performed by village barbers or men who are held in repute in the village for curing small-pox." The statistics compiled annually show a steady increase in the number of successful vaccinations, viz., from 37,980 representing 32 per mille of the population in 1900-01 to 46,240 or 37 per mille in 1910-11.

CHAPTER V.

AGRICULTURE.

The whole district, with the exception of the small portion which lies to the north of the entrance of the Bhāgīrathi, is divided into two tracts of nearly equal size by that river. The characteristics of these two divisions are quite distinct both as regards the configuration of the country and the kind of crops cultivated, as well as the sort of weather required for their cultivation. The Bāgri or eastern half is, as a rule, low and subject to inundation, but the alluvial soil is very fertile. The principal crops are *aus* or early rice and jute, and when they are off the ground abundant cold-weather crops are raised; but in the low lands to the south-east, over the tract known as the Kālantar, practically the only crop is *āman* or winter rice, which depends on floods for successful cultivation. In the Rārh or western portion, on the other hand, and also in thana Shāmsherganj and the northern part of thana Suti, the land is generally high, but intersected with numerous *bils* and old beds of rivers. Winter rice is the main staple grown on the hard clay of the Rārh, and the cold-weather crops are few, but sugar-cane, mulberry, tobacco, potatoes and various vegetables are also grown. GENERAL CONDITIONS.

Owing to differences of situation and surface, and of the nature of the crops grown, these two portions of the district are differently affected by the weather. Thus, for the eastern half, early rains are needed in April and May for the proper cultivation of the *aus* crop, and steady but not too heavy falls until the crop is reaped in August; a premature break-up of the rains is undesirable, as also are very heavy falls when the cold-weather crops are in the ground; finally, some rain is wanted during the cold season. For *āman* rice, the great staple of the western half of the district, it is not so important that there should be early rain, though it is of advantage that the land should be prepared in good time for the reception of the seed. What is wanted above all is steady rain in the months of July, August, September and the early part of October, without long intervals of dry scorching weather : this is especially the case when the seedlings have been transplanted from the nurseries.

The country to the west is highly cultivated and, except for *bils* and marshes and a few patches of jungle, there is comparatively little waste land : even the beds and banks of the nullahs and *bils*, as they dry up, are tilled to the fullest extent. The fields of the high lands are almost exclusively devoted to the production of rice. The land, where sloping, is terraced each field having a bank round it to retain the water for the rice crop. When rain is deficient, the fields in the vicinity of tanks, which abound in the western portion of the district, are irrigated from them. This part of the country is prettily wooded with mango, banyan, *pīpal, sakua* and palm trees; and on some uncultivated patches of land custard apple and *gāman* bushes form a thick underwood. The produce of the northern low lands consists of abundant and luxuriant crops of different kinds of paddy, gram, peas, mustard, different kinds of pulse, mulberry, *pān*, yams, and in the vicinity of villages different sorts of vegetables. In the Bāgri or eastern half large crops of red chillies are grown. The principal trees are those above enumerated, together with *bābul*, jack, *safriām*, tamarind, *papaya, bel, kath, guluria*, plantain, *jamalgota*, *āsan*, fan-leaf and date palm trees and mangoes.

In the vicinity of the *bils*, *boro dhān*, a coarse grained rice, is planted largely. As the *bil* water dries up, this is transplanted into the *bil* lands, and is harvested in the latter end of March and April. The long sloping banks of nullahs and *khāls* yield good crops of mustard, wheat, and other grains. The richest soil and that least liable, from height or locality, to inundation, is, chosen for the cultivation of mulberry and is called *tut* land. The fields thus selected require a fresh layer of good earth every second year. In the course of time they thus become raised above the surrounding country five or six feet high, still further securing the young plants from being drowned by the lodgment of water. The average rent of such land is from three to five times that of any other, except *pān* gardens: these command the highest rent of all, for very rich soil, well raised, is required for the growth of *pān*. Sugar-cane cultivation is carried on to a small extent in the west and south-west. Date palm trees are chiefly cultivated for the preparation of toddy, but little date-sugar being made in the district.

IRRIGATION. Artificial irrigation is largely practised in the Rārh, and but seldom in the Bāgri. In the former tract, owing to the conformation of the country and the quality of the soil, the crops are almost dependent upon an artificial supply of water; whereas, in the alluvial land between the Ganges and the Bhāgīrathi, the rainfall and the annual inundations of the rivers furnish sufficient moisture for the crops. Irrigation is conducted either from the *bils* and tanks, or by leading the water from natural channels. Irrigation wells and artificial canals do not exist.

The machinery employed is of a simple character. Where the dip is great, a bucket is slung at one end of a long bamboo, and the other end is weighted, generally with a lump of stiff clay. This machine, which is known as *dhenkli*, is dipped and worked by a single man. For a small lift the *dongā* or hollowed-out palm-tree is used. The smaller end is fixed on a pivot between two posts, on a level with the channel into which the water is to be poured, the larger end being dipped into the water below. To this is attached, from above, a long bamboo, weighted with clay at the further end, in order to counterbalance the water in the dip-end of the *dongā*. This engine can be worked by one man. The *siuni*, or small bamboo and reed basket, is also used for the same purpose. It is made of a very flat shape, and is slung by four strings. Two men, one on either side of the water-cut, take a string in each hand, and by alternately lowering and raising the basket swing up the water expeditiously into the fields above.

Several kinds of soils are recognised. *Māthāl* or *methel* is a clayey soil, which splits up in the hot weather, and is tenaciously muddy after rain. There are various sub-divisions according to colour, consistency, etc., *e.g.*, *hende māthāl* is black and tenacious, *bāgh māthāl* is brown, and *ranga māthāl*, which is found on the west of the Bhāgīrathi is red with a tinge of yellow. The common name for loamy soil is *doash*, of which several varieties are recognized, such as *pali* (light brown), *shampali* (ash-coloured), *doma* (dark red), etc. These are all very fertile and produce all kinds of crops. *Metebāli* is the name for a sandy loam: if it has a large percentage of sand, it is called *domabāli* *Bāli* or *bele* is a sandy soil found on the banks or in the beds of rivers. It is unprofitable till a clayey silt has been deposited, when it bears a high value, and is chiefly used for vegetables.

Cultivated *land*, as distinguished from *soil*, is arranged in three classes with reference to their degrees of fertility, viz., *āwāl* or first class, *doem* or second class and *siyum* or third class. Apart from these generic groups, six distinct classes are recognised, viz. —(1) *sāli*, (2) *do*, (3) *jedānga*, (4) *olan*, (5) *dihi tut*, (6) *māthāl tut* and (7) *gohuni*.

Of *sāli* land there are three kinds. First class *sāli* land will bear three crops in the year—a crop of rice, a crop of *khesāri* (Lathyrus sativus) and a crop of *til* (*kashta til*): this *til* has a seed somewhat lighter in colour and larger than that of the *krishna til* or black *til* (Sesamum orientale). *Sāli* land of the second class is a little poorer in quality. The best *sāli* land lies a little lower than that of second class, and therefore, when rain falls, gets all the silt of the higher levels. It is also easier to irrigate. *Sāli* land of the second class yields two crops, *āman* rice and *til*, the out-turn being about one-third less. Third class *sāli* land is situated still higher. The yield of rice is still smaller than that of second class *sāli* land and about half that of first-class land. High lands capable of bearing cold weather crops are called *sona* in distinction from low *sāli* rice lands.

Do land bears *aus* or autumn rice, and also the following crops:—*būt* or gram, *musuri*, peas, wheat, *tisi* or linseed, mustard, *khesāri*, *til* (Sesamum orientale) and sugar-cane. *Do* land is more coveted than *sāli*, and commands a higher rent, because there is a greater choice of crops and therefore less risk of total failure. It is divided into two classes. In the first class, rice is either sown broadcast or (more usually) transplanted from the nursery. The process is the same as for *āman* rice; but the *aus* rice ripens earlier, and is cut in September or October. The land is then manured and again ploughed, and a cold-weather crop (any of those mentioned above, except *til* and sugar-cane) is sown broadcast and ploughed in. After the cold-weather crop is taken off the ground, the land is frequently manured again and ploughed, and is then sown with *til*. When this has been reaped, the time for rice sowing has come round again. Sugar-cane is grown on *do* land as a single crop.

Second class *do* land is not so easily irrigated as the first class, and is also inferior in yield. The same crops may be grown in this as in *do* land of the first class; or, instead of the cold-weather crops mentioned above, onions or garlic may be raised.

Jedāngā is a high, poor land—*niras*, or juiceless, is the word used to describe it: it is found near homesteads, and also in the open plains. The crops grown upon it are *arhar* (Cytisus cajan), *son* or Indian hemp (Crotolaria juncea), and *bāigun* or brinjal (Solanum melongena). Orchards or groves of mango, jack and other fruit trees are also to be found on this land. Other crops are not grown. The land is difficult of irrigation, and bears but one crop in the year.

Olan is land covered with silt along the river banks. It is very fertile, but liable to inundation, as its name (*olan*, low) indicates. It is generally devoted to the growth of cucurbitaceous plants, such as the following:—*tarmus* or water-melon, *kānkur*, *lāu*, *uchhe*, *karalā* and *khero*.

Mulberry lands are of two kinds, known as *dihi tut* and *māthāl tut*. The first is high land near the village, and is particularly favourable to mulberry cultivation. *Māthāl tut* is high land in the open, away from the villages; it is not so strong as the *dihi tut*.

AREA UNDER CULTIVATION. According to the statistics for the year 1911-12, the net cultivated area is 906 square miles, or two-fifths of the district area. A considerable portion of the soil bears double crops in the year, the area cropped more than once amounting to 332 square miles or over a third of the cultivated area. Current fallows account for 582 square miles and cultivable waste (other than fallow) for 417 square miles, while the area not available for cultivation is 235 square miles.

PRINCIPAL CROPS. Rice is by far the most important crop, being raised on 788 square miles or 87 per cent. of the cultivated area. Other cereals and pulses occupy 248 square miles, the greater part of which is under gram, wheat and barley. Murshidābād is one of the few Bengal districts in which wheat and barley are produced to any considerable extent. Oilseeds, such as linseed, *til* or gingelly, rape and mustard, have a total area of 56 square miles, and jute of 43 square miles. The area sown with jute varies according to the seasons and the price obtained for the fibre; and the figure quoted is considerably below the normal, which is 62 square miles. Sugar-cane and tobacco are cultivated to a small extent.

Rice. The rice crop is divided into two great classes, known as *āman* and *aus*. The *āman* or *haimantik* is the principal crop of the district, and constitutes the bulk of the rice that is consumed by the well-to-do classes, and exported to foreign markets. It is sown in July and August, occasionally as late as September, and reaped in December and January. It generally undergoes one transplantation, but sometimes it is allowed to grow up as it is sown broadcast. Well-watered or marshy lands are best suited to its cultivation, though it can be grown on high lands. The *aus* crop, which is sometimes also called *bhadai*, from the name of the month in which it is reaped, is sown in April and May and harvested in August and September. It is a coarser kind of rice, and is chiefly retained in the district as the food of the lower classes. It is usually grown on dry land, and never in the marshes. Convenience of irrigation is the circumstance that mainly governs the selection of land for its cultivation: fields which border on rivers or *khāls* are most frequently chosen. It is sown broadcast and not transplanted. There is one variety of the *aus* crop, the cultivation of which differs considerably from that which has been just described. It is distinguished from the common *bhadai* by the name of *kārtiki*, and is also known as *jhanti*. It is sown in July and reaped in October. It grows for the most part on moist lands, and is sometimes transplanted.

There are two minor crops known as *boro* and *jāli*. The *boro* is a coarse kind of marsh rice, sown in January or February and reaped in April, May or June. It grows on swampy lands, the sides of tanks, or the beds of dried-up water-courses. The *jāli* rice is not much cultivated. It is sown in spring and reaped during the rainy season. It grows on low river banks, which remain moist even during the hot months owing to subsoil percolation.

Rice, when in the seed, is called *bij* or *bichān;* when it germinates, *ankur;* the young plant is *jāwāli;* the full-grown plant, *gāchh-dhān;* just before it is in the ear, *thor;* when in ear, *phulā*. The grain until it is husked is known as *dhān;* after husking it becomes *chāul;* and when cooked it is *bhāt* or *anna*.

The preparations made from rice are—(1) *khai*, which is paddy or unhusked rice merely parched, the husks separating from the grain during the process of parching; (2) *murki*, which is *khai* dipped in boiled *gur* or molasses; (3) *muri*, a peculiar kind of husked rice, fried; (4) *chirā*, unhusked rice which, after being boiled, is husked and beaten flat; (5) *chāul bhājā*, or ordinary parched rice; and (6) *pistak*, or home-made cakes of parched or husked rice ground into flour. *Pistak* or *pithā* includes the following varieties:—(1) *puli;* (2) *saru chākli*, which consists of ground rice made into thin *chapātis;* and (3) *mālpuā*, which is composed of ground rice fried in oil or *ghi*, together with plantains and sweetmeats.

Other cereals and pulses.

Cereals other than rice comprise wheat and barley (both of which are sown in October and November and reaped in March and April) and the following coarser grains—(1) *bhura*, (2) *chinā*, (3) *kodo*, (4) *maruā*, (5) *kowāin*, (6) *sial neja* and (7) *syāmā*. These seven are all sown in April or May and reaped in August or September. For eating they are either boiled entire like rice or ground into flour. Maize (*bhutta*), oats (*jāi*) and *bājra* are also cultivated, but only to a small extent.

Gram (*chānā*, *chholā*, or *but*) is sown in October and November and reaped in February and March. The pulses cultivated are of various sorts, and include (1) common *kalāi*, which is sown in October and reaped in January, (2) *mās-kalāi*, sown in September and reaped in January, (3) *mug*, sown and reaped at the same time as the preceding, (4) *arhar*, sown in April and reaped in March and (5) *musuri*, sown in October and reaped in February and March. *Kurti kalāi* is sown in August and reaped in December and January. *Khesāri* is also sown in October and reaped in February and March. The *khesāri* crop is sown among the rice, as it begins to ripen, in moist and muddy land. This crop requires no care, and ripens in Phālgun (February-March), when it is cut and threshed.

Mustard (*sarishā*) is sown in October and reaped in December and January. Linseed (*tīsi*) is sown in October and reaped in February and March. Sesamum (*til*) is sown in July and August and reaped in December and January. Oil-seeds.

The actual quantity of land given up to jute varies considerably according to the prices which the produce commands in the market, but on the whole it shows a steady tendency to increase. In 1901-02 the normal acreage under jute was only 21,700 acres, the actual area under the crop in that year being 24,000 acres, whereas the corresponding figures for 1911-12 are 39,800 and 27,700 acres respectively. Jute.

The seasons for sowing and growth are the same as for *aus* or early rice. After the usual ploughing the seed is sown broadcast from the middle or end of March to the beginning of June, and the plant is generally cut from the middle of August to the middle of October, by which time it has attained a height of five to ten feet. The stalks, when cut, are made up into bundles and immersed in some pool, tank or stream, and left to steep; this process is called retting. While the bundles are under water, they are examined from time to time to see how far decomposition has proceeded. As soon as it is found that the fibre will peel off easily from the stem, the bundles are taken out, and the stalks are beaten or shaken in the water till the glutinous substance in the bark is entirely washed away. The fibre is then dried in the sun, and, when dry, is made up into hanks (*gānt*) and sold to agents, who consign it to the jute presses and mills.

MISCELLANEOUS.

Mulberry cultivation.

Mulberry cultivation is of considerable importance in Murshidabad. The plant (*Morus indica*) requires a light soil above flood level with good drainage. It is propagated from cuttings and cultivated like a shrub. The plants are arranged in lines 1½ to 2 feet apart and are pruned so as to prevent them reaching a height of more than 1½ to 2 feet. In the way the plants are laid down in lines and regularly pruned, the cultivation resembles that of tea. Plucking of leaves goes on throughout the year, but the chief seasons are April, June and November. The mulberry fields have generally embankments round them, which gives them a curious chess-board appearance. The principal centres of cultivation are called *juārs.*

For mulberry cultivation, the ground is first ploughed three times in Bhādra (August-September), and is afterwards dug up with the hoe, and well manured. In Aswin (September-October) the cuttings are planted, the ground watered, and the earth pressed down; in ten or twelve days the cuttings begin to sprout. In Kārtik (October-November) the ground must be dug and the plants earthed up. In Chaitra (March-April) a top-dressing of mud from the bottom of a tank is spread over the field. During the hot weather irrigation must be kept up, and during the rains the field must be weeded monthly. In Bhādra (August-September), after the first year of growth, the plants should be pruned.

The crop is a risky one, for, should the worms die, the mulberry leaf becomes a drug in the market. Mulberry fields are more valuable than any others, except the little plots on which *pān* is grown; but, as the quality of the silk mainly depends on a full supply of good and fresh leaves to the worms, the demand for mulberry constantly fluctuates according as silk-worms are plentiful or otherwise. When worms are plentiful, the leaf fetches a high price, and the gain to the mulberry grower is great; when the worms fail, it is merely used as fodder for cattle.

Indigo cultivation.

The cultivation and manufacture of indigo used to be an industry of considerable importance in Murshidābād. It flourished in the first half of the nineteenth century, but fell off after the indigo riots of 1860, of which an account is given below. The disturbances were particularly disastrous to this district, which witnessed the most serious case of loss of life which took place in an attack upon a factory. The industry, though badly shaken, survived till the early years of this century, when it was extinguished by the rise in the cost of labour and the competition of the cheaper synthetic dye made in Germany. The proprietors of large concerns have now sold their lands or have become receivers of rent from lands which grow country produce. Many ruined factories may be seen in various parts of the district, but more especially in the Bāgri or eastern half, where the principal concerns were located.

During the first half of the nineteenth century the district became dotted with indigo concerns, owned by European capitalists or by proprietors backed by money advanced by agents in Calcutta. The high prices which the dye fetched in the market ensured large profits, and money was plentiful with the planters. The ryots eagerly took advances to grow the plant, and its cultivation steadily increased. After 1850, however, the prospects of the industry became overclouded. There was a real and widespread discontent among the cultivators, which was the resultant of several combined causes. As the concerns increased in size, the European managers and assistants could give less personal supervision, and their underlings had more independent control, which they used to cheat and fleece the cultivators. The latter sunk into a state of chronic indebtedness to the factories on account of the advances which went on in the books from father to son. These were a source of hereditary irritation, which became inflamed whenever bad seasons obliged the planters to put pressure on the cultivators to make them pay up; and for some years previous to 1860 there had been bad harvests and high prices, which made them feel the pinch. Added to this was the fact that there had been a rise in the price of ordinary country crops, which made their cultivation more paying than that of indigo, while the raiyats were precluded from growing them by their engagements to the factories. At the same time the construction of the Eastern Bengal State Railway line led to a sudden rise in the price of labour, with which the planters failed to keep pace; and some of the badly managed factories had recourse to illegal practices to enforce the cultivation of indigo. The unrest was fanned by agitators, and a rumour having been started that Government itself was opposed to the cultivation, the ryots at length boycotted it.

At first, all the planters suffered equally, the good with the bad, and for some time were at the mercy of the cultivators. Those of them who had acted on their own judgement, and sown their lands with indigo in the terms of the contracts which they had entered into with the factories, were seized and beaten by mobs of angry peasants. The Bengal Government endeavoured to arrest the movement, and eventually passed Act XI of 1860 "to enforce the fulfilment of indigo contracts, and to provide for the appointment of a commission of enquiry." This commission sat during the hot weather of 1860, and its report was submitted in August of the same year. The general conclusion at which it arrived was that the cause of the evils in the system of indigo cultivation as then practised was to be found in the fact that the manufacturer required the ryot to furnish the plant for a payment not nearly equal to the cost of its production, and that it was to the system, which was of very long standing, rather than to the planters themselves, that blame attached. The only remedy recommended by the commission which it was in the power of Government to apply was a good and effective administration of the law as it stood.

The moral effect of the temporary Act of 1860, and the public assurance given to the ryots that proved grievances would be remedied for future seasons, was such that most of the planters were able to complete their spring sowings, but as autumn came on the state of affairs became very critical. Lord Canning wrote:—"I assure you that for about a week it caused me more anxiety than I have had since the days of Delhi," and "I felt that a shot fired in anger or fear by one foolish planter might put every factory in Lower Bengal in flames." Towards the end of September the Government of India authorized the issue of a notification in the affected districts to disabuse the minds of the rural population of the erroneous impression that Government was opposed to the cultivation of indigo. They were assured that in future their right to free action in regard to indigo, as in regard to all other crops, would be respected. All parties were warned against having recourse to violent or unlawful proceedings; and Government announced its intention not to re-enact the temporary law of 1860. Reports that the ryots would oppose the October sowings led Government to strengthen the military police in the indigo districts, and to send two gun-boats to the rivers of Nadiā and Jessore, and Native Infantry to the headquarters stations of these two districts. Further steps were taken to prevent disturbances during the next sowing season. For a long time however there was a complete overthrow of the industry in the indigo districts (Murshidābād, Nadiā, Jessore, Pābna and Farīdpur). By degrees, as the excitement cooled down, those factories which had been most carefully managed before the disturbances recovered; and eventually most of the concerns which were well backed by capital succeeded in weathering the storm. They were, in fact, carried on until the invention of synthetic indigo reduced the price of the natural dye to such an extent as practically to destroy the industry.

PASTURAGE. In the south-west of the district, at the confluence of the Mor and the Dwārka rivers, there is a tract of low-lying country, known as the Hijāl, which is used for pasturing cattle. During the rains it is covered with water, and produces *aus* and *boro* rice; but during the dry season the Goālas drive thither numerous herds of cattle. Besides the Hijāl, there are numerous smaller spots of pasturage ground scattered over the district.

Cattle fairs are held at Pānchāmdi and Tālibpur in the Kāndi subdivision and occasionally at Bhābta, Lālgala and Beldānga in the Sadar subdivision.

AGRICULTURAL EXHIBITION. An agricultural and industrial exhibition is held at Banjetia every year in the middle of February, at which prizes are awarded to successful exhibitors. The cost is borne by Maharaja Manindra Chandra Nandi of Cossimbazar, and the Government Agricultural Department generally makes a grant of Rs. 250.

CHAPTER VI.

NATURAL CALAMITIES.

FAMINES.
Famine of 1769-70.

THE first famine of which there is any detailed record is that of 1769-70, which was a calamity of the first magnitude in this and the neighbouring districts. The following account is taken mainly from the statements made at the time by Mr. Becher, Resident at the Darbār of Murshidābād, which are quoted in Sir George Campbell's *Memoir on the Famines which affected Bengal in the Last Century*. The first allusion to the impending distress was made in August 1769, when Mr. Becher reported "the alarming want of rain which has prevailed throughout all the upper parts of Bengal, both the last and this season, and particularly the latter, to a degree which has not been known in the memory of the oldest man." On 26th August he added, "There is great reason to apprehend that in all the districts to the northward of Nadia the crops of rice will be very short indeed. Since the season for rain began, they have hardly had any; and if God does not soon bless this country with plentiful showers, the most fatal consequences will ensue—not only a reduction in the revenues, but a scene of misery and distress that is a constant attendant on famine." All through the closing months of 1769 the drought continued, and the worst anticipations were realized.

In the beginning of February 1770, the Resident, in conjunction with the authorities of Murshidābād, arranged to have rice distributed daily in the city at six places, at half a seer to each person. The Government, in reply, informed him that he might be assured of their concurrence in measures for the relief of the poor, and earnestly recommended his taking every step towards that purpose. On the 30th March he stated that the districts which had more particularly suffered by the unfavourableness of the season were Purnea, Rājmahāl, Bīrbhūm, and part of Rājshāhi. The measures of relief which he adopted were advances to ryots, remissions of revenue, and distributions of food. A little later he said that he had intended to proceed on tour, but was deterred for the present, being "persuaded that, though my humanity may be shocked at the numberless scenes of distress that would present themselves to my view, little would remain in my power to contribute to their comfort, while God pleases to hold from them the blessing of rain, and the country remains parched and unfit for cultivation. The distress of the inhabitants does not only proceed from scarcity of provisions, but in many parts they are without water to drink." His Assistants were out in their districts, and all told the same painful story.

In the beginning of June we have another report from the Resident at Murshidābād. "Up to the end of March," he says, "the ryots hoped for rain, but God was pleased to withhold that blessing till the latter end of May. The scene of misery that intervened, and still continues, shocks humanity too much to bear description. Certain it is, that in several parts the living have fed on the dead; and the number that have perished in those provinces which have suffered most is calculated to have been within these few months as 6 to 16 of the whole inhabitants." On the 18th of June he writes, "Misery and distress increase here daily; rice at six and seven seers for the rupee, and there have been several days lately when there was not a grain to be purchased. A happy precaution it was, ordering a supply of rice from Backergunge; without it, many of the Company's immediate attendants even must have starved."

In July the distress reached its climax. On the 12th of that month the Resident reported as follows:—"The representations I have hitherto made from hence, of the misery and distress of the inhabitants for want of grain and provisions, were faint in comparison to the miseries endured in, and within 30 miles of, the city. Rice only three seers for a rupee, other grain in proportion, and even at these exorbitant prices, not nearly sufficient for the supply of half the inhabitants; so that in the city of Murshidâbâd alone, it is calculated that more than five hundred are starved daily; and in the villages and country adjacent, the numbers said to perish exceed belief. Every endeavour of the Ministers and myself has been exerted to lessen this dreadful calamity. The prospect of the approaching crop is favourable; and we have the comfort to know that the distress of the inhabitants to the northward and eastward of us is greatly relieved from what they have before suffered. In one month we may expect relief from our present distresses from the new harvest, if people survive to gather it in; but the numbers that I am sensible must perish in that interval, and those that I see dying around me, greatly affect my feelings of humanity as a man, and make me as a servant to the Company very apprehensive of the consequences that may ensue to the revenues."

Rain came at the end of July; but, as often happens, the long-continued drought was succeeded by disastrous floods. The excessive rainfall caused much sickness among the people; and at the height of the famine small-pox had broken out, to which the young Nawāb himself fell a victim. As late as September, it was reported that the people near Cossimbazar were suffering from want of food. In October the prospect brightened; and on the 14th December the Government could inform the Court of Directors that the famine had entirely ceased.

The measures adopted to relieve the starving population in the city of Murshidābād appear very inadequate when judged by the modern standard. The account of the Backergunge rice received shows only Rs. 1,24,506 expended on its purchase. A further sum of Rs. 87,000 was sanctioned for the gratuitous distribution of rice; but of this sum the Company was to pay only Rs. 40,000, or less than half, the remaining portion being defrayed by the Nawāb and his Ministers. This sum was however, far exceeded; and Mr. Becher writes pathetically to beg the Council to believe that "neither humanity nor policy would admit of a stop being put to the distribution earlier than was done." He continues, "I have only to observe that these gentlemen (Muhammad Reza Khān and his officers), independent of this distribution, helped to preserve the lives of many by their charitable donations, as, I believe, did every man of property in these parts. Indeed, a man must have had a heart of stone that had the ability and would have refused his mite for the relief of such miserable objects as constantly presented themselves to our view. I understand it to be esteemed good policy in all Governments to preserve the lives of the people; on this principle of humanity the distribution of rice took place."

Famine of 1866.

In the famine year of 1866 the district of Murshidābād lay just outside the limits of extreme suffering. The neighbouring districts to the south, Nadia and Burdwān, experienced all the severity of the dearth; but in Murshidābād itself no lives were lost from starvation, and Government relief was never required. The following paragraphs are taken from the Report of the Famine Commissioners:—

"The pressure of high prices was much felt in this district, rice selling at from 7 to 9 seers per rupee in part of June, July, and part of August; but very great relief was afforded by native liberality. The rich Hindustāni merchants settled in the neighbourhood of Murshidābād (Rāi Dhanpat Singh and others), and several of the wealthier residents of that city and of the sister town of Berhampore distributed food largely to the poor; and a rich and benevolent widow, the Rāni Swarnamayi, distinguished herself by great liberality at several different places. Up to a certain date it was hoped that there would be no actual famine; but in the course of July it was found that much local distress was beginning to appear in the south-eastern corner of the district adjacent to Nadia. The local committee, presided over by the Commissioner, immediately sent out food, and an active native officer was specially deputed to ascertain the facts and superintend the operations. The distress was for a short time very considerable, but it was relieved by an ample distribution of food. Eight feeding centres were established, and at one of these the number receiving rations was at one time as high as 1,800 persons, mostly women and children. The plan was adopted of giving to each three days' uncooked food at a time, and thus much of the inconvenience of the feeding centres was avoided; but, of course, this required fuller supplies and better superintendence than was available in the districts where the famine was most severe. The indulgence does not seem to have been abused, for as soon as the early rice crop was cut, the distress ceased, and the relief operations were discontinued. The relief in this district was entirely supplied from private funds, without any aid from the North-West fund, the Government, or any other external source."

Famine of 1874.

The famine of 1874 was also felt only to a slight extent in the district of Murshidābād, which again lay on the border-land of the distressed area. The price of rice undoubtedly rose very high, and the export of this grain from the river marts of the district towards the north-west entirely ceased; but the crisis was tided over without recourse to relief operations on a grand scale. The intervention of Government was limited to the grant of an extraordinary sum of Rs. 75,000 to the District Road Cess Committee, which was devoted to constructive works wherever a demand for labour arose. Charitable relief was also given indirectly from this source, and no further operations were required to mitigate the distress. Further references to the conditions obtaining in this famine are given, for comparative purposes, in the following account of the famine of 1897, which is condensed from the final report of the Collector (Mr. E. V. Levinge, I.C.S.).

Famine of 1897.

The conditions prevailing prior to the commencement of distress in 1897, and the causes which led up to it, were somewhat similar to those which preceded the famine of 1874. There were the same antecedent failures or partial failures of crops, and the same conditions as to rainfall, but prices at the latter end of 1896 and in 1897 were much higher than in 1874. There was this further difference, that in 1874 the distress affected chiefly the Rārh country on the western side of the Bhāgīrathi, on which *āman* or winter rice is grown, whereas in 1897 the affected area was that portion of the Sadar subdivision which lies to the east of the Bhāgīrathi and is known as the Bāgri, together with a narrow strip on the west of the river in the Kāndi subdivision. Over the greater part of this tract the chief crops are the *aus* or early rice, followed by a cold-weather crop, but on the low land to the south-east of the district, over what is known as the Kālantar, the only crop is *āman* rice, which here depends entirely on floods.

Short rainfall and the lowness of the rivers in 1895 led to a partial failure of the autumn and winter crops of that year and of the *bhadoi* crop of 1896, the average outturn of which did not exceed 8 annas, while in parts of the affected tract it completely failed. In 1896 there was an early cessation of the rains, and the rivers were so low that only a small portion of the Kālantar was flooded. The result was an almost complete failure of the rice crop over a portion of the Kālantar and a partial failure in the Rārh, which was only saved from being a complete failure by a good fall of rain in the middle of September. Owing to this rain, the outturn of winter rice in the Rārh was about 9 annas, but the average outturn for the district did not exceed 7 annas. The difficulties of the people were increased by the failure of the March "bund," which kept many of the silk filatures in the affected area closed at a time when distress was becoming acute, and by the almost total failure of the mango crop, the outturn of which did not exceed 2 annas.

The statement below compares the outturns of the various crops in 1895-96 and 1896-97 with those of 1873-74:—

Crop.	1895-96.	1896-97.	1873-74.
	Annas.	Annas.	Annas.
Āman paddy	8	7	6
Aus "	9	8	12
Wheat	8	3	12
Pulses	14	7	12
Other *rabi* crops	10	8	12

There is no doubt that conditions in 1897 were worse than in 1874, for not only had the previous failure of crops been greater, but prices were much higher than in 1874. The poor *aus* crop in the Bāgri in 1896 was practically exhausted before the *āman* harvesting commenced, and in many villages the people had to draw on the Rārh for their supply of rice even as early as November. The first indications of distress appeared, about December, in an increasing number of beggars, in numerous petitions for employment or relief, and in thousands of applications for agricultural loans, which poured in continuously for the next three months.

Test-works were opened in February, the maximum wages which the workers were allowed to earn in a day being 1½ annas for a task of 66 cubic feet. In spite of the severity of the task and the small wages allowed, the numbers rapidly increased, and people who had never done this sort of work before came to the relief works. Towards the end of April it was found necessary to convert the test-works into ordinary relief works under the Famine Code. The distribution of gratuitous relief was commenced in March in Barwa and Bharatpur thanas, the most severely affected portion of the district. The distress was felt chiefly by the landless and labouring classes, and by those who in ordinary years depend on the charity of their richer neighbours for subsistence. The closing of several of the silk filatures in the Barwa and Bharatpur thanas also deprived numbers of labourers of employment at a time when it was most needed.

By the middle of June the distress was at its height, and the price of common rice ranged from 6 to 7½ seers per rupee in the affected area. New relief centres were opened at Nawāda at the end of April and later on at Jalangi. The whole of the Sadar subdivision was more or less affected, and where circles were not opened, relief was administered by private persons and members of the Relief Committee. It was not until the prospects of the *aus* crop were assured at the end of July that the pressure began to abate, and the relief operations were gradually relaxed. By the end of August when the new *aus* came into the market, prices began to fall, and the necessity for relief was virtually at an end.

The seriously affected portion comprised an area of about 205 square miles, with a population of about 125,000. The percentage of the population of this tract in receipt of gratuitous relief was 2·29, while in the most affected portion, viz., the Dādpur circle, nearly 4 per cent. were thus relieved. Test and regular relief works helped to maintain an aggregate number of 384,000 adult male units at a cost of Rs. 66,000, inclusive of establishment charges, which amounted to Rs. 6,000. The work consisted of the raising and repairs of main roads, the construction of village roads and the excavation or re-excavation of tanks. Substantial relief was given by private persons whose public spirit the Collector acknowledged as follows:—"This district is fortunate in possessing many wealthy and public-spirited zamīndārs who are always ready to co-operate liberally in any measures for the relief of distress. A large number of tanks have been excavated all over the district, and specially in the Sadar subdivision, by private individuals; and, although I have no statistics of the amount expended and the number of persons employed, it is probable that some 5,000 or 6,000 persons have thus found employment at a time when the distress was at its greatest. Where so many have been conspicuous for their charity, it is difficult to particularize, but I may specially mention the late Mahārāni Swarnamayi, whose death occurred on the 25th August, the very day on which the relief operations closed in this district; the Nawāb Bahādur of Murshidābād, Rai Sitāb Chand Nahar Bahādur, Rai Budh Singh Dudhuria Bahādur of Azīmganj, Bābu Jogendra Nārāyan Rai of Lālgola, Bibi Rāni Mena Kumāri and Bābu Narpat Singh and many others. There can be no question that, had it not been for all this private charity, Government relief operations would have been required on a far more extensive scale."

No non-working dependants were relieved on the relief works, and no Government funds were expended in gratuitous relief. The whole of the gratuitous relief and of the relief in exchange for work was conducted by the members of the District Charitable Relief Committee, assisted by official agency, and was met from subscriptions raised within the district, supplemented by a grant of Rs 10,000 from the Central Committee in Calcutta. The total expenditure of the Committee on gratuitous relief, in round numbers, was Rs. 46,000, of which rather more than Rs. 13,000 represented the sale-proceeds of jute string and silk and cotton cloth worked up in return for the relief granted. The total number of persons relieved by the Committee was about 720,000, which is equivalent to 120,000 persons relieved for 30 days. Regarding the work of the Committee, the Collector wrote:—"The relief of spinners and weavers of coarse silk is a special feature of the Committee's operations. These are among the poorest of the population of the district, and even as early as November last the probability of great distress among them was specially brought to my notice. The coarse silks, called *matkas*, are worn chiefly in the Marātha country, but, owing to the prevalence of the plague in the Bombay Presidency, the *matka*-weaving industry suffered an almost total collapse. As these weavers are not cultivators and have no other means of livelihood, the distress among them was very great. The Committee gave employment to 150 families of weavers (consisting of about 700 persons), and through them, directly and indirectly, to 1,200 spinners. To Mr. Mukharji is due the credit of the uccess of these operations. He induced the weavers to weave coarse silks in imitation of Assam silk, and these have been readily bought up both locally and in Calcutta."

The following statement gives the salient statistics of this famine and of the famine of 1874:—

Months.	Daily average number of persons relieved.				Average price of common rice per rupee.		Rainfall in inches.	
	Gratuitous relief.		Relief works.					
	1874.	1897.	1874.	1897.	1874.	1897.	1874.	1897.
1	2	3	4	5	6	7	8	9
January ...	Nil	Nil	1,892	Nil	12·5 seers ...	10 seers ...	0·31	0·01
February ...	Nil	Nil	2,338	32·2	12 seers ...	10-2 to 10-8 seers.	1·13	0·29
March ...	367	361·59	2,834	1,451·5	12-7 seers ...	9-8 seers ...	·84	0·01
April ...	520	1,555·41	3,134	2,704·9	12 seers ...	8-8 to 8-12 seers.	1·59	0·12
May ...	2,446	6,069·43	3,103	3,425·5	11 seers ...	8-8 seers ...	3·66	3·78
June ...	6,319	6,233·25	3,347	1,914·1	11 seers ...	7-12 to 8 seers.	9·67	10·68
July ...	16,159	6,328·76	2,765	3,033·8	12 seers ...	7-4 to 7-8 seers.	10·16	9·21
August ...	21,592	4,823·06	6,171	1,656·8	12 seers ...	7-8 seers ...	9·47	7·02
September ...	12,854	Nil	1,967	Nil	11-5 seers ...	9 seers ...	10·39	8·22
October ...	Nil	Nil	Nil	Nil	13-5 seers ...	...	5·80	...
Total ...	60,257	25,371·50	27,551	14,218·8	Average 12-2 seers.	Average 7½ to 8 seers.	53·02	39·34

Floods are of common occurrence in the district, especially in the low-lying Bāgri or eastern half, which is situated between the Bhāgīrathi and the Ganges. These inundations are caused, not by excess of local rainfall, but by the rising of the rivers before they enter the district. Owing to the course of the rivers and the general slope of the country, which is on the whole towards the rivers, a rise in their waters can rarely affect the whole of the district; and the floods that occur have seldom been so serious as to cause a general destruction of the crops. FLOODS.

In the western part of the district, where the rivers partake more or less of the nature of hill torrents, and are subject to sudden and dangerous freshets, they often overtop their banks, and flood the adjoining land in a single night, their fall being as rapid as their rise. During the latter end of August 1884 the Mor burst one of its embankments, and flooded the town of Kāndi and the surrounding country, creating considerable alarm but doing little damage, except to the roads. The inundation lasted only twenty-four hours, during which time the greater part of the town was under water to a depth of two to three feet. There is no doubt, however, that the action of the flood, apart from the slight inconvenience and damage to property inseparable from such a sudden inrush of water, was distinctly beneficial. The drainage channels, which are very imperfectly cleansed in ordinary years, were thoroughly flushed, while many tanks were purified by an accession of fresh water. The cultivators also benefited largely and reaped such crops as they had not had for years.

The earliest flood of which I have been able to find a detailed record is described as follows in the *Calcutta Gazette* of 29th September 1785:—"We are sorry to learn by letter from Murshidabad that, in consequence of the unusual height of the river (which has been such as was never known in the memory of man), the great river had overflowed its banks and laid the country between the city and Bogwangola entirely under water; and had, by the channel of Ackbarpore Lake, even penetrated the eastern parts of the city; that from the same unfortunate cause some of the dykes on the Cossimbazar river had likewise given way below the Berhampore cantonments; and that the water from these two sources having joined, had overflowed all that part of the country and had come up to the walls of the Cossimbazar filature."

Serious floods are known to have occurred in the years 1823, 1834, 1838, 1848, 1856 and 1866; but the flood of 1823, which the Collector described as the most destructive on record, was the only one that may be said to have caused any general destruction of the crops. No definite information, however, is now forthcoming as to its extent. Such is also the case with the inundations that occurred in subsequent years until 1870.

In that year the embankments at Lalitākuri on the Bhāgīrathi gave way, and the flood water swept across the district into Nadia. In the Bāgri, or eastern half of the district, a great portion of the *aus* rice crop was destroyed by the floods; and nearly all the *āman* rice growing in the low lands was submerged and lost. The rice crop, however, in the Rārh or western half of the district was good, and the outturn is stated to have been above the average. The cold-weather crops in many parts of the district were destroyed by a third rise in the rivers. Although the crops, especially rice, were deficient, there was plenty of food in the district for those who could procure it. This, however, was by no means an easy matter for many of the suffering cultivators, who were living on *māchāns*, or bamboo platforms raised above the waters. It was found necessary to undertake relief operations. These, however, only entailed an expenditure of Rs. 3,000, for the land in many parts was benefited by the rich deposit of silt left by the receding waters. While the crops in low-lying places were almost entirely destroyed by submersion, the peasants elsewhere were congratulating themselves that the floods had brought down an abundant supply of water, which enabled them to raise a larger quantity of rice from their lands than they had obtained for several years past. On the more exposed lands in the north, the destruction of the growing crops was great, but the southern part of the district, which is by its situation inaccessible to any overwhelming rush of flood water, bore an unusually fine harvest.

There were also high floods in 1885 and 1890. In the former year the embankment breached at Lalitākuri on the 23rd August, and water passed through it until the end of September. For three weeks the discharge through the breach was at the enormous rate of 50,000 cubic feet per second, and on 11th September the Jalangi rose nearly 29 feet above its lowest hot-weather level. In 1890 there was a similar inundation due to the Lalitākuri embankment bursting again. There were also heavy floods in 1904, when the whole of the Lālgola thana in the Jangipur subdivision, the Bhagwāngola thana in the Lālbāgh subdivision, and parts of the Sadar and Kāndi subdivisions were affected. Some fifty villages in the west of the Lālgola thana and the whole of the Bhagwāngola thana were submerged owing to breaches in the embankment, and the water did not subside till after a month. Great damage was done to the *aus* and *āman* crops, and grants of money and advances of agricultural loans had to be made for the relief of the distressed. The last severe inundation occurred in 1907, when the Lalitākuri embankment gave way in the Lālbāgh subdivision, and there was a partial failure of the winter rice crop.

EMBANKMENTS.

The Public Works Department maintains a long line of embankments along the Bhāgīrathi, the object of which is to prevent the country on the east bank from being flooded by the spill of that river. It cannot be gainsaid that both the railway and the country are protected from inundation by these embankments, but the propriety of maintaining them has been called in question on the ground that the land which would otherwise be flooded is thereby deprived of its supply of fertilizing silt, while the river, being confined to its bed, deposits its silt there, and thus gradually raises itself above the level of the surrounding country. It is also reported that water-logging occurs in the north of the Lālbāgh subdivision during the rainy season, when water rises above the level of the houses in villages below the Government embankments. The principal embankment extends from Bhagwāngola to Plassey and is 57 miles long. Other lengths of embankments maintained by the Public Works Department are from Kulgāchi to Bhagwāngola, 15 miles, and from Bhagwāngola to Dadmāti, 10½ miles.

There are also a number of marginal embankments maintained by zamīndārs in order to prevent the rivers overflowing their banks and flooding the country below them. They are occasionally breached; but great as is the immediate injury caused by such accidents they are often accompanied by compensations. Fresh and rich deposits of silt are usually brought in by the inundation, fertilizing and raising the soil. The reverse effect, however, is sometimes produced, for a layer of sand may impoverish what was before productive land.

That the private embankments are not always in an efficient state, and that breaches are easily caused in them, is apparent from the description given in Colonel Gastrell's *Report on Murshidābād*:—"Accidents to these *bāndhs* often occur; rats are particularly destructive to them; cattle passing and repassing cut them; and the inhabitants neglect to repair the breach in time. The fishermen of the interior *bils* and *khāls* have also often the credit of coming in the night and making small cuts in them, to secure a fresh influx of fish from the large rivers to supply their fishing grounds. A very small injury suffices to destroy a *bāndh* in a single night; the end of a sharp bamboo thrust through is quite enough."

The early MS. records of the Board of Revenue are full of letters concerning the embankments of Murshidābād. It was, in theory, the duty of the neighbouring landowners to maintain them in good order, and to repair the breaches which were caused by the floods almost every successive year. As a matter of fact, the Government was habitually compelled by the default of the zamīndārs to undertake the work, and was left to recover the expenditure from the parties primarily liable as best it could. On some occasions money was advanced to the zamīndārs, but more commonly a special officer was told off to make the requisite repairs. In the year 1800, the Collector was directed to furnish the Superintendent of Embankments with Rs. 32,788 for the necessary repairs of that year; and was authorized to put up for sale the lands of the zamīndārs, in order to recover the balance due on this account for the preceding year. In the same year, the Government undertook the construction of a new embankment at Kālīgāchha at its own cost, and gave compensation to the zamīndārs for the land thus acquired. It would appear that this was the first embankment in Bengal constructed with *pakkā* (masonry) sluices, for it was represented as a model on this account to the Collector of Jessore. In those days extraordinary measures were demanded to protect the exposed city of Murshidābād. The banks of the Bhāgīrathi just above the city were the especial charge of the Superintendent of Embankments, who seems to have been in some sense independent of the ordinary executive official, whether called Chief or Collector, and to have been entrusted with the general sanitary supervision of the city.*

* In 1800, the Superintendent of Embankments wrote a letter to the Board regarding the removal of certain houses; and in the following year he presented a report respecting the filling up of hollows in the city of Murshidābād.

CHAPTER VII.

RENTS, WAGES AND PRICES.

RENTS. THE rents paid by the cultivators vary according to the fertility and situation of their land, and also according to the crops grown. They differ widely in different parts of the district, being lowest in the Sadar and Jangipur subdivisions and highest in the Kāndi subdivision, where rice and wheat lands bring in from Rs. 7-8 to Rs. 18, and mulberry and sugar-cane lands from Rs. 12 to Rs. 24 an acre. In the Sadar subdivision, on the other hand, the rent of rice and wheat lands ranges between Re. 1-2 and Rs. 9, of land growing pulses between Rs. 2-4 and Rs. 3, of sugar-cane land between Rs. 3 and Rs. 7-8, and of mulberry land between Rs. 1-12 and Rs. 12 an acre. The rents paid in the other two subdivisions are as follows. In the Jangipur subdivision, rice and wheat land fetches from Rs. 3-12 an acre upwards, mulberry land from Re. 1-12 to Rs. 6-8, and land bearing pulse crops from Rs. 3 to Rs. 3-12. In the Lālbāgh subdivision, the rent of rice and wheat land ranges from Rs. 6 upwards, while the average rent of mulberry land is Rs. 7-8 and that of pulse land Rs. 2-4. As there has not yet been a general settlement of the district, which would furnish accurate information regarding the actual rents paid, these figures are only approximate. The average incidence of rent throughout the district is about Rs. 3 per cultivated acre.

The *utbandi* tenure, which is also known under the expressive name of *fasli jama*, is found in the south of the district, mostly in *diāras*. The peculiarity of this tenure consists in the circumstance that the cultivator only pays rent for the quantity of land that he may happen to have cultivated during the year; if it lies fallow, no rent is paid. These tenures are usually created for short terms, and are then renewed, often at rack rents.

Produce rents are also paid under the *barga* or *bhāg* system. The *bargāits*, who abound in every part of the district, form a special class of the agricultural population. They possess rights, which amount almost to a metayer species of tenure, in the lands which they cultivate. The conditions of their holding are, that they retain a fixed share of the produce, which is usually one-half, and supply both seed and cattle for cultivation. Such is the general outline of the *bhāg* system, which admits of many variations of detail. The owner of the land and the *bargāit* may contribute in varying proportions to the expenses of cultivation, and their shares of the outturn may vary in a corresponding proportion.

WAGES. The marginal table, showing the daily wages paid for different classes of labour during the second fortnight of March in the last twenty years, sufficiently indicates that in the first ten there was a sharp rise, but that during the last ten there has been practically no difference except in the case of unskilled labour, which receives a much higher wage. With these figures may be compared those of 1872-73, when the daily rate of wages was—masons 3 to 4 annas, carpenters 4 annas, blacksmiths 4 annas 9 pies, male coolies 2 to 2½ annas, and female coolies 1½ anna. Half a century ago the scale of wages was even lower, for the returns for 1858 show that coolies received about Rs. 3 per month; agricultural labourers, Rs. 4, paid partly in food; smiths for agricultural implements, Rs. 6; smiths in towns, Rs. 6-8; bricklayers, Rs. 6-8; carpenters in the country, Rs. 6, and carpenters in the towns, Rs. 6-8.

Class of labour.	1893.	1903.	1913.
	As. P.	As. P.	As. P.
Mason, superior ...	6 0	8 0	8 0
" common ...	3 0 to 4 0	6 0	6 0
Carpenter, superior ...	6 0	12 0	12 0
" common ...	4 0	6 0 to 8 0	8 0
Blacksmith, superior	5 0	12 0	12 0
" common	4 0 to 5 0	8 0	8 0
Cooly, male ...	2 6	4 0	6 0 to 8 0
" female ...	1 6	2 3	3 6 to 4 0

Agricultural day-labourers, who are largely employed in cultivating the lands of others, are paid money wages in the majority of cases, and always in the sowing season; but at harvest time they receive a certain share of the crop. When so remunerated, they are called *krishāns*. The *krishāns*, though receiving a portion of the produce, supply their manual labour only, and do not contribute in furnishing either the cattle or any portion of the seed, nor have they any interest whatever in the land. They are to be carefully distinguished from the *bargāits* already referred to.

PRICES. Statistics of the prices paid for various articles of food in each subdivision during the last fortnight of March from 1893 to 1912 will be found in the B volume, which forms a statistical appendix to this volume. As is well known, there has been a general rise of prices during the present century, with one notable exception, the price of salt having fallen considerably owing to the reduction of the duty. Prices were particularly high in the five years 1906-10, after which they fell, and reached the maximum in 1908, when common rice sold at 7 seers 15 chittacks per rupee (during the last fortnight in March) in the Sadar subdivision, at 7 seers 12 chittacks in Lālbāgh, at 9 seers 8 chittacks in Jangipur and at 8 seers 4 chittacks in Kāndi. The average price was but little higher in the famine of 1897, when it was 7½ to 8 seers, and was much less in the famine of 1874, viz., 12 seers 2 chittacks.*

That the people should be able to withstand the pressure of such prices without any relief being necessary appears to show that their resources and staying power have increased greatly. If further proof of this statement be needed, it may be mentioned that in 1871 the Collector reported that famine rates would be reached when ordinary rice was selling at 10 seers per rupee: at that point the ordinary rate of labourers' wages (Rs. 4 a month) would, he considered, be insufficient to provide the necessaries of life, and Government aid would be required. The rate of 10 seers per rupee was, however, reached in each of the years 1907-09 without any scarcity ensuing.

Previous to 1870 the price of rice stood at what now seem extraordinarily low figures. If a line be drawn at the year 1855-56, it will be found that the average price of common rice for the twenty years preceding that date was 43 seers 1 chittack for the rupee, while in the subsequent fourteen years the price averaged 27 seers 5½ chittacks for the rupee. It may not be out of place to mention here that, according to the Muhammadan chroniclers, the price of unhusked paddy in the city of Murshidābād during the rule of Murshid Kuli Khān, in the early part of the seventeenth century, was four maunds for the rupee.

WEIGHTS AND MEASURES. The standard of weight is universally the seer, of which the fractions and multiples are always constant. The seer itself, however, varies greatly in different parts of the district. These variations are commonly expressed in terms of the *tolā*; the *tolā* is the weight of a rupee, and is thus ultimately the theoretical unit of weight. The standard seer, which is equivalent

* For the prices in each month during these two famines, see the table in the preceding chapter.

to 2·205 pounds avoirdupois, and contains 80 *tolās*, is in use in the towns. In the villages, the seer is usually estimated to contain 82½ *tolās;* but in some parts of the Kāndi subdivision it contains only 58½ *tolās*, and in other parts 60 *tolās*. The denominations of the seer are as follow:—4 *kānchās* = 1 *chhatāk;* 4 *chhatāks* = 1 *poā;* 4 *poās* = 1 seer; 5 seers = 1 *paseri*; 8 *paseris* = 1 maund.

The measure of distance is:—18 *buruls* (inches) = 1 *hāth* (cubit); 2 *hāths* = 1 *gaz* (yard); 2 *gazes* = 1 *nal* or *kāthā;* 20 *kāthās* or 80 *hāths* = 1 *rasi* or *bighā;* 88 *rasis* = 1 *kos* (two miles); 4 *kos* = 1 *joyon*. The above terms are primarily applicable to linear measure. The table of square measure, which is based upon them, is:—16 *chhatāks* = 1 *kāthā;* 20 *kāthās* = 1 *bighā*. The standard *bighā* is precisely equivalent to 14,400 square feet, or 1,600 square yards, which is one third of the English acre. This *bighā* is reported to be the one most commonly adopted in all parts of the district. In *pargana* Plassey (Palāsi), however, a second *bighā* is in use by the side of the standard *bighā*, which is estimated to contain 17,666 square feet, or 1,963 square yards, equivalent to ·405 of an acre. A second local *bighā* is said to be in force in certain villages of *pargana* Kumārpratāp, composed in the regular way of 80 *hāths*, but each of these *hāths* is 19½ instead of 18 inches. This *bighā* would therefore contain 16,888 square feet, or 1,878 square yards, equivalent to ·388 of an acre.

Measures of quantity proper are not much in use, as commodities, almost without exception, are sold by weight and not by quantity. Paddy is however sold by quantity, in baskets, each of which contains a certain recognised volume or capacity. The denominations of the paddy baskets are as follow:—20 *hātuās* or *aris* = 1 *bis;* 16 *bis* = 1 *pauti* or *kahān*.

The European measure of time is in use in the towns. The Indian measures of time are these: 7½ *dandas* = 1 *prahar;* 8 *prahars* = 1 *dibā-rāt* (a day and night); 7 *dibā-rāt* = 1 *saptāha* (a week); 2 *saptāhas* = 1 *paksha* (a fortnight). The *mās*, or month, varies from 29 to 32 days. The *batsar*, or year, consists of twelve months or 365 days. When compared with English standards, the *danda* is made equal to 24 minutes, and the *prahar* to 3 hours.

CHAPTER VIII.

INDUSTRIES, MANUFACTURES AND TRADE.

OCCUPATIONS. The returns of occupations made at the census of 1911 show that 953,000 persons or 70 per cent. of the population are supported by agriculture, 157,000 or 11 per cent. by industries, 106,000 or 8 per cent. by commerce (including transport) and 18,000 or 1 per cent. by the professions and liberal arts.

Of those maintained by agriculture, 12,000 subsist by income derived from the rent of agricultural land, *i.e.*, consist of landlords and their families, 673,000 are cultivators and 251,000 are farm servants and field labourers, or their dependants. Taking the figures for actual workers only, there are 3,000 landlords, 195,000 cultivators and 94,000 agricultural labourers: in other words, there are 15 landlords and 482 agricultural labourers to every thousand cultivators. In addition to these, there are 52,000 persons supported by the allied pursuits of pasturage and cattle-keeping, including all those engaged in the care and keep of farm-stock, such as breeders and herdsmen, and also those who sell milk, *ghī* and butter—for it is usually a matter of chance whether a man who keeps cows is returned as a cattle-keeper or a milkman. The aggregate of those who obtain a livelihood by fishing is 34,000, viz., 23,000 who were returned as fishermen and 11,000 as fish-dealers. The two latter groups may be taken as connoting the same occupation, for though some live by fishing only, and others retail but do not catch fish, the great majority, at least among the Hindus, catch fish and also sell them. The Musalmāns, though they catch fish, are usually not fish vendors.

Altogether 46,000 persons, or over a fourth of those supported by industrial occupations, are engaged in, or are dependent on those engaged in, textile industries. By far the most important textile industry is silk spinning and weaving, which is the means of livelihood of 27,000 persons: of these, 14,000 are actual workers. Cotton spinning and weaving, once so important a factor in the economic life of the peasantry, now supports only 16,000 persons, of whom 6,000 are workers. The domestic work of rice pounding and husking, which is carried on almost exclusively by women, accounts for 31,000 persons. The total number of those who come under the head of "Transport" is 20,000, of whom 5,000 are boat-owners and boatmen and their families. Work on the roads, *e.g.*, as cartmen, *pālki*-bearers and labourers engaged in road construction and repair, with their dependants, provides for 13,000. Service in the public force and in different branches of the public administration furnishes nearly 12,000 persons with their daily bread, or 6,000 less than the professions and liberal arts.

The returns for actual workers under this latter head are interesting as showing how small a fraction of the population are engaged in professional, artistic and scientific pursuits, either because they are not sufficiently well educated or because they are debarred by want of means, opportunity or training, or by traditional custom, from following them, or because they do not find them sufficiently attractive or lucrative. The total number of workers in the professions and liberal arts is only 7,447, nearly a third (2,123) of whom consist of persons having some religious avocation, such as priests, religious mendicants, temple servants, etc. A larger number (2,557) is returned as engaged in medical pursuits, but 1,500 of them are ordinary midwives; the actual number of medical practitioners, including dentists, oculists and veterinary surgeons (who may be ignorant cattle-doctors), is only 921.

The legal profession has only 384 adherents, including lawyers' clerks and touts, in addition to barristers, pleaders and mukhtārs, while those who are grouped together under the head "Letters, Arts and Sciences" aggregate 1,294. This latter figure cannot be regarded as a large one, considering that there are over $1\frac{1}{3}$ million persons in the district, and that the head comprises a wide range of pursuits, *e.g.*, music, painting, acting, dancing, architecture, engineering, etc. It may be noted, moreover, that the great majority of those returned under this head consist of musicians, actors, dancers and singers, many of whom have attained no high level in art, and that the total of the remainder, including authors, artists, photographers, astrologers, astronomers, botanists, architects, surveyors, engineers and their employés, is only 65.

Domestic service provides for 32,000 persons, while the number of those living on private income is 2,000 and of those engaged in or dependent on unproductive pursuits, such as beggars and prostitutes, 12,000.

INDUSTRIAL CENSUS.

The statistics of occupation compiled from the returns made at the census, while indicating the main functional distribution of the people, furnish meagre information concerning individual industries and manufactures. To remedy this defect, an industrial census was held in 1911, concurrently with the general census, *i.e.*, the owners, managers and agents of industrial works, employing 20 persons or more, submitted returns in which, *inter alia*, the number of their employés at the date of the census was entered. These returns, of course, only referred to the state of affairs on that date, when some concerns may have been closed and others not in full work, while others, on the other hand, may have had a larger number of operatives than usual.

Even so, the results are sufficient to show, beyond possibility of a doubt, that there are few large organized industries in the district, and that, with the exception of the silk industry, their operations have no pretence to magnitude. Altogether, there were only 26 concerns employing 5,080 hands, and of these 23 were silk filatures with 4,907 employés. The remaining three concerns consisted of an oil mill, a brick and tile manufactory and a factory which was classified under the head of iron and steel works; the aggregate number of their employés was only 173.

INDUSTRIES AND MANUFACTURES.

Silk manufacture.

The silk industry has been the principal non-agricultural industry in Murshidābād for the last three centuries. It was this which attracted the East India Company to the district, where its enterprise was stimulated by competition with the Dutch, French and Armenians. The centre of the industry was Cossimbazar, where the Company started a factory at about 1658. At first the operations were on a small scale: according to Bernier, the Dutch employed 700 or 800 persons in their factory at Cossimbazar, and the English and other merchants as many more. It soon began to develop with European capital and organization. In 1670 a factor "well skilled in silk" was sent out from England to Cossimbazar, and in 1681, when the Chief was Job Charnock, the future founder of Calcutta, out of £230,000 sent out by the East India Company as "investment" to Bengal, £140,000 was assigned to Cossimbazar. From this time forward the Company made unremitting efforts to foster sericulture and extend the trade in silk, until by 1776 "Bengal silk drove all competitors, except Italian and China silks, out of the English market.*"

The value of the trade to this district may be realized from the fact that, in the time of Alī Vardi Khān, raw silk to the value of 87½ lakhs was annually entered in the Custom House books at Murshidābād. This is exclusive of the European investments, which were not entered there, as being either duty

---

* Geoghegan's *Silk in India*, p. 5.

free or paying duty at Hooghly. As regards the European investments, we find that, in 1763, out of a total of 40 lakhs required as "advances for investment," the Cosimbazar *aurangs* or filatures demanded 9 lakhs, or as much as any other two agencies excepting Calcutta itself. Colonel Rennell again wrote (*cir.* 1779) as follows:—"Cossimbazar is the general market of Bengal silk, and a great quantity of silk and cotton stuffs are manufactured here, which are circulated throughout great part of Asia; of the unwrought silk, 300,000 or 400,000 lbs. weight is consumed in the European manufactories." The filatures and machinery of the Company at this time were estimated to be worth twenty lakhs of rupees. Another important centre was Jangipur, where silk filatures were established as early as 1773; it was described by Lord Valentia in 1802 as "the greatest silk station of the East Indian Company with 600 furnaces and giving employment to 3,000 persons." The Company continued its operations until 1835, when it gave up its commercial monopoly. After this, large European firms, such as Messrs. Watson & Co., James Lyall & Co., Louis Payen & Co. and the Bengal Silk Company, came into the field.

The following account of the industry, which was given in the *Statistical Reporter* for May 1876, is of interest as showing the proportions it had then attained: it must, however, be remembered that at that time the district contained the Rāmpur Hāt subdivision, which has since been transferred to Bīrbhūm.

"There are 45 filatures belonging to or under the management of Europeans in Murshidābād district, and 67 filatures belonging to natives. The number of basins in the former is not less than 3,500; and in the latter not less than 1,600, making a total of 5,100 basins. In addition to these, there are some 97 small filatures worked by natives in their homes, containing about 200 basins. Computing according to the house valuations recorded under the Road Cess Act, the value of the whole of the filatures may be set down at not less than Rs. 4,50,000. Each basin is worked by two persons; the total number of persons employed is thus 10,600. One-half of these represent the skilled workmen; there is besides a large number of peons, overseers and clerks. The quantity of silk manufactured yearly cannot be accurately ascertained, but it probably amounts to 3,000 maunds (246,000 lbs.) in an ordinary year. Estimated at a low price, say, Rs. 14 per seer, owing to the unfavourable state of the market, the value of the silk produced will be found to amount to the large sum of Rs. 16,80,000. The amount paid to rearers of silk-worms on this quantity of silk is about Rs. 10,80,000, and to the spinners about Rs. 1,80,000. If to these sums is added the cost of establishment, Rs. 2,40,000, the expenditure involved in manufacturing the product of an ordinary year will be found to amount to about Rs. 15,00,000. The figures refer to spinning only.

"The weaving of silk cloths forms another branch of the industry of considerable importance. Looms are found in no less than 137 villages, and the number of weavers in the whole district may be computed at 1,900, besides the adult members of their families, who generally assist them in weaving. Last year from eighty to one hundred thousand pieces of silk were woven, the value of which could not have been less than Rs. 6,00,000. The amount spent amongst weavers for wages was about Rs. 1,00,000.

"The extent of the mulberry cultivation may be estimated at 50,000 *bighas* (17,000 acres), an estimate more probably under than above the mark."

The *Statistical Reporter*, in giving this account, stated that the industry was rapidly declining, and this view is borne out by a comparison of the figures with those of 1872 when the total number of filatures, both large and small, including those worked by Indians as well as those under European management, was estimated at 334 (of which no less than 110 were in the Barwa thana): the Collector, while giving these figures, reported that the industry had greatly declined during the previous thirty or forty years.

The decline of the industry has not been arrested, but has proceeded still further. In 1903 Mr. N. G. Mukharji (in his *Monograph on the Silk Fabrics of Bengal*) estimated the annual production of silk fabrics at 20 lakhs, and concluded that its prospects were brightening, but the census shows this expectation has not been realized. In 1901 there were, according to the returns of occupations, 28,950 persons supported by silk spinning and weaving, while 10,041 subsisted by rearing silk-worms and gathering cocoons. The number was reduced at the census of 1911 to 27,338 and 6,803 respectively: as already shown, there were, at the time of this census, 23 filatures at work, in which 20 or more persons were employed, and the aggregate number of their employés was 4,907. European firms are finding it more difficult to pay their way even with power looms, and in 1908-09 the Bengal Silk Company was obliged to close its factories and stop work.

The industry has suffered from the heavy protective tariff against manufactured silk imposed by the French Government since 1892, which has affected the export trade in *korāhs* very prejudicially; other contributory causes have been extensive importations to Europe from Japan and China, the abundant yield in Italy and the indifferent quality of the local silk. The competition of foreign silk has also affected the internal trade. The most potent cause of the falling off in the manufacture is believed to be disease among the silk-worms. From the end of 1886 to 1896 Mr. Nritya Gopāl Mukharji was engaged in inquiries and experiments with the object of combating silk-worm epidemics and introducing healthier methods of rearing silk-worms. He was successful in rearing seed-cocoons under the Pasteur system, which were far superior to the native seed, and his pupils in charge of private nurseries which he started were able to make the business pay. In 1899 the work was taken over by a committee of silk merchants, but in 1908 the control was resumed by the Director of Agriculture. The operations were then placed under the supervision of the Bengal Silk Committee presided over by him, the officer in immediate charge being the Superintendent of Sericulture, Bengal, whose headquarters are at Berhampore.

A central nursery with seven rearing houses and a mulberry plantation of 62 *bighas* has been started at Berhampore, which is under the management of an Assistant Superintendent, and there are other central nurseries at Chandanpur, Kumārpur, and Mahmudpur. The Government nurseries provide pure seed, and supervisors are sent round to the rearers' villages to show how silk-work epidemics can be checked by the disinfection and fumigation of the rearing houses. By these means considerable progress has been made in eradicating diseases among silk-worms, in distributing healthy seed and so improving the quality of the silk produced. The chief kinds of Indian silk-worms that are now being reared under the Pasteur system are the *Nistāri* and *Chotapālu*. In order to ascertain whether better results can be obtained with other species, a French expert, Mr. F. D. Lafont, was appointed in 1912, under the title of "European Professor in charge of Sericultural Research," to conduct experiments in hybridizing European with Indian seeds ; the experiments were carried on by him for a year, and since then have been continued by the Superintendent of Sericulture. A school of sericulture has also been opened at Berhampore with the object of diffusing scientific methods of rearing silk-worms among the rearers. The sons of *bonâ fide* rearers only are admitted to the school and receive a year's training. They are then examined, and, if successful, are given Rs. 250 for the purchase of microscopes, for the construction of a rearing-house according to the new methods, etc.

Though the industry has declined and European silk merchants are being forced (by competition and hostile tariffs in Europe) to wind up their business, the small local filatures (*bānaks*) owned by the class known as *khangru*-reelers still have a large outturn. They are said to take up all the cocoons produced at higher rates than the European filatures can afford to pay, and turn out a large quantity of cheap piece-goods called *korāhs* and *matkas* which find a market in India, and more especially in the Punjab and the Marātha country. The weavers in the village of Mirzāpur alone produced 34,750 yards, valued at Rs. 1,32,790, in 1909-10, and the produce of their looms was even greater in 1907-08, amounting to 40,000 yards, valued at Rs. 1,89,850. Mulberry-growing and cocoon-rearing are carried on chiefly in thana Barwān in the Kāndi subdivision, thana Raghunāthganj in the Jangipur subdivision and thana Rāninagar in the Sadar subdivision. The chief centres of the weaving industry are thana Mirzāpur in the Jangipur subdivision and thanas Hariharpāra and Daulatbazar in the Sadar subdivision. The best silks are made at Mirzāpur. Other important centres are Bāluchar, Islāmpur, Kadai, Saidābād, Beldānga and Hariharpāra. Though Bāluchar has given its name to a special class of silks, the weavers do not live in the village itself, but in the surrounding villages. The principal centres of the trade are Berhampore and Jiāganj.

Cocoons and *bands*.

There are three branches of the industry, viz., cocoon-rearing, silk-reeling and cloth-weaving. As regards the first, there are three seasons, locally termed *bands*, for hatching the eggs, spinning and gathering the cocoons, viz., the November *band*, from 1st October to end of February, the March *band*, from 1st March to 30th June, and the July (or *barsāt*) *band*, from 1st July to 30th September. The first is the most important, for the silk worms thrive best in the cold season, and the silk is then better in quality and much more valuable. The March *band* is not so good, and the rainy season *band* the worst. Cocoon-rearing is a "small-holding" industry, each rearer having a few *bighas* under mulberry in addition to the land growing ordinary crops.

After they have finished spinning, the cocoons are either (1) taken to the nearest *hāt* for sale or (2) killed by exposure in thin layers to the sun and reserved for sale until the *paikārs* or agents of the filatures come round, or (3) steamed (in baskets covered up with cloth under which a pot of water is kept boiling) and reeled off into silk, or (4) if formed in a very healthy manner, they are bought up for seed by travelling rearers going about in quest of seed.

Matka spinning.

Matka cloth is made from the silk pulled off before the cocoon is reeled and that left after reeling, and also from pierced cocoons. Empty cocoons accumulate in every cocoon-rearer's house after seeding is finished, *i.e.*, after the moths have cut out of the cocoons and laid eggs. These empty cocoons cannot be reeled off into silk in the same manner as whole cocoons with dead chrysalids inside them. Their number is great, for each cocoon-rearer makes, on an average, four attempts every year to rear cocoons, and it is estimated that he uses an average quantity of one *kāhan* (1,280) of seed-cocoons each time. Many rearers use as much as five or six *kāhans* of seed each time, but the majority use only half a *kāhan* of seed, and the average is taken to be one *kāhan* per crop or four *kāhans* per annum. The greater portion is spun into a course thread and utilized for weaving *matka* cloth. *Matka* spinning and weaving give occupation to the poorest women and the least artistic of the weavers. The spinning is only carried on for a few days in every *band*, and women are never employed on it all the year round.

Khamru spinning.

More than half the quantity of mulberry cocoons is spun into thread by the country method of reeling; this is called *khamru*, *khangru* or *bank* silk. *Khamru*-reeling prevails chiefly in the Jangipur and Kāndi subdivisions. The *khamru* silk is produced for the Indian market.

Filature silk.

Silk reeled in filatures according to European methods is called filature silk and is nearly all exported to Europe. Evenness of size throughout the skein, elasticity of thread, colour and appearance are looked to. Many small filatures, producing silk of nearly as good quality as that produced in European filatures, are owned by Indian merchants. The principal filatures of the Bengal Silk Company were situated at Babulbona and Rāngamāti, and those of Messrs. Louis, Payen & Co. at Gadi in the Jangipur subdivision (now closed), Bājarpāra in the Kāndi subdivision, Gauripur, Sujāpur and Nārāyanpur.

As regards the general position of the weavers, the following review is quoted from a district monograph prepared in 1903:—

"The method on which many of the rearers carry on their business is industrially a bad one. The filature-owners and their employés in many cases advance money to them, and buy their cocoons at a price fixed according to the current rates in the silk market. Interest being charged, the rearers frequently get into financial difficulties. Those who work on their own capital are in a much more favourable position. There seems no doubt that the silk-weaving industry is on the decline. The importation of foreign stuffs has, of course, a great deal to do with this. Another reason lies in the lack of enterprise displayed in disposing of native fabrics. Where there is an attempt at advertisement, it usually meets with great success. It would be a splendid thing for the trade if middle-class Bengalis with a small capital were to hawk round the silk products of Mirzāpur and other places. At the time of the famine the sufferings of some of the weavers of this district were much alleviated by the efforts of a native gentleman, who advantageously disposed of their goods in Calcutta. It is a pity that more energy is not displayed in this direction. There is no doubt that as a class their condition is not prosperous, and that they are deeply involved in debt. They do not, as a rule, work for themselves, but for dealers who advance them material and pay them so much for their labour. Some of these dealers employ a very large number of weavers. I am told that in Kāndi subdivision some weavers found the industry so little profitable that they have entirely given it up, and in many cases taken to agriculture. Others in the same subdivision have abandoned the weaving of silk for that of cotton."

Silk fabrics.

The following description of the principal kinds of Murshidābād silk fabrics is given by Mr. N. G. Mukharji in his *Monograph on the Silk Fabrics in Bengal*:—

"*Class A.*—Fabrics made with ordinary looms, such as may be used for weaving cotton cloths also. Under this class come—(*a*) plain fabrics, either bleached, unbleached or dyed; (*b*) striped fabrics; (*c*) checks; (*d*) bordered fabrics; (*e*) printed fabrics; (*f*) *bānhus*.

"*Class B.*—Fabrics made with *naksha* looms for weaving figured silks."

"*Class C.*—Embroidered and other hand-worked fabrics."

"*Class A.* (*a*).—*Plain fabrics* are usually made with *khamru* silk and rarely with filature-made silk. *Matka* silk is also made use of for special purposes. Mirzāpur weavers usually obtain Mālda *khamru*, and sometimes very high class native filature-reeled *dhāli* or *barapālu* silk. The best fabrics are made of this latter kind of silk. The following silk fabrics fall under this class:—

"(1) *Gown-pieces.*—The raw silk used for gown-pieces is twisted and bleached, and sometimes dyed, before weaving. White gown-pieces are woven in four different styles—(*a*) plain, (*b*) twill or drilled (*terchi* or *ālpāli*), (*c*) striped and (*d*) checked. Coloured gown-pieces are usually made either plain or of drill. The dimensions are usually 10 yards by 42 inches. Sometimes the width is made 44 inches, 45 inches or even 54 inches. The price of gown-pieces varies from Rs. 12 to Rs. 40 per piece. An extra thick gown-piece, 10 yards by 42 inches, made out of filature-reeled *barapālu* silk, is valued at Rs. 45 or even Rs. 50. The cheaper kinds are made of untwisted thread, and should be styled *korāhs* rather than gown-pieces. The only difference between a *korāh* and a gown-piece made of untwisted thread is, that for the latter bleached thread is used, while for the former unbleached thread, *i.e.*, raw-silk as it comes from the *ghai*, is used. Gown-pieces are in use among European ladies for making dresses, and by Bengali gentlemen for making coats, *chapkans* and *chogās*.

" (2) *Korāhs.*—These are the cheapest silk fabrics, which form the staples of export to Europe, where they are used mainly for lining purposes. *Korāhs* are generally woven 7 yards by 1 yard, and sold at a rupee per square yard. They are made out of unbleached and untwisted thread, and they are bleached in the piece after they are woven. *Korāhs* are also woven 10 yards by 42 inches like ordinary gown-pieces, and worn as *sāris* by females. Like gown-pieces, *korāhs* are valued by the number of warp threads (called *shānā*), 2,400 warp threads per yard making the best gown-pieces and *korāhs*, while, 1,200 or 1,000 warp threads per yard make the poorest gown-pieces and *korāhs*. The price of *korāhs* varies from 6 annas to Re. 1-8 per square yard. High class *korāhs* are used for making ladies' blouse-jackets and other garments, usually after dyeing.

" (3) Silk muslins or *hāwāi* pieces are very fine fabrics made with filature-reeled *dhali* silk. Silk muslins are locally used by rich men for making shirts, coats or *chapkans*, which they wear in the hot weather, *hāwāi sāris* being similarly used in the zenāna. It is only highly skilled silk weavers who can turn out superior silk muslins.

" (4) *Handkerchieves.*—These are made either with twisted yarn or with raw silk, and are sometimes made with dark blue or red borders. A high class Mirzāpur handkerchief 2 feet square costs a rupee. Poor *khām* hankerchieves 18 inches square may be had for 4 annas each.

" (5) *Alwāns* or thick *chādars* are usually worn double by Bengali gentlemen of means. Each *chādār* is 3 yards long and $1\frac{1}{3}$ or $1\frac{1}{2}$ yards wide. They are, as a rule, twilled, and sometimes they are coloured. The price varies from Rs. 25 to Rs. 35 per pair. An ornamental bordered *ālwān*, first woven for Mahārāja Sir Jotindra Mohan Tagore by Mrityunjay Sarkār of Mirzāpur, now sells for Rs. 50 a pair.

"(6) *Plain white dhotis* and *jors* (*i.e.*, *dhotis* and *chādars* woven in the same piece alternately) have a considerable sale throughout Bengal, as they are required for ceremonial purposes. The father of a bride or bridegroom wears a *jor* at the marriage ceremony of his child. High-class priests also wear *jors*. *Jors* are worn at the *srādha* (funeral feast) ceremony also. Plain white *dhotis* are worn by rich widows when they go to see their friends. A *jor* usually cost Rs. 16, and a *dhoti* Rs. 8 to Rs. 10. The length of a *dhoti* is 10 cubits and of a *jor* 15 cubits, and the width 45 inches.

"(7) *Mekhlas.*—These are a special kind of *korāh* which are exported to Assam. There they are converted into women's skirts, sometimes after being embroidered with gold thread.

"(8) *Matkas.*—The *matka dhotis* and *sāris* made in Murshidābād are much coarser than those made in Rājshāhi. They are largely exported to the Marātha country, but locally they are also worn by elderly men, by widows and by the poor women of the villages where they are woven. They are made 4 to 8 yards long and 40 to 45 inches wide, and they can be had for Rs. 3 to Rs. 5 per piece. They are also woven into the *chādar* size (3 yards by 1½ yard), and in this state exported to Assam. Locally these *chādars* are worn dyed to a very limited extent.

"(9) *Matka* and *khamru* yarns are sometimes used mixed, *i.e.*, twisted *khamru* silk going to make the warp and the *matka* silk going to make the weft, for weaving thick pieces suitable for making men's suits. These are sold for about Rs. 2 a yard. There are two styles of these mixed fabrics—one plain and the other twilled and striped (*i.e.*, of *khejurchhari* pattern).

"(10) *Imitation Assam silk.*—These were introduced in this district by Mr. N. G. Mukharji in connection with the famine operations of 1897. About 150 families of poor *matka*-weavers came for relief, and the only kind of work they were capable of was coarse weaving. About Rs. 11,000 were spent for their relief, including cost of materials, and the fabrics they were made to weave realized by sale about Rs. 10,000. Messrs. Whiteway, Laidlaw & Co. patronised these silks largely, and they have since become very popular. About Rs. 50,000 worth of these silks are now exported annually from Berhampore, and the importance which this new industry has already achieved has given rise to a hope that under fostering care the silk-weaving industry of Bengal may be developed in other directions also. The imitation Assam silks, or Murshidābād *endis* as they are now called, are sold specially by one Berhampore firm (S. S. Bāgchi & Co.). The pieces are usually made 7 yards by 27 inches, as originally advised by Messrs. Whiteaway, Laidlaw & Co., and they are sold for Rs. 6 or Rs. 7 per piece. They are just sufficient for making one ordinary suit of clothes. They are also woven double the width.

"*Class A(b).—Striped fabrics.*—Gown-pieces with coloured stripes are made in two styles, called respectively *rekhis* and *dharis*. *Rekhis* are plain white or coloured gown-pieces (usually 10 yards by 40 inches) with some dark coloured lines or double lines. The ground of *rekhis* may be either plain or twill. *Dharis* have broader stripes, usually of more than one colour. According to the colour of the widest stripe, a *dhari* may be either (*a*) red, (*b*) yellow, (*c*) green, (*d*) purple or (*e*) *banesh* (chocolate coloured). These five standard kinds of *dhari* are woven for the Arabian market. The kind of *dhari* appreciated locally is not so highly coloured. Like *rekhis*, *dharis* are woven in 10 yards by 40 inches pieces, and are sold for Rs. 16 to Rs. 18 or Rs. 23 to Rs. 25 per piece, the heavily-starched, high-coloured pieces being sold cheaper, while the thick woven, lighter-coloured pieces made for the local market are sold for the higher price.

"*Class A(c).—Checks* are divided into five kinds of fabrics—

"(1) *Chārkhānas* or checks where the squares or oblongs are of diverse colour. These, like *rekhis* and *dharis*, are made in two styles—one suited to Arab taste and the other suited to local taste. The former (called *chaukaras*) are more highly coloured and heavily starched, and are cheaper fabrics sold for Rs. 18 to Rs. 19 per piece, while the latter are closer woven superior fabrics, sold for about Rs. 25 a piece. Fine flimsy checks are woven in the Bāluchar circle for the use of Jain ladies and Jain children of Bāluchar and Azīmganj, who are habitually to be seen in *kurtas* and *pāijāmas* made of such cheap silk. They are made 40 inches wide and are sold for Re. 1-8 per yard. These fine and flimsy checks used to be made at Chandrakona and other villages in the Arambāgh subdivision of Hooghly, and the Bāluchar weavers have simply taken over the industry.

"(2) *Chārkhānas* or checks, which consist of white ground and coloured square outlines, the squares being of various sizes as in the previous case. The lines are either double, triple or single, and the ground is either plain or twill. The dimensions and prices are the same as in the previous case, *i.e.*, they are usually made 10 yards by 40 inches and priced at Rs. 20 to Rs. 40 per piece.

"(3) *Matras.*—These are of a standard Arabic pattern, like *dharis*, *rekhis* and *chaukaras.* They are striped like *dharis*, but all along the edges of the stripes are studded rows of little squares or oblongs. The dimensions are the same as in *dharis*, *rekhis* and *chaukaras*. *Matras* exported to Arabia cost a rupee more than the other styles also made for the Arabian market.

"(4) *Phulikat checks* are woven for the Rangoon market. The lines are white, and the ground is either red or yellow or green or purple or *banesh* (chocolate), which are the five standard colours for the goods that are exported. *Phulikat* checks are considered suitable only for handkerchieves. They are made a yard square, and fifteen are woven together, which cost about Rs. 19.

"(5) *Check matkas* are a very coarse class of fabrics woven for the Marātha country. A check *matka sāri* 8½ yards long and 45 inches wide may be had for Rs. 5 or Rs. 6. The trade with the Marātha country in plain and check *matkas* is pretty extensive.

"*Class A(d).—Bordered fabrics.*—The demand for Murshidābād bordered *sāris*, *dhotis*, *jors*, *chelis* and *matkas* is very considerable. The upper middle classes of Bengal patronize these fabrics very largely, and *chelis* and *matkas* are in demand among the lower middle classes also. The price of a *sāri* of two or three borders varies from Rs. 10 to Rs. 18. White silk *sāris* made out of *dhali* silk with *dhākka tājpār*, or border of *kamlea*-orange colour, are considered very fashionable by Bengali ladies. A *sāri* with spotted ground has been recently produced by Mrityunjay, which is sold at Rs. 30 a piece. This is the very best fabric produced in Murshidābād. But *tājpār*, *kalkāpār*, *padmapār* and *bhomrāpār sāris* with plain white ground are the common styles in use. *Dhani katkāpār*, *phitāpār*, *ghunsipār* and *churipār* are the common styles of border adopted for men's *dhotis*. The borders of *dhotis* are made narrower, and there are never three but always two borders at the two edges. Silk *sāris* and *dhotis*, when they have coloured grounds, are called *chelis*. *Chelis* of very flimsy texture have a large sale. They are used for making ceremonial presents at various religious festivals. Parsis also use cheap *chelis* for making ceremonious presents in celebrating funeral rites. A seven-yard piece of *cheli* of this sort may be had for Re. 1-10 to Rs. 2, and when it is considered that the material used is pure silk, the worthlessness of the stuff can be very well imagined. A *cheli jor* (*i.e.*, *dhoti* and *chādar*) of superior quality, such as is worn by a Bengali bridegroom of good family, may cost as much as Rs. 25.

"*Reyias* have also coloured borders. They are sent to Assam, where they are worn by Assamese women to cover the upper part of their bodies, somewhat in the same way as *chādars* are worn. They are woven in the Bāluchar centre. They are 4½ yards long and 22 inches wide, the two ends (*ānchlās*) being ornamented with coloured borders. The gold embroidering of *reyias* is done after their arrival in Assam. Handkerchieves are sometimes woven with coloured borders. *Matka dhotis* and *sāris* are also made with black or red borders, the borders of *sāris* being wider than those of *dhotis*.

" *Class A(e).—Printed fabrics.*—The art of printing *korāhs* for making handkerchieves, door-curtains, scarves and *nāmābalis* (or *chādars* containing religious texts) is almost extinct in Murshidābād. The industry has transferred itself to Serampore and Chandernagore, though silk pieces are taken to these places from Berhampore for the purpose. The dyers of Khāgra are chiefly employed in dyeing yarns, but they still do printing to special order. The price of these fabrics depends on the quality of *korāh* used.

" *Class A(f).—Bānhus* or *bāndhāna* (tie-and-dye) silks are dyed *korāhs* or *matkas* with spots or rings, coloured or white. These spots and rings are made by tying strong knots at small distances, according to the required pattern, and dyeing the pieces of *korāh* or *matka*. The word *bāndhāna* in Sanskrit means tying, which is the origin of the term *bandannah*.* The pieces after patient knotting are dyed and washed and dried, and the knots loosened. White spots or rings are formed at the points where the knots were made. When coloured spots or rings are desired, the strings with which the knots are made are first dyed in that particular colour before the tying of the knots. The colour of the strings is imprinted on the cloth at the points where the knots are made. Pieces with rings instead of spots are called *churis*. When the rings are small and close together, they are called *matichurs*. Skirts and turbans are made of these materials, and there is a considerable trade with the United Provinces and the Punjab in *bānhus* and *churis*. The price of a piece depends entirely on the quality of *korāh* or *matka* used, about eight annas per piece being added for the dyeing process.

* In his paper on " Art as applied to the Weaving and Printing of Textile Fabrics," Sir Thomas Wardle, in alluding to the tie-and-dye work, says:—"It is extensively practised in India, particularly in Jeypore and Ulwar. It was the precursor of printing in the silk handkerchief trade in Calcutta and Berhampore, and is a very remarkable means of producing designs in spots, round, oval or square."

"*Class B.—Fabrics made with naksha looms.*—(1) Under this class we have first of all the Bāluchar *butedār sāris.* These *sāris* with ornamental ground, ornamental border, ornamental corner figures (called *kunjas*) and a more highly ornamental end-piece or *ānchla*, were at one time very highly prized by the upper middle-class people of Bengal. Now the ladies of this class go in for the more costly fabrics of Benares. The ordinary Bāluchar *butedār sāri* is rather an ugly fabric to use for personal decoration, but some are very neatly made and deserve encouragement. These *sāris* are made 10 cubits long and 42 to 45 inches wide. The price varies according to quality from Rs. 10 to Rs. 50. For the cheaper articles untwisted and ill-sorted raw silk is used; the number of threads used for the warp is also less, the weft is loosely woven, the dyes used are fugitive and the appearance is maintained by heavy starching, sugar being mixed with the starch used to add to the gloss. A cheap Bāluchar *butedār sāri* can be woven in a week, but a valuable one takes three or four months weaving. Sometimes these *sāris* are made without *ānchlas*, but only with four *kalkas* or *kunjas* (conventional lotus buds) at the four corners. Such *sāris* of the same size are somewhat cheaper (Rs. 8 to Rs 40 instead of Rs. 10 to Rs. 50).

"(2) *Rumāls* (square shawls) and shawls with ornamental borders and corners, in imitation of Kashmir *rumāls* and shawls, are occasionally made to order. Table-cloths are also turned out from *naksha* looms. The ground is of twilled pattern and white, the ornaments either grey or more highly coloured. The shawls are made 6 cubits long and 3 cubits wide, and the price asked is Rs. 40 or Rs. 50, there being no inferior articles of this class in demand. The high-class *sāris*, *rumāls*, shawls and table covers used to be woven until lately by only one man in the district, or rather the looms turning out these could have been set only by Dubrāj, the weaving being done by others working under Dubrāj's direction. Dubrāj would not set looms for making these high-class fabrics for anyone else. He used also to weave at one time shawls with religious texts in the place of the ground ornament, but he gave up this work in his old age, as the operation of weaving required that the cloth-beam should be below the naval, which is considered a sacrilege when one is dealing with a cloth containing religious texts.

"(3) *Scarves and sashes* were also woven by Dubrāj to order. The width of these is always 1 foot, and the price varies with the length, a rupee being charged for every foot of length. The quality of silk (which is twill) is the same, and there is no variation made in the price. Dubrāj's loom for weaving sashes has been acquired by the Râmpur Boalia Sericultural School, and it is in working order and actually in use in this school. The products of Dubrâj's looms are inferior only to the best products of the Kashmir and Benares looms. The competition with Kashmir products would not affect the sale of these, as rich men who use Kashmir shawls and scarves in the cold weather could use Dubrâj's shawls and scarves in warmer weather, as locally they are so used. But the competition with Benares gold-embroidered *sāris*, shawls, etc., is too strong even for Dubrâj's goods. A Hindu lady who can afford to wear a Benares *sāri* will not look at even a high-class Bāluchar *sāri* on high days and holidays. One thing, however, should be mentioned in favour of these ornamental silks. They stand any amount of washing, which Benares goods do not. It is too late, however, to think of reviving the industry of weaving ornamental silk fabrics, as the only man who could be used as a lever to uplift the industry is now dead. The Society for the Promotion of Indian Arts in London interested itself in the matter and raised some money also, but the local people were extremely apathetic and the scheme fell through. The only hope of reviving the art now rests on the fact that Dubrāj's looms are still in existence.

"*Class C.—Embroidered and other hand-worked fabrics.*—Embroidering on silk is chiefly done in rich Jain families and also in some Muhammadan houses for domestic purposes. The few professional embroiderers there are in the district live in City Murshidâbâd, and they come to Bāluchar for embroidering *reyiās* and *mekhlas* that are exported to Assam. A piece of embrodered *reyiā* or *mekhla* costs Rs. 40 to Rs. 50. Foreign silks, satin and velvet are usually chosen by Jain and Muhammadan ladies for their domestic work, in which they often exhibit great skill and taste. Hand-embroidered wearing apparel cannot be had in the district in shops or markets; and the fabric used being usually foreign, the art need only be mentioned here. . .

"Knitting of silk socks was an industry of some note in Murshidâbâd in days when there were English military officers in the district. The industry is now extinct. . .

"The costliest silk fabrics are used in Bengal. Some costly fabrics are exported to Assam also, but the quantity is insignificant. The fabrics used in Bengal are *sāris*, *dhotis*, *jors*, Bāluchar *butedār sāris*, *chelis*, gown-pieces, *hāwāi* goods, *rekhis*, *chārkhānas*, scarves, shawls and plain and bordered handkerchieves. Individual weavers may be seen hawking them about in the towns, and sometimes carrying bundles of silk cloths down to Calcutta as personal luggage by train. Many such weavers come to Calcutta before the Puja time, in September and October, when there is always a brisk sale of silk *sāris* in the Calcutta market. To Europe, *korāhs*, printed handkerchieves and gown-pieces, also *tâsars* and *bāftās* (*tasar* mixed with cotton), are exported. To Rangoon are exported *phulikā'* handkerchieves and *bānhus*. To the United Provinces and the Punjab are sent *matichurs* or *churis* made out of *maktas* and *korāhs*. To Arabia are exported *dharis*, *chaukaras* and *matras*. *Chelis* go to most parts of India, also *korāhs* for printing. *Matka dhotis* and *sāris* (plain and check) go to all parts of India where there are Marāthas."

Ivory carving.

Another industry for which the district is famous is ivory carving. The skill of the carvers and the high estimation in which their work has been held are sufficiently attested by the remarks of Professor Royle in *Lectures on the Arts and Manufactures of India (1852)* with reference to the exhibits sent to the London Exhibition of 1851:—

"A variety of specimens of carving in ivory have been sent from different parts of India and are much to be admired, whether for the minuteness of size, for the elaborateness of detail, or for the truth of representation. Among these the ivory-carvers of Berhampore are conspicuous. They have sent a little model of themselves at work, and using, as is the custom of India, only a few tools. The set of chess-men carved from the drawings in Layard's 'Nineveh' were excellent representations of what they could only have seen in the above work, showing that they are capable of doing new things when required; while their representations of the elephant and other animals are so true to nature, that they may be considered the works of real artists and should be mentioned rather under the head of fine arts than of mere manual dexterity." In 1888 again the Murshidābād carvers were declared to be perhaps the best in India, "fully displaying the finish, minuteness and ingenuity characteristic of all true Indian art."

The industry dates back to the time when the Nawābs of Bengal had their court at Murshidābād. The legend of its introduction is quaint. The Nawāb, it is said, one day called for an ear-pick or scratcher, and when one made of grass was brought, said that it was not worthy of the dignity of a Nawāb and that one must be made of ivory. An ivory carver was therefore brought from Delhi to make one. While he was at work, a Hindu Bhāskar spied on him through a hole in the wall and learnt his art, which he taught his son, Tulsi Khatumbar. The latter soon excelled his father and was made carver in ivory to the Nawāb. He was a pious Hindu and anxious to go on pilgrimage, and, this being known, a guard was set over him, for fear that he might leave the city. At last he managed to escape and went on pilgrimage to various places, paying his way by his work. After an absence of 17 years, he returned to Murshidābād and was summoned before the Nawāb, who ordered him to make from memory a carving of the late Nawāb. The statue he produced was so life-like, that the Nawāb, in admiration of his genius, gave him his salary in full for the 17 years he had been away and presented him with a house in Mahājantuli. To this day, it is said, "the ivory carvers of Murshidābād bend their heads and raise their hands in veneration whenever the name of Tulsi is mentioned." Whatever be the truth of the legend, the art appears to have been from the first the monopoly of the Bhāskars, whose original hereditary occupation is the manufacture of clay and wooden images, wood carving and wall painting. It was an industry which depended for its prosperity on the support of a luxurious court and wealthy noblemen, and when the Nawābs lost their power and their court disappeared, it languished.

The causes of its decline are stated as follows by Mr. G. C. Dutt in his *Monograph on Ivory Carving in Bengal* (*1901*):—

"For lack of encouragement the Murshidābād carvers have been obliged to sacrifice quality to quantity. Established during the declining days of the Nawābs of Murshidābād, the encouragement the art received from them was but limited and sporadic. During the palmy days of Cossimbazar, when many Europeans belonging to the cotton and silk factories of the old East India Company lived there, the ivory carvers carried on a brisk business, both in the district and out of it. Even in 1811, when the place was fast sinking into the obscurity from which it had temporarily emerged, it was still noted for silk, hosiery, *korāhs* and inimitable ivory work. Similarly, when Berhampore rose into importance as the chief military station in this province, the art flourished there for a time, but with the decline of the military importance of the town it began to wane, and had it not been for the railway communication which has made a trade with Calcutta and Bombay possible, the art would have died out long ago. Formerly the ivory carvers used sometimes to get large orders from Government for supplying specimens of their work for the various exhibitions in England and other European countries, as also in India, but this has been discontinued in recent years, as collections for exhibitions are now generally made on loan from noblemen and zamīndārs, like the Nawāb of

Murshidābād and the Mahārāja of Cossimbazar, who have the very best specimens in their possession.

"Within the last 30 years the industry has altogether died out from Mathra, Daulatbazar and Ranshagorgrām, all three villages near the city of Murshidābād. Thirty years ago there were over 50 families of ivory carvers at Mathra, and even so recently as 12 years back there were about a dozen houses left. Many of them died of malarious fever, and the few survivors have migrated to Bāluchar, Berhampore and other places. At present there is not a single Bhāskar in Mathra, and there are not more than 25 ivory carvers, principal and apprentices all told, living in the district."

The best workers, it may be added, live in Khāgra, a quarter of Berhampore. The Murshidābād Art Agency has been started for the advertisement and exhibition of specimens of the art.

The peculiar features of the work are the minuteness of the carving, which requires 70 to 80 different tools, and the absence of joins. The carvers hate joins, and would rather make a small image in which none are required, than a large article which would sell at double or treble the price, because in the latter they would have to join the pieces together. The tools are of a simple character, being mostly ordinary carpenters' tools, though some are far smaller and finer. They use Assam or Burma ivory for the most part, as it is light and soft and yields easily to the chisel without any preliminary process of softening. For the solid end of the tusk, which is called the *nakshidant*, they pay generally Rs. 8-8 to Rs. 10 per seer; for the middle portion, known as *khordidant*, Rs. 15 to Rs. 16 a seer; and for the thick end, which is hollow (*galhardant*), Rs. 7 to Rs. 8 per seer. African ivory, which the carvers say is hard, and therefore liable to crack under the chisel, sells at Rs. 2 to Rs. 3 per seer less.

The first thing the carver does is to cut a block of ivory of sufficient bulk for the article required. On this a tracing of the object to be carved is drawn in pencil, but sometimes the design is sketched on paper. A clever workman can carve without any preliminary sketch, if the article to be manufactured is one which he is accustomed to carve. After this, the model is roughly shaped by means of chisels, large and small, according to the size of the parts to be chiselled off. Then files of different sizes and fineness are employed to work the model into a finer shape, and drills of different sizes are used to drill holes for perforated work. Finishing touches are given with an iron stylus, which the carvers call by the common name for a pen, *kalam.* The *kalams* are of various degrees of fineness, some as fine as needles and others like knives or sketch-erasers. When the model has been brought exactly to the designed shape, it is soaked in water for some time, and the surface is polished, first with fish scales and lastly with common chalk. For fastening figures into stands and for joining parts, small ivory pegs are used. For turning, a heavy lathe is used. When they have to carve from a new pattern, and they find that none of their existing tools are suitable or fine enough for the work, the Bhāskars will at once improvise a suitable tool, in the middle of their work.

The following list of the articles produced by the carvers is given in Mr. G. C. Dutt's *Monograph on Ivory Carving in Bengal.* Formerly they supplied a local demand for images of the gods, but now for the most part turn out an assortment of table ornaments and knick-knacks, mainly for the European market:—

No.	Articles.	Prices.	REMARKS.
1	2	3	4
1	Alphabet	1 to 1½ annas per letter.	
2	Durga (the ten handed goddess, with her attendant gods and goddesses, in the act of fighting with the giant Mahisasura).	Rs. 50 to Rs. 300	The best article that can be made from one block of ivory can be had for Rs. 150.
3	Kāli standing on the body of Siva with two attendant goddesses.	,, 40 to ,, 120	
4	Jagaddhātri standing on the lion and elephant with two attendant goddesses.	,, 50 to ,, 125	
5	Jagannāth's car procession ...	,, 50 to ,, 150	
6	Palanquin, single or with bearers and attendants.	,, 15 to ,, 100	
7	Chessmen	,, 25 to ,, 250	
8	Work-box...	,, 25 to ,, 300	
9	Elephant, single or caparisoned, or fighting with tiger.	,, 5 to ,, 150	
10	Horse, plain or with rider ...	,, 2 to ,, 30	The price varies according to the size of the pieces, and also according to the quality of the work.
11	Bullock-carts	,, 8 to ,, 50	
12	*Maur-pankhi,* or peacock state barge.	,, 10 to ,, 100	
13	Camel, single or with driver ...	,, 4 to ,, 40	
14	Cow, single or with calf ...	,, 3 to ,, 20	
15	Dog	,, 2 to ,, 8	
16	Pig	,, 2 to ,, 10	
17	Buffalo	,, 3 to ,, 20	
18	Crocodile	,, 5 to ,, 20	
19	Deer	,, 2 to ,, 15	
20	Plough, with ploughman ...	,, 3 to ,, 20	
21	Locket and chain (with or without gold or silver mounting).	,, 5 to ,, 50	

No.	Articles.	Prices.	Remarks.
1	2	3	4
22	Earrings	Rs. 4 to Rs. 10	The price varies according to the size of the pieces, and also according to the quality of the work.
23	Figures of zanana ladies, Hindu priests, washermen, water-carriers, peons, porters, tailors, sepoys, *fakirs*, policemen.	" 2 to " 5 each.	
24	Paper-cutter	" 1 to " 30	
25	Bangles, bracelets with or without gold or silver mountings.	" 25 and upwards	
26	Card case	" 6 to " 15	
27	Knitting needles	Annas 8 for a set of four.	
28	Crochet needles	Re. 1-8 each	
29	Napkin rings	Rs. 2-8 each	
30	Photo frames	" 15 to Rs. 60	
31	Caskets	" 30 to " 100	
32	Walking sticks	" 25 to " 75	
33	*Chāmur* or fly-flap	......	
34	Combs	......	

"The above list," writes Mr. G. C. Dutt, "is by no means exhaustive. The Murshidābād carvers turn out various other toys and trinkets, and of mythological subjects there is, perhaps, no end. Only one mythological figure the Murshidābād Bhāskars will not carve or sell, and that it is that of Krishna, as they are his followers * and cannot create or sell the deity they worship. Although the Murshidābād carvers can carve any practicable model of almost every useful and ornamental object, it must not be supposed that there is a regular supply of all these things in the market, nor should one expect to find many such objects in daily use anywhere, except, perhaps, the bangles and combs which are worn by up-country and Deccan women generally. There is usually but a limited and fitful outturn."

Other manufactures.

Oil is manufactured at an oil mill in Dayānagar (in the Berhampore Municipality), which was formerly called the Sambhu Mill, but has been renamed the Manindra Oil Mill after its owner, Mahārāja Manindra Chandra Nandi of Cossimbazar.

The manufacture of steel trunks, boxes, safes, etc., is a newly introduced industry. There are three manufactories at Jiāganj, another at Bhagwāngola and a fifth at Khāgra in Berhampore: the last was started by a man who learnt the art in Calcutta and established agencies both in Berhampore and Rāmpur Boalia. Rolled steel is obtained in Calcutta and worked up by Indian artisans under Indian supervision. These small factories are doing well, and the prices are cheaper than those of English-made goods.

* They belong to the Vaishnava sect.

Textile industries.

Cotton weaving survives as a village handicraft, bedsheets, *gāmchas*, *lungis*, etc., being woven on hand looms. Blanket weaving is carried on by colonies of Gareris, or up-country sheep-rearers and blanket-weavers, in the Jangipur subdivision, the principal seat of the industry being Aurangābād. The blankets, which cost Rs. 7 to Rs. 8, are exported to Calcutta and elsewhere. They are also made in the Kāndi subdivision, but for local sale only. Dyeing of cotton and silk is confined to a few families at Khāgra, Bālucbar and Mirzāpur. There are skilled embroiderers in the town of Murshidābād, who embroider caps, slippers and clothes with gold and silver wire.

Metal industries.

Gold and silver work is carried on in Khāgra, Berhampore, Pulinda and Kāndi; malaria is said to have depleted the families of workmen. Bell-metal and brass utensils are manufactured in considerable quantities at Khāgra, Berhampore, Kāndi, Baranagar and Jangipur; they are exported as well as sold in the local markets. Locks and betel-nut cutters of a superior kind are made at Dhuliān and iron chests at Jangipur. *Bidri*-ware is produced by a few workmen at Murshidābād; the process consists of inlaying silver in pewter, which is blackened with sulphate of copper. The Murshidābād Art Agency has endeavoured to foster this latter industry by advertising and exhibiting specimens.

Wood and bamboo work.

This district is one of the few in Bengal in which lac turnery is carried on. Bamboo work is a fairly extensive handicraft; chairs, *moras*, screens (*chiks*), boxes and waste-paper baskets are made and sold locally.

Clay models.

Clay models and figures are made at Khāgra. The specimens shown at an exhibition which was held at Banjetia a few years ago to encourage local industries compared very favourably with those made in the Nadia district, the workmanship of which has long been held in high estimation.

Fishing.

Last but not least of the district industries may be mentioned fishing, which, as already stated, is the means of subsistence, directly and indirectly, of 34,000 persons. It must, moreover, be borne in mind that a certain number subsist partially by fishing and partly by agriculture, and at the census return the latter as their principal means of livelihood. Altogether 1,158 cultivators and 698 agricultural labourers returned fishing or boating as a subsidiary occupation in 1911, and these were workers only; their dependants would account for nearly 3,000 more persons.

The Ganges abounds with fish at all times of the year, and a large number of fishermen live along its banks. The Bhāgīrathi and Jalangi also furnish a large supply during the rainy season. The Bhāndārdaha Bil is the most valuable fishery among confined waters, containing nearly all the fresh-water varieties that are found in Bengal. Its resources have, however, been reduced materially since communication with the Bhāgīrathi was cut off by the construction of an embankment. The *bil* formerly extended another five miles northward to near Lalitākuri, but the embankment at that place being constantly breached, another was built from Digha Ghāt to Bhagwāngola. The latter has cut off the northern portion of the *bil*, which is known as the Bura Thākur Bil and effectually prevented inundation. Prior to this, the *bil* was full of fish, even *hilsa* being found in it.

Other *bils* also give employment to a considerable fishing population. The Bishtupur (Vishnupur) Bil, which is replenished with fry from the Bhāgīrathi, contains carp of four varieties, Siluridae, etc., which are caught with nets shot from boats as well as with fish-traps. Conditions are the same in the Chaltia Bil. The Chanda Bil is well stocked with the fish known as *kātmācha*, *e.g.*, *Anabas scandens*, *Sacchobranchus fossilis*, *Clarius magur* and the *Ophiocephalidae*, but contains very few carp, probably because they are destroyed by the *kātmācha*, which are all predatory fish. This *bil* is full of weeds and lotuses, which preclude the use of nets, and fish have to be caught in traps or speared with the *kauch* or fish-spear. The Boālia Bil, being a shallow marsh, is chiefly used for cultivation, but the north-eastern portion, which is called the Putijol Bil, abounds with *kātmācha*, which are caught in the same way as in the Chanda Bil. Fishing is also carried on in the Northern Drainage Cut, fixed nets being placed at the entrance of the Putijol Bil; the fishery rights are let out annually by the Public Works Department.

From the end of July till the beginning of October the greater part of the Suti and Shamsherganj thanas is under water of varying depth. The shallow portions are covered with rice, jute, sugarcane and other high-growing crops, and constitute a prolific spawning ground for *ruhi*, *mirgal*, *kātla* and other Gangetic fish. At the village of Bohotāl in thana Suti, which is surrounded by water on three sides and distant only about three miles from the Rājgaon station of the East Indian Railway, a daily market is held for the sale of fry, which are exported in earthen jars (*gharas*) to Bīrbhūm, Burdwān and elsewhere to stock tanks with. Another daily market is held at Bendahāt, 7 miles from Raghunāthgang, from July to October. The boats used are all of one description, and apparently peculiar to this part—long, rakish, narrow, gondola-shaped craft, beautifully put together and very speedy. The fry, when caught, are thrown into the boats, which are kept with four or five inches of water in them. Two holes are bored in the bottom, one at either end, through which a continual stream of fresh water keeps bubbling up, the depth being regulated by baling. On reaching the shore where the market is held, the fish are placed in small tanks cut in the ground and filled with muddy water. They are first, however, washed in large sheets submerged in the *bil* or river water; and, as far as possible, all predatory fish, such as *bouil*, are removed. When purchased, the fry are carried away in *gharas*, which are filled with water, thickly impregnated with mud. The *gharas* are suspended from *bânghy* sticks, which are kept constantly oscillating, because the fry will die if the mud is allowed to settle and the water to clear. Even when standing still, the bearers keep up a jerking motion of their shoulders, so as to keep the water constantly agitated. When carried by rail, the water is stirred with sticks continually with the same object. The fry are sold by measure, a small wicker-work measure containing about half-a-seer being used. The price is in inverse ratio to the size of the fish it contains, for the smaller the fish, the greater the number. Five or six annas per measure seems to be an average price, which would be something like a rupee a thousand; they fetch more than double that price in the districts to which they are exported.

The limits of space preclude a description of the large variety of fishing implements, nets, traps, etc., in use, but mention may be made of a few ingenious contrivances employed. Some of the nets are of very large size. The *dore jâl*, for instance, which is stretched between places on the banks, is sometimes 2,000 or 3,000 feet long. The *kachal* nets, again, are 2,100 feet long by 66 feet deep and require two boats to work them. When they are being shot, the fishermen make a peculiar noise by rubbing a hollow piece of bamboo against the side of the boat, and also strike the water with the hollow side of half split bamboos in order to drive the fish into the net. The smaller fish are kept in the hold, but the larger varieties are strung through the eye cavities (not the eyes) by a string, which is attached to a rope hanging from one end of the boat to the other; they thus remain in the fresh water of the *bil*, and can be kept alive a long time and sent fresh to the markets. Another net, known as the *moi jâl*, is used in pairs, which require four boats to manipulate them. The boats, which are 18 or 19 feet long, are tied in pairs end to end with a couple of bamboos. The nets are let down from each pair of boats, which then draw near each other, sweeping the intervening space. Two men dive down and join the ends of the nets under water, after which they are drawn up.

Another peculiar device is employed with the long narrow boats called *sarangas*, which are about 42 feet long and $2\frac{1}{2}$ feet broad. On one side of the boat a net is raised to a height of five feet; on the other a split bamboo grating is placed. As the boat is rowed into the bank, a noise is caused by the grating passing through the water. The fish, anxious to escape, endeavour to jump across the boat and are caught in the outstretched net. This method of fishing is only carried on at night-time. Not less curious is the method of catching fish with the *bishāl jāl.* This is a fine-meshed net in the shape of an isosceles triangle, with sides about 10 or 12 feet long, which is kept stretched by bamboos tied at the apex. A man lowers the net into the water, while a woman with a floater (generally a jar or *hāndi*, which is used afterwards to hold the catch) swims about in front of him to drive the fish into the net.

In the Bhāndārdaha Bil and other *bils* it is the practice to place "bushes" in the water, composed of large heaps of twigs and the trunks of trees with large branches. The fish collect in these bushes, which are enclosed twice or thrice in the year. Bamboo enclosures are erected, with nets fastened to the bamboos, and are gradually made smaller as the bushes are approached, the bamboos being taken up and re-erected each time. When the circle is sufficiently small, *i.e.*, about 30 or 40 feet in diameter, the fishermen dive in and begin to take up the twigs and branches, using their hands and also hooks attached to bamboo poles. When all have been removed, two or three of them dive down and bring together the lower ends of the nets, which are then lifted up, brought to the boats, and hauled in with all the fish in them. The tops of the nets are 10 feet above the water, but some fish, especially *kātla* and *ruhi*, manage to escape by jumping over them. This method of fishing takes from two to four days, according to the area to be enclosed.

There are numerous kinds of fixed traps, but, perhaps, the commonest are the *khatans* or *chalis*, which are gratings made of split bamboos placed across *bils* or drains that have a current of water. They are fixed into the ground, and the top, which is five or six feet above the water, has a net attached to it. The fish, which in their way up against the stream try to jump over any obstacle they encounter, are caught in the net when they leap over the grating. A large number of fish are obtained in this way, which is open to the objection that it is a serious impediment to the upward passage of fish. A simple contrivance for catching eels is the *bānchonga*, which is a tube of bamboo, two or three feet long, with both ends open; it is made by splitting a bamboo in two and cutting away the knots inside till it is quite smooth: the two halves are then tied together with a piece of string. The tube is put in the mud, at a depth of seven or eight feet, and fixed there by a pin of bamboo. After 24 hours the fisherman dives to the bottom, and, closing the open ends of the tube with his two hands, takes it to the surface. In weedy waters a fish-spear, called *kauch*, is used. This is a sixteen bladed spear with a bamboo shaft, which is thrown from palm tree dug-outs.*

Pearl fishing.

Pearl fishing, a somewhat rare industry in Bengal, is carried on in this district. The pearl fisheries exist in a series of *bils*, marking the line of an old river, which stretch from the Gobra Nullah to Rukimpur, a distance of about 38 miles. The pearls are found in a mussel, which is a species of *Unio*, probably a variety of the pearl-bearing *Unino margaritifera*. The Motijhil and the *bils* in thanas Bhagwāngola, Barwa and Nawāda yield the greatest number. The majority are seed pearls, and usually have a golden tint. Valuable pearls are occasionally found, fetching as much as Rs. 200 each, but such finds are rare, and the largest pearls seldom exceed Rs. 15 or Rs. 30 in value. The fishery season is in the hot weather, when the water is low and almost stagnant. The various branches of the industry furnish employment to about 300 persons during this period, and its annual value is estimated at Rs. 3,000.

TRADE

The district is favourably situated for trade, having several lines of railway and also being served by the two first deltaic off-shoots of the Ganges, viz., the Bhāgīrathi and Jalangi, through which there is boat communication with Calcutta. The eastern half of the district, enclosed by the Ganges, Bhāgīrathi and Jalangi has, from time immemorial, been the seat of large commercial towns, and the railway has opened up the western half. The principal seats of trade are Azīmganj, Jangipur, Jiāganj, Khāgra and Dhuliān on the Bhāgīrathi; the Jain merchants of Azīmganj are among the richest traders in Bengal. Other important markets are Bhagwāngola, Beldānga, Saktipur, Jalangi, Kāndi, Gokarna, Lālbāgh, Sāgardighi, Bāluchar and Chhāpghāti. Periodical fairs are held at Dhuliān, Jangipur, Chāltia, Saktipur and Kāndi. The external trade is mainly with Calcutta. The chief imports are European piece-goods, salt, coal and kerosene oil; the chief exports are silk and agricultural produce, such as rice, wheat, gram, oil-seeds and jute.

* I am indebted for the above information to a report on the fisheries of Murshidabād by Mr. B. Das, Superintendent of Fisheries, Bengal, who carried out a survey of the fisheries in April 1912.

CHAPTER IX.

MEANS OF COMMUNICATION.

RAILWAYS.

Azīmganj branch.

THE district is served both by the East Indian Railway and the Eastern Bengal State Railway and contains three lines of railway. The oldest is the Azīmganj branch line of the East Indian Railway, which runs almost due east from Nalhāti, a station in the Bīrbhūm district on the Loop Line of the East Indian Railway, to Azīmganj, a town in this district situated on the Bhāgīrathi directly opposite to Jiāganj. Its total length is 27¼ miles, of which 15 miles lie in this district. The stations in Murshidābād, proceeding from west to east, are Bokhara, Sāgardighi, Barala and Azīmganj. The line, which was constructed by a private company in 1862, was acquired by Government in 1872, when it was known as the Nalhāti-Azīmganj State Railway. Through communication with Suri, the headquarters of Bīrbhūm, and thence with the Burdwān district, has been established by the Ondāl-Sainthia line (from Ondāl in Burdwān to Sainthia in Bīrbhūm). This connects the Chord and Loop Lines of the East Indian Railway, and was opened to traffic in 1908.

Rānāghāt-Murshidābād branch.

The Azīmganj branch line was the only railway in the district until 1905, when the Rānāghāt-Murshidābād branch of the Eastern Bengal State Railway was opened. The latter takes off from the main line of the Eastern Bengal State Railway at Rānāghāt and runs northward through the districts of Nadia and Murshidābād (which it enters a little north of Plassey) to its terminus at Lālgola Ghāt on the Ganges. The length within the district is 44½ miles, and there are 13 stations within district limits, viz., proceeding from south to north, Rajinagar, Beldānga, Bhābta, Sargāchi, Berhampore Court, Cossimbazar, Murshidābād, Nāshipur Road, Jiāganj, Bhagwāngola, Krishnapur, Lālgola and Lālgola Ghāt. An additional station is being opened between Jiāganj and Bhagwāngola.

Barharwa-Azimganj-Kātwa line.

The latest addition to the railway lines of Murshidābād is the Barharwa-Azīmganj-Kātwa branch of the East Indian Railway line, which is an extension of the Hooghly-Kātwa and Burdwān-Kātwa branches of the East Indian Railway. It runs from Kātwa in Burdwān through Azīmganj and Dhuliān to Barharwa, a station on the Loop Line in the Sonthal Parganas, and has a length, approximately, of 100 miles. With the exception of 6 miles at either end, which lie in the Sonthal Parganas and Burdwān, it lies entirely in Murshidābād, following the western bank of the Bhāgīrathi.

A proposal for the construction of a light railway from Krishnagar to Jalangi in this district (*viâ* Meherpur), a distance of 56 miles, was made by the District Board of Nadia several years ago. A survey was authorized in 1905 and was carried out by the agency of the Eastern Bengal State Railway. In 1911-12 a concession was granted to Messrs. H. V. Low & Co. to float a branch company for its construction. The line, which is to be on the 2 feet 6 inches gauge, will be subsidized by the Nadia District Board. Light railways.

The District Board maintains 55½ miles of metalled roads and 515 miles of unmetalled roads, in addition to which fair-weather tracks, known as "village roads," have an aggregate length of 872 miles. The following is a brief description of the principal roads. ROADS.

1. *The Bhagwāngola Road*—This is a metalled road, 19¾ miles long, from Berhampore to Bhagwāngola, with a branch to Jiāganj. It connects the Bhāgīrathi with the Ganges and the headquarters station with Jiāganj Ghāt, opposite the Azīmganj railway station. Prior to the construction of the Rānāghāt-Murshidābād Railway line, it was one of the most frequented trade routes, the goods consigned to Azīmganj merchants being brought along it from the Ganges. It passes through Manullābazar and Kalukhāli, where the road used to be periodically swept away when the Lalitākuri embankment was breached; there is an inspection bungalow at Jiāganj, 14 miles from Berhampore.

2. *The Jalangi Road*—Is the most important of those in the eastern portion of the district. It is 28 miles long and connects Berhampore with Jalangi, passing through Daulatābād, Islāmpur and Damkul (Azīmganj). There are inspection bungalows at Kālādānga on the Bhairab 16 miles from Berhampore, and Bhāduripāra, 8 miles from Kālādānga and 24 miles from Berhampore.

3. *The Kāndi-Sainthia Road*—Starts from Rādhārghāt opposite Berhampore, and runs through Gokaran, Kāndi, Kulli and Belgrām to Sainthia in Bīrbhūm, where there is a station on the Loop Line of the East Indian Railway. The portion from Rādhārghāt to Belgrām, 30 miles long, lies in Murshidābād. It is metalled as far as Kāndi (16½ miles), and is bridged throughout except at the Mor and Dwārka rivers, where ferry boats are kept in the rains; at the crossing of the Dwārka a temporary bridge with a causeway is erected in the dry season. There is an inspection bungalow at Kāndi.

4. *The Krishnagar Road, or Calcutta Road*—Extends from Berhampore to Krishnagar, the headquarters of the Nadia district, passing through Barwa, Dādpur, Loknāthpur and Debagrām. The large village of Beldānga is also in the vicinity of the road. Its length within the district is 21½ miles. There is an inspection bungalow at Dādpur, 15 miles south of Berhampore. This is an old military road, along which the troops marched from Calcutta to Berhampore, when troops were stationed at the latter place. Its importance has diminished since the construction of the railway.

5. *The Bādshāhi Road*—Is another old road, for, as its name implies, it was an Imperial road in the Mughal days; the name is now commonly corrupted into Bādshi. It was reconstructed during the famine of 1874, previous to which it had almost disappeared, so much so that there were scarcely any carts in the country traversed by it, all merchandise being conveyed by pack bullocks. This road, which is 45 miles in length, stretches from Jarur on the Murarai Road, near Jangipur, due south to the Nāwada station on the Azīmganj branch of the East Indian Railway in Bīrbhūm, and thence to the south-western boundary of the district at Naugāon, where it joins the Burdwān Road. Seven miles of the road, from Thākurpur to Gambhira, lie in the Bīrbhūm district. It crosses the Pānchgrām Road at Pānchgrām, the Kāndi-Sainthia Road at Kulli and Belgrām, and the Pānchthupi Road at Barwan; the police-stations of Mīrzāpur and Khargrām are also situated on it. The road is carried across the Nāgar or Janka Bil, between Sherpur and Khargrām, on a high embankment. There is an inspection bungalow at Khargrām, which is situated 9 miles south of Kāndi and 12 miles south of Pānchgrām.

6. *The Patkābāri Road*—28 miles long, starts from the western bank of the Bhāgīrathi nearly opposite Berhampore and passes through the villages of Hariharpāra, Choa, Nawāda and Patkābāri on the south-eastern boundary of the district. There are inspection bungalows at Hariharpāra, 13 miles south-east of Berhampore, and at Amtola, 21 miles from Berhampore. The road is of importance, as it connects the headquarters station with the productive thanas of Hariharpāra and Nawāda in the east and south-east. It is metalled as far as Narainpur, 6 miles from Berhampore. From Amtola another important road runs to Beldānga station.

7. *The Pānchgrām Road*—16¼ miles long, extends from Dahapāra, opposite the town of Murshidābād, to Pānchgrām, close to the western boundary of the district, where there is an

inspection bungalow. It crosses the large Bassia Bil between Nabagrām and Pānchgrām.

8. *The Jangipur-Murarai Road*—Is an important feeder road, 14 miles in length, connecting the subdivisional headquarters of Jangipur with the East Indian Railway Loop Line at Murarai. Seven miles of the road from Raghunāthganj on the western bank of the Bhāgīrathi opposite Jangipur to Mitrapur (Sāhebnagar) lie in this district, and the remainder in Bīrbhūm.

9. *The Purānadeori-Murcha Road*—17 miles long, connects Berhampore and Murshidābād with the north-eastern portion of the district and with Rāmpur Boalia, the headquarters station of Rājshāhi.

10. *The Jiāganj-Jangipur Road*—Is a portion of the old Rājmahāl Road, 28 miles in length. It leads from Jiaganj, northwards through Diwānsarai and Khamrasarai, to Jangipur.

11. *The Rāmnagar-Dhuliān Road*—80½ miles in length, runs along the right bank of the Bhāgīrathi from Rāmnagar in the extreme south of the district, opposite Plassey to Suti in the north, and thence along the bank of the Ganges to Dhuliān. It is an unmetalled road passable by wheeled traffic for only nine months in the year. The chief places which it passes, proceeding from south to north, are Saktipur, Rāngāmāti, Dahapāra, Azīmganj, Gadi, Nutanganj, Raghunāthganj, Suti and Shamsherganj.

There are a number of important feeder roads which have a heavy cart traffic, such as those from Raghunāthganj to Bokhara (11½ miles), from Amtola to Beldānga (14½ miles) and from Rajinagar to Garhduāra (3½ miles).

The Ganges or Padma is navigable throughout the year, and steamers regularly ply along it to and from Goalundo. The other big rivers are navigable by country boats except in the dry season, *i.e.*, the hot weather and latter part of the cold weather. The most important of them are the Bhāgīrathi and Jalangi, which, as shown in Chapter I, have long been silting up. During the eighty years, 1822–1902, the Bhāgīrathi was closed during the dry season in 20 years; in 18 years a lowest depth of 1½ to 2 feet was maintained, and in 28 years the lowest depth was 2 to 3 feet. In the last fourteen years of this period it was practically closed during the dry season except in 1895, when there was a depth of 3½ feet. The portion opposite to Berhampore is the worst of all. In spite of the efforts of the Public Works Department to keep it open, nothing is to be seen during the dry season but a long expanse of sand. When the river is navigable by steamers, which is only from about the middle of June to the

WATER COMMUNICATIONS.

middle of October, the Calcutta Steam Navigation Company runs river steamers and keeps up a regular service to Calcutta. As regards the Jalangi, it was closed in the dry season during the last 45 years of the same period, and was open to a minimum depth of about 1½ feet in 11 years, and to a minimum depth of 2 to 3 feet in 24 years. The measures which are taken to keep these rivers open to traffic have already been mentioned in Chapter I.

CHAPTER X.

LAND REVENUE ADMINISTRATION.

It is not possible to compare the present land revenue of the district with that realized under Muhammadan rule, for there was no fiscal unit corresponding to the area now included in the district. Changes of jurisdiction also preclude any comparison of the collections at different periods of British rule until a recent date, *e.g.*, a large part of Bānkura was comprised in the district till 1787, and thana Barwān was transferred to it from Bīrbhūm in 1879, while the Rāmpur Hāt subdivision was detached from Murshidābād and added to Bīrbhūm. LAND REVENUE.

In Todar Mall's rent-roll of 1582 the present district area formed part of several *sarkārs*. The greater part fell within *Sarkār* Tānda or Audambar, but some of the country to the east was in *Sarkār* Mahmudābād, a small tract to the extreme south was in *Sarkār* Sātgāon, and part also was in *Sarkār* Sharīfābād. By the financial reforms of Murshid Kulī Khān, Murshidābād was constituted one of the thirteen *chaklāhs* into which the whole of Bengal was divided. The area of the old *chaklāh* of Murshidābād cannot, however, be compared with the present district, for it seems to have been co-extensive with the whole of the present districts of Rājshāhi, Bogra, Pābna and Murshidābād, and to have covered also the larger portions of Mālda, Bīrbhūm and Nadia. It is evident, therefore, that the revenue raised from this tract can not be brought into comparison with the revenue of Murshidābād district under British rule. According to the assessment of 1722, which is given in detail in Grant's *Analysis of the Finances of Bengal*, the revenue of Murshidābād *chaklāh* amounted to 30 lakhs or more than one-fifth of the revenue of the entire Province of Bengal. This total, however, included not only the land revenue, but also the mint duties of Murshidābād, which yielded 3 lakhs, and the Chunakhāli taxes, which produced the same sum. The last item represented all the varying imposts on houses and trade that were levied within the city of Murshidābād, of which the export duties on silk formed a considerable portion.

The rent-roll of 1722 furnishes some interesting information regarding the value of the *jāgīr* or rent-free grant of land, which was attached to the office of the Nawāb and formed his recognized official income. It consisted of 296 entire or broken *parganas*, scattered throughout the country, of which the annual rent was estimated in the imperial books at 16 lakhs but, according to the principles of valuation adopted for the assessment of other zamīndāris, the estimate falls to 10¾ lakhs. This *jāgīr* formed the viceregal establishment, out of which had to be defrayed a large portion of the military expenses of Government, the whole of the Nawāb's household expenses in his private and public capacity, together with the greater part of the civil-list charges, inclusive of those usually incurred in the Faujdāri or High Court of criminal judicature.

In 1880-81 the collections of land revenue in Murshidābād amounted to Rs. 13,05,000, but in the next decade some estates were transferred to other districts, and the realizations consequently fell to Rs. 10,68,000 in 1890-91. They were Rs. 10,66,000 in 1900-01, but rose to Rs. 10,74,000 in 1910-11. In 1911-12 there were 2,329 permanently settled estates with a current demand of Rs. 10,12,635, sixty-four temporarily settled estates with a demand of Rs. 25,919 and 30 Government estates held directly by Government with a demand of Rs. 38,584. Altogether 4,077 revenue-paying estates, 246 revenue-free estates and 1,327 rent-free lands were assessed to roads and public works cesses in the same year, the aggregate current demand being Rs. 1,82,544. The recorded share-holders of these 5,650 estates were 39,909 in number. There were also 17,022 tenures assessed to cesses with 23,112 recorded share-holders. The gross rental of the district when road-cess was first assessed under Act X of 1871 was Rs. 32,83,057, and it has now risen to Rs. 35,92,604.

COURT OF WARDS. Only one large estate, known as the Cossimbazar estate, is under the management of the Court of Wards. This is the second time it has come under management, for it was administered by the Court of Wards during the minority of the late Raja Ashutosh Nāth Ray of Cossimbazar, and was released only ten years before his death. He died intestate on 17th December 1906, leaving an infant son, only a few months old, since named Kamala Ranjan Ray, as the sole heir of his property. The child was declared a minor, and his person and property were taken charge of by the Court. The properties belonging to the estate lie for the most part in Eastern Bengal; there are 74 revenue-paying and revenue-free estates, 113 *patni* and other permanent leases, nine temporary leases and nine rent-free holdings in the districts of Murshidābād, Bīrbhūm, Hooghly, Monghyr and Calcutta. The total rent and cess demand amounts to about four lakhs; nearly one-third of the rental is derived from properties held under direct management. The liabilities of the estate, as ascertained after assumption of charge by the Court of Wards, were Rs. 2,30,000, but this amount had been reduced to Rs. 49,000 in 1913.

LAND TENURES.

Revenue-paying estates.

At the time of the Permanent Settlement there were four classes of zamīndārs in Bengal. They are thus described in the introduction to Hunter's *Bengal Manuscript Records*. "The first class of Bengal zamīndārs represented the old Hindu and Muhammadan Rājās of the country, previous to the Mughal conquest by the Emperor Akbar in 1576, or persons who claimed that status. The second class were Rājās or great landholders, most of whom dated from the seventeenth and eighteenth centuries, and some of whom were, like the first class, *de facto* rulers in their own estates or territories, subject to a tribute or land tax to the representative of the Emperor. These two classes had a social position faintly resembling the Feudatory Chiefs of the British Indian Empire, but that position was enjoyed by them on the basis of custom, not of treaties. The third and most numerous class were persons whose families had held the office of collecting the revenue during one or two or more generations, and who had thus established a prescriptive right. A fourth and also numerous class was made up of the revenue farmers, who, since the *diwāni* grant in 1765, had collected the land tax for the East India Company, under the system of yearly leases, then of five years' leases, and again of yearly leases. Many of these revenue farmers had, by 1787, acquired the *de facto* status of zamīndārs." The original differences in the holdings of these four classes of zamīndārs were obliterated by the Permanent Settlement, and from 1793 onwards all estates, whatever their origin, were placed on a uniform basis.

Aimas.

In this district the only revenue-paying estates with any peculiar features are those known as *aimas*. They are generally of extremely small area, and though they are borne on the tauzi and pay revenue, its amount is always small and often only nominal. They are believed to have been originally charitable grants for Muhammadan uses, and abound in *pargana* Fatehsingh to the south-west. It is not clear why *aimas* should be so plentiful in this part of the district. The grantees are usually resident Musalmāns; but there is no reason to suppose that the grants were made directly by the Muhammadan Governor of Murshidābād. The estate of Fatehsingh is one of the oldest in the district, and so far back as its history can be traced, it has almost always been in the possession of a Hindu family. It is known also, as a matter of fact, that *aimas* have been created by the

Hindu zamīndārs. It has been conjectured, therefore, that they owe their origin to fear rather than to favour.

Revenue-free estates. Revenue-free estates are largely represented in Murshidābād, but possess few features which are not common to the rest of Bengal. The *lākhirāj* estates are most common in *pargana* Asadnagar, which contains the greater part of the city of Murshidābād. The Nawāb Bahādur of Murshidābād is the largest *lākhirājdār* in the district. His *ramnas* or deer parks, which come under this category, are very extensive, and he owns, besides, several large revenue-free *mahāls* called *zimān*.

Mazkuri and *shikmi tāluks*. The Muhammadan Government, for objects of administrative convenience, sometimes entered into engagements with small proprietors to pay their land revenue through the zamīndārs within the limits of whose estates their properties lay. The zamīndārs again occasionally made unauthorized transfers of land, and to conceal the fact from the Muhammadan Government stipulated that the tranferees should pay their quota of land revenue through them. Partly at their own request, in order that they might obtain protection from the exactions of the zamīndārs, and partly for other reasons, the majority of the *tāluks*, as such estates were called, were separated from the parent estates at the Permanent Settlement and recognized as separate estates with land revenue payable direct to the State. Some, however, were not separated, but continued as dependent tenures, known as *mazkuri tāluks*. They were especially numerous in the old zamīndāri of Rājshāhi, which included some portion of the present district of Murshidābād. They are not now very common, and are chiefly to be found in the *pargana* of Mahālandi, which formerly belonged to the Rājā of Rājshāhi: they continue to be dependent upon the larger zamīndāris of which they form a part, to the extent of paying their Government revenue through the superior zamīndār. In other respects they confer full rights of proprietorship. *Shikmi* seems to be merely another name for the *mazkuri* or dependent *tāluk*, being usually adopted in *parganas* to the west of the Bhāgīrathi, especially Khārgrām and Murāripur.

Istimrāri. Another tenure, dating back to a period anterior to the Permanent Settlement, is the *istimrāri*, which is a hereditary and transferable tenure, held at a fixed rate of rent: it is, in fact, a tenure granted in perpetuity before the Permanent Settlement. It is, however, rare in Murshidābād.

Patni tāluks. Many other tenures have been created since the Permanent Settlement, of which perhaps the commonest are *patni tāluks*. This tenure had its origin in the Burdwān Rāj estate, which was assessed very highly at the Permanent Settlement. In order to ensure easy and punctual realization of the rental, a number of leases in perpetuity, to be held at a fixed rent, were given to middlemen, and this device was soon adopted in other estates. The tenure, which was legalized by Regulation VIII of 1819, consists of a *tāluk* held in perpetuity at a fixed rent. It is liable to sale for arrears of rent; but its chief peculiarity is that the tenure may be altogether extinguished by the sale of the parent estate for arrears of Government revenue. Beneath the *patni* comes a series of subordinate tenures created by successive sub-infeudations, each with rights similar to those of the original *patni*. These are known as *dar-patnis*, *se-patnis*, *daradar-patnis*, and so on. It would appear that this mode of sub-infeudation is especially common in Murshidābād. Most large estates are let out to one or more *patnidārs*; under each *patnidār* flourish *dar-patnidārs*; under whom again are to be found *se-patnidārs*, and sometimes a fourth class of *daradar-patnidārs*. Nor is this the end of the chain. Under the *daradar-patnidār*, there often crops up the *ijārādār*, the *maurusidār*, the *gānthidār*, or other subordinate tenant. Indeed, it is not uncommon to find the mere *gānthidār* or *jotdār* subletting the land to a fresh tenant, whom he miscalls a *patnidār*; and thus the entire series may commence anew.

This process of infeudation is due, in great part, to the urgent need of ready money at certain times. The temptation to get rid of the trouble and uncertainty of collection, and to obtain a lump sum of money for the celebration of a wedding ceremony, *pūja*, etc, is naturally strong; and it is almost invariably the case that when a lease of the *patni* series is given, the lessor receives a cash bonus or *salāmi*, as well as an agreement for the payment of a fixed annual rent.

The term *gānthi* is used loosely to designate tenures generally and is also specifically applied to tenures dating from the time of the Permanent Settlement, which are known by the name of the original grantee, even though they may have passed to another family. Such tenures are entered in the *zamīndar's* accounts under the name of the original grantee, and the actual possessor is shown as paying rent (*gānthi jama*) on his account. *Gānthis.*

Jot is another name applied in this district to hereditary and transferable tenures held at a fixed rate of rent, which are elsewhere called *maurasis*, *gānthis*, *hāwālas*, etc. The origin of the tenure, as the name of *jot* implies, is to be found in cultivators' holdings at a definite rent; but the holders have ceased from various reasons to till the soil themselves, and have sublet to the actual husbandmen. The prosperous peasant always attemps to *Jots.*

leave the cultivator's sphere of life, and to rise into the next higher rank. As soon as he finds he can afford it, he sublets his land, and the industrious worker sinks into the respectable annuitant.

Maurasi. The *maurasi* proper differs somewhat from the *jot*. It is a hereditary tenure, but the right to alienate depends upon local custom, which in Murshidābād is favourable to alienation. Unless protected by express stipulations in the lease, the *maurasidār* remains liable to enhancement of rent. These tenures are sometimes granted for cultivation, but more often for the erection of dwelling-houses, for the laying out of gardens, plantations and similar purposes.

Mukarari. The *mukarari* is also a tenure held at a fixed rate of rent, and the chief difference between it and a *maurasi* is that the former is not necessarily transferable and does not descend to heirs unless it is also *maurasi*. The two terms have, however, come to be synonomous, the *mukarari* leases having, as a general rule, the privileges of *maurasi* grants attached to them.

Ijāras, zarpeshgis and *katkinas.* The *ijāra* is a lease of a temporary character, of which the conditions are almost always governed by a written contract. The term is usually short, and the *ijāradār* cannot create subordinate tenures to endure longer than his own lease nor can he alienate in any way. *Zarpeshgi ijāras* and *katkina* are terms applied to leases of land on usufructuary mortgages.

Service tenures. Village officials and common servants were formerly paid for their services by service holdings (*chākrān*) held rent-free. The old village community has now so entirely decayed, that it is difficult to find any class of public servants holding rent-free lands, except *kotwāls* or village watchmen, and very rarely *mandals* or headmen. It is by no means uncommon, however, to find private servants, *i e.*, servants of particular families of landowners, holding service grants of rent-free land. The services have now in many cases ceased to be performed or even demanded, but the lands remain rent-free. In addition to the *paiks* or zamīndār's retainers, whose lands are called *paikan*, the family priest was often thus paid; so was the family barber, the potter who furnished crockery, the drummer who beat the tom-tom at *pūjās*, the sellers of flowers, vegetables and plantain-leaves and the painter by whose aid Durga was annually enshrined in the halls of her votaries; these, and others used to be, and occasionally still are, paid in land for their services or their goods. The *chākrān* lands are most numerous in the western half of the district, in tracts which once formed parts of the old *zamīndāris* of Bīrbhūm, Rājshāhi and Fatehsingh.

Tenancies.

Except for the *gānthi jot* and *utbandi* tenancy, there are no peculiarities in the holdings actually held by cultivators in Murshidābād. The old classification of cultivators' holdings was into those of the *khudkāsht* or resident raiyats and those of the *paikāsht* or non-resident raiyats. In the early history of British land legislation in India, this distinction was of primary importance. After the desolation caused by the great famine of 1770, there was in every village more land than the survivors could properly cultivate, and migratory bands of peasants had to be invited to settle on the deserted tracts. From the necessities, probably, of this situation, there resulted the superior privileges granted to the resident cultivators. But a century and a half of peace and plenty has obliterated the real meaning of this classification, which now survives only as a legal tradition.

Another classification of cultivators' holdings might be made, according to the form in which the rent is paid. The great majority of peasants pay in hard cash, and their tenure is then called *hari;* but payment in kind is not uncommon, in which case the tenure is known as *bhāg* or *bārga*. This tenure is of a metayer character, the produce being shared in a fixed proportion (frequently in equal moieties) between the cultivator and the landlord.

The classification, which is now generally recognized, is that based on the Bengal Tenancy Act of occupancy raiyats, non-occupancy raiyats and under-raiyats, who are called *korfā* raiyats.

Gānthi jots.

Along the Padma river it is common for a number of raiyats to cultivate *diāra* land under a sort of joint occupancy, the names of one or two only being entered in the zamīndār's books. Such holdings are called *gānthi jots.*

Utbandi.

The *utbandi* is pre-eminently a Nadia tenure, and is found for the most part in the southern part of the district, and especially in *pargana* Plassey, which was formerly included within the district of Nadia. Its essential feature is that the husbandman only pays rent for the actual quantity of land which he has cultivated during the year, and, if paid in kind, the amount of his rent is determined by the outturn of the crop he has grown. It apparently had its origin in the Nadia district, from which it spread to neighbouring districts, though in no district is it as common as in Nadia, where about five-eighths of the cultivated lands are held under it. The literal meaning of the term is "assessed according to cultivation."

In 1861 Mr. Montresor, who had been deputed to investigate certain complaints of European proprietors in the Nadia district, described the system as follows :—" The *utbandi* tenure apparently has its origin in this district and is peculiar to Nadia. There is, in almost every village, a certain quantity of land not included in the rental of the raiyat, and which, therefore, belongs directly to the recognized proprietor of the estate. This fund of unappropriated land has accumulated from deserted holdings of absconded tenants, from lands gained by alluvion, from jungle lands recently brought into cultivation by persons who hold no leases, and from lands termed *khās khamar*, signifying land retained by the proprietor for his household. In other districts lands of the three first descriptions are at once leased out to tenants, but in Nadia it appears to be different. Owing either to the supineness of the landlord or to the paucity of inhabitants, a custom has originated from an indefinite period of the raiyats of a village cultivating, without the special permission of the landlord, portions of such land at their own will and pleasure. This custom has been recognized and established by the measurement of the lands at the time the crop is standing through an officer on the part of the landlord, styled *halsana*, and the assessment is accordingly made.

In the report of the Government of Bengal on the Bengal Tenancy Bill (1884), the *utbandi* holding was described as follows :—" A tenancy from year to year, and sometimes from season to season, the rent being regulated not, as in the case of *halhāsili*, by a lump payment in money for the land cultivated, but by the appraisement of the crop on the ground, and according to its character. So far it resembles the tenure by crop appraisement of the *bhāoli* system, but there is between them this marked difference, that while in the latter the land does not change hands from year to year, in the former it may."

When the Tenancy Bill was under consideration, the Bengal Government proposed to treat *utbandi* lands as ordinary raiyati lands were treated, *i.e.*, to presume that tenants of *utbandi* lands were settled raiyats if they had held any land in the village for 12 years, and to declare that they had, as settled raiyats, occupancy rights in all lands held by them in the village. The Select Committee did not, however, agree to this proposal, and applied the provisions relating to *char* and *diāra* lands to *utbandi* lands also. Accordingly by section 180 of the Bengal Tenancy Act it was laid down that an *utbandi* tenant can acquire no rights of occupancy until he has held the same land for 12 years continuously, and that, until he acquires such a right, he is liable to pay the rent agreed on between him and the landlord. Under these circumstances it is practically impossible for a tenant to acquire a right of occupancy, except with the consent of the landlord.

The most authoritative ruling of the law courts as to the nature of this tenancy is that delivered by the Chief Justice (Sir W. C. Petheram) and Tottenham, J., in the case of Beni Mādhab Chakravarti *versus* Bhuban Mohan Biswās (I. L. R. 17, Cal. 393). This ruling concludes with the following words:— "The description of *utbandi* seems to refer rather to particular areas taken for cultivation for limited periods, and then given up, than to holdings of which parts are cultivated and other parts lie fallow, while the rent for the whole is assessed year by year with reference to the quantity within the holding under cultivation in that year. A holding of the latter description hardly seems to answer to the general conception of *utbandi*."

The subject of this particular tenure came before the Government of Bengal during the years 1900-03. In the annual report for the year 1900 the Collector of Nadia remarked that advantage had been taken of the prevalence of the *utbandi* system to extort excessive rents. The remark attracted the attention of Government, and an enquiry was held chiefly with a view to ascertain whether any amendment of the law was necessary. After considering the matter in all its bearings, the Lieutenant-Governor came to the conclusion that "the system, though theoretically unsound, is practically unobjecionable; it is of great antiquity; it has its champions; and no one contends that the need for change is acute." There was, it was declared, no need for immediate legislation, but the Commissioner was instructed to keep his attention to the system, and promptly bring to the notice of Government any signs of its abuse.

CHAPTER XI.

GENERAL ADMINISTRATION.

ADMINISTRATIVE CHARGES AND STAFF.

THE district was included in the Rajshahi Division or Commissionership (the headquarters of which were at Berhampore) until 1875, when it was transferred to the Presidency Division. It is divided into four subdivisions, the area and population of which are shown in the margin. The present Lālbāgh subdivision is of recent creation, having been constituted in 1900 from portions of other subdivisions. Thanas Bhagwāngola, Manullabazar and Asanpur were transferred to it from the Sadar subdivision, Sāgardighi from the Jangipur subdivision and Nabagrām from the Kāndi subdivision.

SUBDIVISION.	Area in square miles.	Population, 1911.
Sadar ...	834	517,728
Lālbāgh ...	365	195,128
Jangipur ...	509	357,930
Kāndi ...	435	301,493

The sanctioned staff under the Collector at Berhampore consists of three officers with first class magisterial powers and two officers with second or third class powers. The Subdivisional Officers of Kāndi, Lālbāgh and Jangipur have each a Sub-Deputy Collector under them. There is also a Kānungo attached to each of the four subdivisions for land revenue work.

PUBLIC WORKS DEPARTMENT

The headquarters of the Nadia Rivers Division of the Public Works Department, which is under an Executive Engineer, are at Berhampore. The district is divided into three subdivisions, all under the control of the Executive Engineer, viz., the Berhampore, Upper Bhāgīrathi and Akriganj subdivisions.

CRIMINAL JUSTICE.

There is a District and Sessions Judge for the district, whose headquarters are at Berhampore. In addition to the stipendiary Magistrates there are Benches of Honorary Magistrates at the following places—the numbers in brackets indicate the number of Honorary Magistrates on the Bench at each place:—Berhampore (6), Dhuliān (3), Lālbāgh (11), Kāndi (6) and Jangipur (5).

The number of criminal cases disposed of by the different courts in 1911 was 3,203, viz., 2,369 by stipendiary Magistrates, 816 by Honorary Magistrates and 18 by the Sessions Court. This number is less by 256 than that recorded in 1901.

Civil justice is administered by the District Judge, a Subordinate Judge at Berhampore and nine Munsifs. Two of the Munsifs hold their courts at Berhampore, two at Jangipur, two at Kāndi and one at Lālbāgh. The ninth Munsif is an Additional Munsif appointed for Kāndi, Lālbāgh and Jangipur. CIVIL JUSTICE.

In 1911 there were 14,428 suits disposed of under the ordinary procedure and 8,588 under the Small Cause Court procedure, while 263 appeals were disposed of by the District Judge and 87 by the Subordinate Judge. Civil litigation is increasing steadily, for since 1901 the number of suits disposed of under the ordinary procedure has risen by 2,764, and of those under the Small Cause Court procedure by 1,106, representing an increase of 24 and 15 per cent., respectively, in ten years.

For police purposes the district is divided into 23 thanas, as shown in the statement below, which also gives the other police-stations which form independent investigating centres :— POLICE.

Thana.	Police-station.	Thana.	Police-station.
Sadar subdivision.		*Lālbāgh subdivision.*	
Beldānga ...	Saktipur.	Asanpur.	
Damkul ..	Jalangi.	Bhagwāngola.	
Daulatbazar.		Manullabazar.	
Hariharpāra.		Nabagrām.	
Nawāda.		Sāgardighi.	
Rāninagar ...	Harshi.	Shāhānagar.	
Sujāganj.			
Jangipur subdivision.		*Kāndi subdivision.*	
Lālgola.		Barwan.	
Mirāapur.		Bharatpur ...	Kāgrām.
Raghunāthganj.		Gokaran.	
Shamshirganj ...	Farakka.	Kāndi.	
Suti.		Khargaon.	

Before 1890 Barwan and Nabagrām, which used to be called Kaliānganj, were in the Sadar subdivision. In consequence of the creation of the Lālbāgh subdivision there were further changes in 1900, which have already been mentioned in the first paragraph of this chapter. Gorābazar used to be a thana, but was amalgamated with Sujāganj and retained only as a town outpost. The headquarters of what is now the Rāninagar thana were formerly located at Goās, and there used to be an outpost at Rāngāmāti, which was abolished, part of the charge being added to Sujāganj and part to Saktipur.

According to the returns for 1912, the sanctioned strength of the district police is:—a Superintendent, one Assistant Superintendent, 7 Inspectors, 70 Sub-Inspectors, 87 head-constables and

678 constables—in all, 844 men. The village police force in the same year consisted of 220 dafadārs and 2,550 chaukīdārs.

JAILS. There is a District Jail at Berhampore and subsidiary jails at each of the outlying subdivisional head-quarters. The accommodation in each, according to the returns for 1911, is shown in the margin.

JAIL.	Males.	Females.	Total.
Berhampore ...	360	9	369
Jangipur ...	23	3	26
Kāndi ...	17	2	19
Lālbāgh ...	10	2	12

The chief industries in the District Jail are oil-pressing, *surki*-pounding, carpentry, *dari*-weaving and cane and bamboo work. The District Jail used to be located at Maidāpur, about 4 miles distant from Berhampore, but the buildings, being on a damp, low-lying site, were unhealthy. In 1871-72 it was decided to transfer the jail to the former hospital of the European troops within the cantonments at Berhampore and on the bank of the Bhāgīrathi. This change was effected in 1873 and 1874, the majority of the prisoners being removed in the former and the remainder in the latter years.

REGISTRATION. There are 8 offices for the registration of assurances under Act II of 1877, as shown in the following statement, which gives the salient statistics for the year 1912:—

OFFICES.	Number of documents registered.	Receipts.	Expenditure.
		Rs.	Rs.
Asanpur	1,828	2,286	2,314
Aurangābād	3,394	3,563	2,234
Berhampore	4,180	8,997	5,765
Bharatpur	3,847	3,817	2,834
Damkul (Azimganj) ...	1,849	1,966	1,511
Jangipur	2,678	2,862	2,384
Kāndi	5,921	6,410	3,387
Lālbāgh	1,477	1,607	1,535
Total ...	25,174	31,508	21,964

REVENUE. Details of the revenue of the district during the decade ending in 1910-11 are given in the B Volume, which is published separately as a statistical appendix to this volume; and it will be sufficient to state that the collections in 1910-11 amounted to Rs. 19,66,443, and were made up as follows:—Rs. 10,73,919 from land revenue, Rs. 4,12,747 from stamps, Rs. 2,05,379 from excise (including opium), Rs. 1,86,444 from road and public works cesses, Rs. 87,707 from income-tax (which was paid by 1,006 assessees) and Rs. 247 from other sources.

CHAPTER XII.

LOCAL SELF-GOVERNMENT.

The District Board consists of 21 members, of whom six are *ex-officio* members, five are appointed by Government and ten are elected. The District Magistrate is the Chairman of the Board. Details of the receipts and expenditure of the Board during the ten years ending in 1910-11 are given in the B Volume (published separately as a statistical appendix to this volume), from which it will be seen that the annual income has varied from Rs. 1,07,659 in 1900-01 to Rs. 1,90,379 in 1908-09. In 1911-12 the receipts amounted to Rs. 1,46,469, excluding the opening balance. DISTRICT BOARD.

The District Board gives grants-in-aid to 19 middle schools, 140 upper primary schools, 486 lower primary schools and 59 other schools; its educational expenditure in 1911-12 aggregated Rs. 26,774. It also aids four dispensaries, the grants to which in the same year came to Rs. 6,920. It maintains 55½ miles of metalled roads, 515 miles of unmetalled roads and 872 miles of village roads; the cost of repairs in 1911-12 was Rs. 63,443. There are 90 pounds under its administration, the income from which was Rs. 11,456. A few years ago the Board carried out a scheme for supplying rural areas with good drinking water, which was initiated by a gift of a lakh of rupees from Rāja Jogendra Narayan Ray of Lālgola.

There are three Local Boards with headquarters at Berhampore, Jangipur and Kāndi. The Sadar Local Board consists of 22 members, of whom 10 are elected and 12 are nominated. The Jangipur and Kāndi Local Boards have each 13 members, of whom one is an *ex-officio* member, viz., the Subdivisional Officer, who is the Chairman. Of the other members four are nominated and eight are elected in the Kāndi Local Board, while three are nominated, eight are elected and one is appointed under section 10 of the Local Self-Government Act, in the Jangipur Local Board. LOCAL BOARDS.

There are five union committees having control over small local areas. They have charge of village roads and pounds in the localities within their jurisdiction, and their income consists of small annual grants from the District Board, which vary UNION COMMITTEES.

from Rs. 125 to Rs. 300. The following statement sufficiently indicates their constitution:—

Union Committee.	Year of establishment.	Area in square miles.	Population.	Number of members.
Aurangābād	1904	5	8,717	7
Choa	1903	20	11,000	8
Mirzāpur	1905	12½	8,906	9
Pānchthupi	1905	10½	10,140	9
Patkabāri	1902	11½	15,207	5

MUNICIPALITIES. Six municipalities have been constituted, viz., Azīmganj, Berhampore, Dhuliān, Jangipur, Kāndi and Murshidābād. The statement below gives the more salient statistics relating to each municipality in the year 1911-12, and a more detailed account of each will be found in the last chapter. This statement may be supplemented by a mention of the taxes by means of which the municipal income is raised in each town.

In Berhampore the chief tax is a rate on holdings at 7½ per cent. on their annual value. Latrine fees are also raised according to a scale, and a water-rate is assessed at 7½ per cent. on the valuation of holdings situated near hydrants, and at 6 per cent. on the valuation of holdings situated in lanes where there are no hydrants close by. In Azīmganj, Dhuliān, Jangipur, Kāndi and Murshidābād the system of taxation is uniform. In all of them a personal tax is imposed, *i.e.*, a tax on persons according to their circumstances and property at the rate of one rupee per hundred rupees of income, while Government and other public buildings are assessed at 7 per cent. on their annual value. Latrine fees are levied in Azīmganj, Jangipur, Kāndi and Murshidābād. In Azīmganj they are assessed at 5 per cent. on the annual value of holdings, in Jangipur at 11 pies per rupee on the annual value of holdings, and in Kāndi at 11 annas per hundred rupees of income, while in Murshidābād they are assessed according to a scale.

Municipality.	Year of establishment.	Number of ratepayers.	Percentage to population.	Number of Municipal Commissioners.	Incidence of taxation per head.	Income (excluding opening balance).
					Rs. A. P.	Rs.
Azīmganj ...	1896	3,030	24·5	15	1 10 5	22,360
Berhampore ...	1876	5,719	21·8	25	2 11 1	97,242
Dhuliān ...	1909	1,406	16·9	9	0 7 3	5,632
Jangipur ..	1869	2,354	20·6	18	1 0 3	16,203
Kāndi ...	1869	2,390	18·8	11	0 11 2	9,372
Murshidābād ...	1869	2,827	22·3	15	1 5 11	26,906

CHAPTER XIII.

EDUCATION.

A FAIR indication of the extent to which education is diffused is afforded by the census statistics of literacy. The test of literacy is ability both to read and write, with this further qualification that a person is only recorded as literate if he can write a letter to a friend and read the answer to it; all persons who are unable to do this are entered in the census schedules as illiterate. The total number of persons in Murshidābād who came up to the prescribed standard of literacy in 1911 was 79,490, representing 6 per cent. of the population. This proportion is below the average for Bengal, viz., 8 per cent., so that the district must be regarded as backward from an educational point of view; but there has been a slight advance since 1901, the proportion of literate males having risen from 106 to 108 per mille, and of literate females from 6 to 9 per mille. The improvement, though slight, is really greater than would appear from the figures, for the criterion of literacy was stricter than in 1901, when no conditions as to ability to read and write a letter were laid down. LITERACY.

How backward the education of woman still is may be realized from the fact that the literate males outnumber the literate females by 12 to 1, the actual figures being 73,427 and 6,063, respectively. There is also considerable disparity between the figures for Hindus and those for Musalmāns. Of the former 56,343, and of the latter 22,392, were recorded as able to read and write, so that there are approximately only 4 literate Musalmāns to every 10 literate Hindus. Taking the proportional figures for each of the two religions, 160 per mille of the Hindu males and only 62 per mille of the Musalmān males are literate, the corresponding ratios for females being 16 and 2 per mille, respectively. Altogether, 10,565 persons (10,291 males and 274 females) can read and write English, the ratio being 15 per mille in the case of males and 4 per 10,000 in the case of females.

EDUCATIONAL INSTITUTIONS.

The number of pupils under instruction at educational institutions of all kinds was only 12,000 in 1883, but was nearly doubled in the next ten years, the aggregate for 1892-93 being 23,000. This advance has been more than sustained, the figure rising to 25,628 in 1902-03 and to 38,186 in 1912-13, when there were 981 educational institutions in the district, as shown in the margin.

Institutions.	Number.	Number of pupils.
Arts College	1	810
Professional college	1	22
High English schools	17	4,723
Middle " "	34	3,019
Middle Vernacular schools ...	12	951
Upper Primary " ...	174	8,566
Lower " " ..	629	17,596
Training schools	8	123
Other "	105	2,376

There has been a very considerable expansion of primary education in recent years, the number of primary schools having increased by 292 or 57 per cent. since 1900-01, while the attendance has risen by nearly 10,000 or 61 per cent. In 1912-13 there were 23 schools (including one High school) with 1,884 scholars managed by Government; while 857 schools (including 9 High, 19 Middle English and 8 Middle Vernacular schools), with an aggregate attendance of 30,661, received grants-in-aid. The number of unaided schools was 101, attended by 6,341 pupils.

According to the statistics of the Education Department, the number of male scholars in 1912-13 represented 34 per cent. of the male population of school-going age, the corresponding proportion in the case of female scholars being 4 per cent. The school-going age, it may be explained, is 5 to 15 years, and the number of children of this age is assumed, in the returns of the Education Department, to be equivalent to 15 per cent. of the population, but the census shows that the actual proportion of children aged 5 to 15 in Bengal is 27 per cent. for males and 25½ per cent. for females. The actual percentage of children under instruction to the total number of those of school-going age is, therefore, much less than that shown in the departmental returns.

The Krishnāth College.

The chief educational institution is the Krishnāth College at Berhampore, which has completed its jubilee. Old gazetteers state that a "British" college was opened at Berhampore in 1826, but it cannot be identified with the present college, which was founded by Government in 1853. It was at first located in one of the old barracks, from which it was transferred in 1869 to the present building, half the cost of which was met by public subscription ; the foundation stone of this building was laid in 1863 by Sir Cecil Beadon and the building was completed six years later. A law department was started in 1864, and the institution became a first grade Arts College in 1869. Three years later its status was reduced to that of a second grade college, and in 1875 the law department was abolished.

In 1886 Government decided to withdraw from the management and accepted the offer of the late Mahārāni Swarnamayi, of Cossimbazar, to maintain it. It was accordingly made over to her next year. By a Government Resolution, dated the 14th May 1887, the administrative and financial control was vested in a Board of Trustees. In 1888 it again became a first-grade college, with a law department attached. Since the Mahārāni's death in 1897 the college has been financed by her nephew and successor, the Hon'ble Mahārāja Manindra Chandra Nandi of Cossimbazar. In 1905 it was handed over to him by a deed of transfer, and a Board of Management was formed with him as President, the other members being the District Judge, the District Magistrate, the Inspector of Schools for the Presidency Division (all three *ex-officio*) and Rai Baikuntha Nāth Sen Bahādur. There is also a Committee of Management consisting of the members of the Board of Management and three members of the college staff.

The college was formerly known as the Berhampore College, and the present name has been given to it in memory of Raja Krishnanāth, the husband of Mahārāni Swarnamayi, who died in 1844. In his will he left property for the establishment of a University in this district, which was to be called the Krishnanāth University after him, but this bequest was never given effect to, as the will was declared void.

There is a large staff under the Principal, consisting of Professors of English, Philosophy, History, Mathematics, Physics, Chemistry, Botany, Political Economy and Sanskrit, besides Demonstrators in Physics and Chemistry, a Lecturer and Tutor in English, a Lecturer on the Vernacular, a Librarian and Laboratory Assistants. In the B.A. classes English, Philosophy, Mathematics, History, Political Economy, Sanskrit, Physics and Chemistry are taught ; honours classes are held in English, Philosophy, Sanskrit and Mathematics. In the B.Sc. classes Mathematics, Physics and Chemistry are taught, honours classes being held in all three subjects. There is a collegiate school which teaches up to the Matriculation standard. The headmaster has a staff of sixteen assistant teachers, three pandits, a maulvi and two drawing masters. Six hostels are attached to the college, which are managed by resident Superintendents under the control of the Principal. The number of students on the rolls of the college on 31st March 1913 was 832.

Other institutions.

The only High school managed by Government is the Nawāb Bahādur's Institution at Murshidābād, which is, to all intents and purposes, on the same footing as a zilla school. It is also known as the Nizāmat school, and is located in a fine building in the north of the city near the river Bhāgīrathi. The high school at Khāgra in Berhampore is maintained by the London Missionary Society, and that at Kāndi by the Paikpāra Rāj family. Sanskrit educaton is given at the Victoria Jubilee Tol at Berhampore, which was founded in 1887 by Srīmati Arnākāli Devi, widow of Rai Annada Prashād Ray Bahādur of Cossimbazar, and is maintained by her estate. The students live in the Tol, which is intended to be a replica of the early Hindu educational institutions.

There is a sericultural school at Berhampore, at which the sons of silkworm-rearers receive instruction in scientific methods of rearing silkworms. An industrial school known as the Rām Krishna Orphanage Middle English Industrial School was opened at Sargāchi in 1899 for teaching carpentry and weaving.

High schools.

The following statement shows the high schools in the district and the number borne on the rolls of each on 31st March 1913 :—

Name of school.	Number of pupils.	Name of school.	Number of pupils.
Managed by Government.		*Aided*—concld.	
		Khāgra	365
Nawāb Bahādur's Institution	472	Salar	246
Aided.		*Unaided.*	
Banwāribād	283	Berhampore Collegiate ...	675
Beldānga	201	Bhagirathpur ...	130
Damkul	118	Gokaran	149
Jangipur	383	Islāmpur	144
Jiaganj	249	Kāndi	404
Kāgrām	162	Pānchthupi	324
Kānchuntala	179	Saktipur	239

CHAPTER XIV.*

GAZETTEER.

Azīmganj.—Town in the Lālbāgh subdivision, situated on the right bank of the Bhāgīrathi 13 miles north of Berhampore. Its population, according to the census of 1911, is 12,327, of whom 9,772 are Hindus, 1,712 are Musalmāns and 795 are Jains: these figures include the population of Jiāganj on the opposite bank of the Bhāgīrathi, which is within municipal limits. The population has been steadily declining since 1872, when it amounted to 21,648. Azīmganj is the terminus of the Azīmganj branch line of the East Indian Railway, which connects it with Nalhāti on the Loop line, and is also a station on the Barharwa-Azīmganj-Kātwa line, which was opened in 1912. A small steamer runs, in connection with the railway, between Azīmganj and Berhampore for about five months, *i.e.*, during the rains. There are also steamer services between Jiāganj and Dhuliān, and between Jiāganj and Calcutta during the rainy season. The town contains a colony of Mārwāri merchants, who profess the Jain religion, and whose handsome temples are conspicuous from the river. Their ancestors are said to have migrated here from Bikaner in the latter half of the eighteenth century. The town was formerly a suburb of Murshidābād and was perhaps so called after Prince Azīmus-shān, grandson of Aurangzeb.

Azīmganj is also an alternative name of Damkul, the head-quarters of a thana in the east of the district.

Badrihāt.—Ancient name of a village situated 7 miles north of Azīmganj, which is more generally known as Ghiāsābād. *See* the article on Ghiāsābād.

Baranagar.—Village in the Lālbāgh subdivision, situated on the west bank of the Bhāgīrathi about 2 miles from the railway station at Azīmganj. In the second half of the eighteenth century it was the residence of Rāni Bhawāni of Natore, whose memory is cherished by the Hindus of Bengal.

* In compiling this chapter, free use has been made of a series of articles entitled *Old Places in Murshidābād*, by Mr. H. Beveridge, which appeared in the Calcutta Review, 1892.

Left a widow in 1748, she spent the remainder of her life in acts of charity and munificent benevolence, which have made her name a household word : a Hindu officer describes her, in a note contributed for the Gazetteer, as "the wisest, most intelligent and most pious Hindu lady who figured in the history of Bengal in the eighteenth century, and whose unrivalled munificence and virtue are still engraved upon every Hindu heart." She spent the last years of her life at Baranagar, and here she died, on the bank of the sacred Bhāgīrathi, about 1795. Her son, Rām Krishna, and her daughter, Tāra, who, like her, was widowed at an early age, also lived at Baranagar. Rām Krishna is said to have been a devout Sākta, and a *bel* tree is pointed out under which he sat, when engaged in meditation, on a seat placed above five human skulls. He was a frequent visitor at the shrine at Kiriteswari, and, tradition relates, had a canal excavated from Baranagar to that place in order that he might go there by boat.

Legends also cluster round Tāra, and to this day stories are told of how she escaped the evil designs of Sirāj-ud-daula through the help of a saint named Mastarām. On one occasion, when the Nawāb came to seize her, he found her suffering from small-pox and retired discomfited. The small-pox, which had been miraculously caused by the saint, at once disappeared in the same miraculous fashion. Mastarām lived at Sadikbāgh on the opposite side of the Bhāgīrathi and had the supernatural gift of being able to walk, or of being transported by invisible agency, across the stream. His bamboo staff is preserved at the *ākhra* at Sadikbāgh, which was founded in 1646 and is known as the *Akhra* of Mahant Mastarām Aulia.

There are several temples at Baranagar built by Rāni Bhāwani, two of which are ornamented with terra-cotta tiles, each containing a figure or a group of Hindu gods excellently modelled and in good preservation. The temples of Bhubaneswar and Rājrājeswari are ascribed to Rāni Bhawāni and that of Gopāl to her daughter Tāra.

Berhampore.—Headquarters of the district, situated on the eastern bank of the Bhāgīrathi, six miles south of Murshidābād and 117 miles (by rail) north of Calcutta. It is connected with the latter by the Murshidābād branch of the Eastern Bengal State Railway, the station being called Berhampore Court. It is situated 65 feet above sea-level, and is 170 miles from the sea and about 30 miles below the point where the Bhāgīrathi leaves the Ganges. It is thus on the edge of the delta, for from a short distance to the west of the Bhāgīrathi the ground rises to the undulating country of Bīrbhūm and the foot of the Rājmahāl Hills. The number of its inhabitants, according to the census of 1911, is 26,143, of whom 21,524 are Hindus, 4,293 are Musalmāns and 288 are Christians. The population has been steadily growing since 1881, when it was 23,605.

The name Berhampore is an English transliteration of the vernacular name Bahrampur, the derivation of which is explained as follows by Mr. Beveridge*:—" Berhampore (Bahrampur) seems to be a corruption of the Hindu name of the place—Brahmapur, *i.e.*, the city of Brahma. Brahmapur is the name which the original mauza, or village, bears on the Collector's revenue-roll. Probably the name comes from the place having been a settlement of Brāhmans. One of the bathing places in the river is called Bipraghāt, or the Brāhman's ghāt. The name does not appear to be in any way connected with the Muhammadan name Bahrām. There is a place about 5 miles to the north-east and on the high road to Murshidābād, which has the very similar name of Bahramganj. Probably this has the same origin as Berhampore, though it may be connected with Bahram Jang, a son of Muhammad Reza Khān, otherwise Muzaffar Jang.†"

Berhampore was proposed as the site of a cantonment a few months after the battle of Plassey—doubtless in view of the fact that the factory at Cossimbazar had been demolished, and its fortifications dismantled, by Sirāj-ud-daula in the previous year; but the proposal was not given effect to for some years. In October 1757,‡ Captain Brohier proposed to Mr. Drake to build a pentagonal fort on " the Berhampore plain ; " and, in January 1758, the Government wrote to the Directors that a fortified place near the capital of the Subahship would be the means of enforcing their influence at the Murshidābād Darbār, and that they had obtained a grant of 400 *bighas* on the Berhampore plain, under a *sanad* granted by Mīr Jafar. The Court of Directors, however, scouted the project, and in a letter, dated March 1759, wrote :—" We cannot avoid remarking that you seem so thoroughly possessed with military ideas as to forget your employers are merchants, and trade their principal object ; and were we to adopt your several plans for fortifying, half our capital would be buried in stone walls." Other counsels prevailed after the war with Mir Kāsim in 1763, when it was realized History.

* *Old Places in Murshidābād*, Calcutta Review, 1892.

† Muhammad Reza Khān was Naib Diwān, and subsequently Naib Nāzim, in the early days of the East India Company's rule.

‡ Long's *Selections from Government Records*, p. 104.

that it was necessary to have a force near Murshidābād to keep the Nawāb in check. Its proximity to the capital determined the choice of Berhampore, but, in addition to this, it was regarded as a healthy locality. The belief in its salubrity appears, however, to have been delusive, for we find that Mrs. Sherwood, the authoress of *Little Henry and his Bearer*, who was living at Berhampore in 1807, describes it as extremely unhealthy, and "as ill suited to Europeans as any place throughout the whole extent of our dominions in India." In her time the parade ground and race-course used to be often covered with water, but the draining of Berhampore has made it much healthier.

According to Hunter's Statistical Account of Bengal—"The barracks took two years in building, being completed in 1767, and were at that time looked upon as the northern frontier station of the Bengal army. The cost amounted to the enormous sum, for those days, of £3,02,270, the price of materials being three times as much as in Calcutta. In 1768 the Chief of Murshidābād appointed a committee to inquire into the exorbitant charges which had been made; and three covenanted officials were suspended, for overcharges amounting to two lakhs of rupees." The researches of the Revd. W. K. Firminger have, however, proved that the barracks cannot have been fully completed by the date mentioned above. A reference to the Press Lists shows that in 1770 estimates for the construction of a palisade and a moat round the cantonments were drawn up, and were followed by the submission of indents, while the Committee of Works at Berhampore wrote a little later about the rate for brickwork In April 1772 orders were issued to the Chief and Council at Cossimbazar that no new foundations were to be laid at Berhampore. The Consultations of 21st August contain three important letters, viz., (1) a letter from the Chief Engineer, Colonel A. Campbell, submitting an estimate of the cost of completing the building of the Berhampore Cantonments, (2) a letter submitting a proposal for making a ditch and stockaded palisade round them instead of a brick wall, and (3) the draft of a letter to the Committee of Circuit inquiring what further buildings are, in their opinion, indispensably necessary for the accommodation of the Brigade at Berhampore, and requesting that steps may be taken to supply the required materials. Finally, on 22nd March 1773, Lieutenant George Russell, Superintendent of Works at Berhampore, reports to the Chief and Council of Cossimbazar the cost of completing the building of the cantonments.* They are described as follows in the *Sair-ul-Mutākharin*

* *Bengal Past and Present*, April 1908, pp. 216-17.

(1786) :—"The barracks of Berhampore are the finest and healthiest that any nation can boast of. They contain two regiments of Europeans, seven or eight sepoys, and fifteen or sixteen cannon. And yet I have heard men say that the Musalmāns are so numerous at Murshidābād, that with brickbats in their hands they could knock the English down."

Berhampore was for a long time a large brigade station, but in 1857 the garrison had been reduced to the 19th regiment of native infantry, a detachment of native cavalry and a battery of native artillery. The story of the rising of the men of the 19th, the first overt act of mutiny in 1857, is well known, but it will not be out of place to quote the following account from the *Red Pamphlet* * which, in addition to being a graphic narrative, has the merit of being contemporaneous and obviously based on local knowledge. After describing how the sepoys had been excited by the story of the greased cartridges, † it goes on to say :— The Mutiny.

"On the 25th February, Colonel Mitchell, commanding the 19th, ordered a parade for exercise with blank ammunition for the following morning. In the evening, the blank catridges were served out to the men. They were of the very same description as those which for a century past had been used by the Bengal Army. These particular cartridges had, in fact, been made up before even an Enfield rifle had reached India, and had been made over to the 19th magazine by the 7th Regiment, Native Infantry, on the latter leaving the station. In ordinary circumstances no objection whatever would have been made by any sepoy to use similar cartridges. But the passions of the men had been roused; their feelings had been so excited that they could no longer control them; they were beyond the power of reason; they felt satisfied that their caste was to be taken away by means of cartridges, and their excitement persuaded them that these were the fatal messengers. They at first refused to receive them, and it was only when their commanding officer threatened all recusants with court-martial that they took them in gloomy silence. That night they held a consultation. The "multitude of counsellors" gave new energy to their fears, and in a moment of fanatical frenzy the regiment rose as one man, and took possession of their arms shouting defiance.

* The pamphlet, which is now rather rare, was published in 1857 under the title of *The Mutiny of the Bengal Army. A historical narrative by one who has served under Sir Charles Napier.*

† A description of the previous proceedings is given in Chapter II, but the events of the night of 25th February are not described in such detail.

"Intelligence of these facts was promptly conveyed to the commanding officer, Colonel Mitchell. Two courses were open to him. The only troops at the station besides the 19th were a detachment of native cavalry and a battery of native artillery. The night was pitch dark, and no movement could be made with any certainty. He might either, therefore, have despatched the cavalry and artillery to guard the public buildings, the treasury, etc., and await the early dawn for ulterior operations, or he might at once march down on the lines and endeavour to coerce the mutineers. The first course seemed the most prudent, and was urged upon him; however, he adopted the other, and moved as quickly as possible on his mutinous regiment. The night was so dark that he was compelled to use torches to enable him to find the way; in this manner, and with difficulty, he moved on. In the meanwhile, the 19th, having seized their arms, remained drawn up in front of their lines, waiting apparently for their European officers to take the initiative. The ground near their lines was interspersed here and there with tanks, and on these, by the light of the torches, they beheld the artillery and cavalry advancing. Had they been thoroughly evil-disposed, it would have been easy for them, in darkness as they were, to have picked off their officers and the artillery-men, whilst the nature of the ground and the darkness of the night would have prevented all idea of danger from the cavalry. They were, however, more excited than ill-disposed, and with arms in their hands they waited the first movement of their officers.

"On his part Colonel Mitchell could not have been insensible to the insecurity of his own position; he was marching at the head of natives against natives. Could he depend upon them? It was at all events doubtful. Were he to give the order to charge or to fire, was he certain that he would be obeyed? And if he were not obeyed, not only would there be three regiments in revolt instead of one, but the lives of the residents of that and surrounding stations would be jeopardized. Besides which, he found, as had been pointed out to him, that the nature of the ground and the darkness of the night would prevent the possibility of his acting efficiently against the mutineers. Something, however, must be done: he felt that. After deliberately weighing every circumstance of his position, he deemed it most prudent to try in the first instance the effect of conciliatory measures. He accordingly addressed the men of the 19th; he pointed out to them the absurdity of their fears and the enormity of their offence, and conjured them to give up their arms and return peaceably to their lines. The 19th on their part were not over-anxious to push matters to extremities; their excitement was beginning to wear off, and many of them felt a little ashamed of themselves. Still they were sensible of the advantage of their position, and seemed resolved not to act under coercion. In reply, therefore, to their Colonel, they expressed their readiness to return to their lines, and to restore their arms to the proper place, provided only the artillery and cavalry were first moved away. To this unmilitary concession, Colonel Mitchell felt averse to accede. However, for the reasons above stated, he was powerless: he did not wish to provoke the 19th into a more open demonstration; he consented then to the proposal, and moved off the artillery and cavalry. The 19th gave up their arms, returned to their lines, and the *emeute* was at an end."

After the Mutiny, European troops were again stationed at Berhampore, and it continued to be a cantonment till 1870, when it was finally abandoned as a military station. After this, the cantonment, which intervened between the two blocks then making up the municipality, viz., Berhampore and Gorābazar to the south, was brought within municipal limits. It is still known as Garh Berhampore. The town was also the headquarters of the Rājshāhi Division until 1875, when the district was transferred to the Presidency Division.

The barracks. The old barracks, which still form the most conspicuous feature of the town, are arranged in a large square on the bank of the river Bhāgīrathi. The range of buildings next the river was reserved for the General and his staff: north and south were ranges of officers' quarters, and on the eastern side, which completes the square, were three ranges of double-storied barracks for the soldiers. The cavalry lines lay a few miles to the east of the barracks, away from the river. The soil there is more sandy and the water better, besides which the horses escaped that fatal malady, so common in Bengal, known as *kamri* or "going in the loins." After the abandonment of the cantonment, the buildings were appropriated for non-military purposes. Those on the west side of the square, next to the river (which were in two blocks, each partitioned into four separate houses), were sold, some being purchased by Messrs. Louis Payen & Co. and others by the London Missionary Society. That at the southern extremity, which is said to have been once occupied by Clive, is used partly as the Collector's residence and partly as a circuit-house; the house next to it has been pulled down and a vacant space left. Of the lines of officers' quarters to the north and south, some were sold to private persons, but the greater portion was kept by Government for the accommodation of officials.

A portion of the east end of the northern range is fitted for public worship and forms the station church, but there is no external indication of its sacred character. A small building close by forms the station club. The three large two-storied barracks to the east of the square are used for the Government offices and magisterial courts, and also accommodate the municipal office; the Judge's Court is about a mile to the south-east. The upper floor of the north-eastern block, which is usually vacant, has more than once been used as a central census office after the decennial census; on such occasions it is occupied by a staff of several hundred men. Another portion of the barracks has been utilized for the lunatic asylum, which was constructed from the materials available, while the military hospital was transformed into a jail.

Both the asylum and the jail were formerly located at the old civil station of Maidāpur, 3 miles to the east (an article on which is given later); the former was transferred to Berhampore in 1874 and the latter in 1873. From the Jails Reports for 1873 and 1874 it appears that the new jail enjoyed an ephemeral popularity among debtors. "In 1873, a wealthy merchant at Jiāganj fell dangerously ill, and his sons announced their intention of releasing on a certain date all those who were incarcerated on account of debt, for the benefit of their suffering parent. The news spread all over the district, and debtors flocked into the jail from every part." A precisely similar story is told for 1874. 'In that year occurred the marriage ceremony of Dhanpat Singh Bahādur, the wealthy banker of Azīmganj; and it was anticipated throughout the district that he would follow the example of his brother, who, on the occasion of his son's marriage, had released all the civil prisoners in the jail by paying their debts for them. Creditors, accordingly, began to press their debtors, until they drove them into prison. As soon, however, as it was discovered that the banker had no intention of paying off other people's debts on this grand scale, the subsistence allowance for the civil prisoners ceased to be paid, and their number fell off as rapidly as it had risen.'

Other buildings.

Of other buildings the finest are those belonging to the Krishnāth College to the north of the barracks, which were completed in 1869; a full account of this institution has been given in the last chapter. There is a Roman Catholic chapel to the east of the barracks, and a chapel of the London Missionary Society, built by public subscription in 1828, a little to the north of them.

The town is the fortunate possessor of water-works, which it owes to the generosity of the late Mahārāni Swarnamayi, who, in 1894, undertook to furnish it with a supply of filtered water. The works, which were opened in 1899, are designed to give a daily supply of 200,000 gallons. The water is pumped up from the Bhāgīrathi into three settling tanks, each with a capacity of 229,000 gallons, whence it passes through filters into clear-water reservoirs, and is distributed to the town by pipes with an aggregate length of 12¼ miles. Gorābazar, the southern suburb, is the quarter in which Musalmāns and Hindustani-speaking immigrants from up-country chiefly reside. About two miles to the east of Gorābazar is the site of a large annual fair known as the Chaltia *mela*.

One of the most interesting spots in Berhampore is the old cemetery at Babulbuna, a mile to the north-east of the barracks, which contains several interesting monuments of the end of the eighteenth and beginning of the nineteenth century. The oldest inscription is in memory of Captain James Skinner (uncle of Colonel Skinner, who raised Skinner's Horse), who died in 1773. Here also was buried George Thomas, one of the most famous of European adventurers in India. He started his career as a sailor in the Navy, deserted his ship at Madras in 1781 and in the course of twenty years carved his way to power, becoming a general under Samru Begum and finally Rāja of Hariāna. He died of fever in his pinnace off Berhampore in 1802, while on his way to Calcutta. The tomb bears no inscription, but has been identified from an old engraving. Other graves of the early years of the nineteenth century are those of Henry Creighton of Goālmāti, an indigo factory in the Mālda district, who was one of the first to explore the ruins of Gaur, and of his friend, William Grant, who lived near him at Chandny and died, three weeks after him, on 23rd October 1807. The epitaph on Grant's tomb records that he left Rs. 40,000 for the purpose of supporting Christianity and for translating the Scriptures into eastern languages. Close by are the graves of a civilian named Robert Creighton (*ob.* 1828), who was perhaps James Creighton's son, and of his wife and daughter. Another noteworthy grave is that of Captain Robert Boileau Pemberton, a distinguished surveyor and cartographer, who died at Berhampore in 1840 when serving as the Governor-General's Agent at Murshidābād. He saw active service in Manipur, was sent as a special envoy to Bhutān in 1838, and was an authority on the north-east frontier.

The cemeteries.

Not the least interesting is the grave of the infant son of Mrs. Sherwood, the authoress of *Little Henry and his Bearer*, a book which had a considerable vogue in early Victorian days. The inscription on the grave reads as follows:—

"To the memory of Henry Sherwood, infant son of Henry Sherwood, Esq., Paymaster, His Majesty's 53rd Regiment, and Mary Martha Sherwood, his wife, who was born at Dinapore on Christmas Day, 1805, and died at Berhamproe, July 22nd, 1807. Suffer little children to come unto me and forbid them not, for of such is the Kingdom of Heaven."

"It is often said," writes Mr. H. Beveridge, "that this Henry was the original of the hero of *Little Henry and his Bearer*; but this cannot be altogether correct, for he died when only nineteen months old, and could never have held conversations with Boosy. The Henry of the story lived till he was eight years and seven months old. There can be no doubt, however, that Mrs. Sherwood was thinking of her own child when she wrote the story, and that this supplied the pathetic note, which otherwise would be wanting. The first word that Little Henry tried to say was Boosy; and when he was only ten months old, he used to put his arm round his neck and kiss him, or stroke his swarthy cheek with his little delicate hand. It is such touches as these that make the book still fresh and beautiful, in spite of the narrowness and rigidity of its religion. Little Henry is represented as being born at Dinapore and as dying at Berhampore, like Mrs. Sherwood's own child. And there is a sequel to Little Henry, called *The Last Days of Boosy*, which has a frontispiece of Boosy before his little master's tomb, where the monument and its surroundings resemble Henry Sherwood's grave."*

There is another large cemetery about a mile to the south, which was the military cemetery. It is comparatively modern and has no inscriptions of particular interest.

Berhampore Subdivision.—Sadar or headquarters subdivision comprising the south-eastern portion of the district. It has an area of 834 square miles and a population, according to the census of 1911, of 517,723 persons, the density being therefore 621 per square mile. It is bounded on the north by the Lālbāgh subdivision and the river Ganges, here known as the Padma, which separates it from the Rājshāhi district; on the east by the Padma and Jalangi rivers, the latter of which separates it from the Meherpur subdivision of the Nadia district; on the south by the Jalangi and the Nadia district (Sadar and Meherpur subdivisions) and on the west by the Lālbāgh subdivision and the Bhāgīrathi, which separates it from the Kāndi subdivision.

* *Old Places in Murshidābād*, Calcutta Review, 1892.

The subdivision is an alluvial plain watered by the Bhāgīrathi, Bhairab and Jalangi (or the Bhairab-Jalangi, as the united river is called) and by their offshoots, such as the Siālmāri and Gobra Nullah. The country is low-lying and subject to annual inundation; some parts have become water-logged owing to defective drainage and the silting up of *khāls* and *bils*. The Bhāgīrathi embankment runs along the whole of the western boundary and protects the country along the river bank from floods. A large variety of crops are raised. The principal are *āus*, or early rice, and cold-weather crops such as gram, peas, *kalāi*, *mug*, *arhar*, wheat and barley; *āman* rice and oil-seeds are also cultivated.

For administrative purposes it is subdivided into eight thanas, viz. Belādānga, Berhampore, Damkul, Daulatbazar, Hariharpāra, Nawāda, Rāninagar and Sujāganj.

Bhagwāngola.—Village in the Lālbāgh subdivision, situated on the Bhairab river, 18 miles north-east of Berhampore. It is the headquarters of a thana and has a station on the Murshidābād branch of the Eastern Bengal State Railway. The name originally belonged to a river mart on the Padma, 5 miles to the east, which served as the Gangetic port of Murshidābād. So important was it as the source of the city's supplies, that, during the wars with the Marāthas, Alī Vardi Khān was forced to keep a garrison in it, "to preserve the communication for supplies open between the Ganges and the city."* In its neighbourhood a battle took place in 1697 between the Afghān rebels under Rahim Shāh and the imperial troops under Zabardast Khān: a brief account of this battle, which ended in the rout of the rebels, will be found in Chapter II. It was here that Sirāj-ud-daula embarked on his flight northwards after the battle of Plassey. The place was visited on 2nd August 1824 by Bishop Heber, who wrote—"I found the place very interesting and even beautiful; a thorough Hindu village without either Europeans or Musalmāns. The small but neat mat-houses are scattered over a large green common, fenced off from the river by a high grassy mound, which forms an excellent dry walk, bordered with mango trees, bamboos, and the date palm, as well as some fine banians. The common was covered with children and cattle; a considerable number of boats were on the beach; different musical instruments were strumming, thumping, squealing, and rattling from some of the open sheds; and the whole place exhibited a cheerfulness and an activity and bustle which were extremely interesting and pleasing."

* Stewart's History of Bengal (1813), p. 480.

The place inspired the good Bishop to a poem beginning—

"If thou wert by my side, my love,
How fast would evening fail,
In green Bengala's palmy grove,
Listening the nightingale."

About half a century ago the main stream of the Padma receded from the village, and in its place sprung up the present village, which in contra-distinction was called New Bhagwāngola or Alātali.

Chunākhāli.—*See* Maidāpur.

Cossimbazar.—Old town in the Sadar subdivision, situated on the east bank of the Bhāgīrathi, a little over a mile north of Berhampore; it is included in the municipal limits of that town. Though little now remains to attest its former greatness, Cossimbazar may lay claim to an historical interest little, if at all, inferior to that of Murshidābād. Even before that city had been given its present name, Cossimbazar was a great emporium attracting the trade of Lower Bengal, and the European nations who traded to India had established factories in it. It even gave its name to the surrounding country, for the triangular tract enclosed by the Padma, Bhāghīrathi and Jalangi was known in the early days of the East India Company as the Cossimbazar Island, while the common name for the Bhāgīrathi in its records, down to the nineteenth century, was the Cossimbazar River.

History.

Its history cannot be traced further back than the seventeenth century, but even then it was a place of commercial importance. In or about 1658 the English established a factory there, John Ken being appointed Chief on £40 a year, while Job Charnock, the founder of Calcutta, was appointed fourth Member of Council on £20 a year. Before the end of the seventeenth century it had become the leading English commercial agency in Bengal; in 1681, when Charnock was Chief, out of £230,000 sent out by the East India Company as investment in Bengal, £140,000 were assigned to Cossimbazar. Five years later the English factory, in common with other factories in Bengal, was confiscated by order of the Nawāb Shaista Khān; and for the first half of the next century, it was exposed to occasional outbursts of hostility or caprice on the part of the Nawābs and their officers.

The factory owed much of its wealth, and all its political importance, to its close neighbourhood to the Muhammadan capital of Murshidābād. But from the same cause it was liable to constant danger. It was easy enough for the Nawāb to order out his troops and blockade the walled factory, whenever he had any occasion of quarrel with the English Council at Calcutta. It followed, therefore, that the duties of the Chief of Cossimbazar were always diplomatic as much as commercial; for it was through him that negotiations were conducted with the Nawāb. In 1757, when Sirāj-ud-daula resolved to drive the English out of Bengal, the Cossimbazar factory felt the first effects of his anger. Its capture was easily effected, according to Broome* (who follows Orme) :—

"The defences at Cossimbazar were of an insignificant description, barely sufficient to render the use of cannon necessary to attack it; the building was a quadrangle having small bastions at the corners, the curtains were only 3 feet thick, built round ranges of warehouses, of which they formed the exterior wall; there was no ditch or outer defence, and the whole was surrounded by buildings which overlooked the factory at the distance of about 100 yards. The guns were of small calibre, and most of them were honey-combed, the carriages more or less decayed, and the whole stock of ammunition not exceeding 600 rounds; but, worst of all, the garrison consisted of only one officer, Lieutenant Elliot, and 44 regular soldiers, of whom twenty were Portuguese and several Dutchmen, together with about 250 matchlock men.† Under such circumstances, a protracted defence could not reasonably be expected. The factory, being untenable, was surrendered on the 4th of June. The property found there was plundered, the soldiers confined and the whole party subjected to such indignities, that Lieutenant Elliot, who commanded the troops, was driven to distraction and shot himself."‡ Among the captives were Watts, the Resident, and Warren Hastings, his assistant, who were sent in custody to Murshidābād, from which Hastings shortly afterwards made his escape.

After the battle of Plassey, Cossimbazar regained its commercial importance, but the political power formerly held by the Resident was transferred to the Agent at the Court of the Nawāb, who lived at Motijhil in Murshidābād. Mrs. Kindersley, who visited Cossimbazar in 1766, wrote that a vast quantity of silk was prepared at the factory, the products including silk pieces, handkerchieves, stockings, gloves, etc. "The Company's

---

* Rise and Progress of the Bengal Army (1850), p. 49. See, however, the contemporary account given in Chapter II.

† Orme, Vol. II, p. 57; Grose Vol. II, p. 240.

‡ Orme, Vol. II, p. 58.

servants," she said, "are fond of being appointed to these out-settlements, because it is more advantageous than the appointments at Calcutta; otherwise, not perhaps so agreeable, as there are sometimes but three or four English amidst a number of black people." Colonel Rennell again wrote (*cir.* 1759)—"Cossimbazar is the general market of Bengal silk and a great quantity of silk and cotton stuffs are manufactured here, which are circulated throughout great part of Asia; of the unwrought silk 300,000 or 400,000 lbs. weight is consumed in the European manufactories." The decay of Cossimbazar dates from the beginning of the nineteenth century, when its climate changed for the worse and fatal epidemics broke out.

At one time the climate was celebrated for salubrity, and Cossimbazar was regarded as almost a health resort. Captain Hamilton, who visited Bengal at the beginning of the eighteenth century, mentions in *A New Account of the East Indies* (volume II, page 21), that "the country about Cossimbazar is very healthful and fruitful and produces industrious people who cultivate many valuable manufactures." Orme, in his *Military History of Hindustan*, treating of the months immediately following the battle of Plassey in 1757, states that of the English troops quartered at Calcutta and Chandernagore, two-thirds were in hospital owing to the intemperance produced by the distribution of prize-money; while of 250 men at Cossimbazar, 240 had been preserved, by the excellence of its climate, from the effects of at least equal intemperance. In 1768, it was recommended that European troops should not be brought nearer to Calcutta than Cossimbazar, on account of the climate lower down the river being so unfavourable to the health of Europeans. The Government Records, edited by Mr. Long, contain an application to the Council from a writer at Calcutta, dated March 1763, "requesting permission to go to Cossimbazar for the recovery of his health." After the famine of 1770, the margin of cultivation receded in all the country round, and wild beasts increased. In 1811, a traveller described Cossimbazar as "noted for its silk, hosiery, *koras*, and inimitable ivory work"; but the greater part of the surrounding country was "a wilderness inhabited only by beasts of prey. At eleven or twelve miles from Berhampore, an almost impervious jungle extends for a considerable space, denying entrance to all but tigers."

Two years later the ruin of Cossimbazar was brought about by a change in the course of the Bhāgīrathi, which took a sudden sweep three miles to the west of its old channel, which was left a desolate stretch of stagnant water. Epidemics of fever broke out, and the population was decimated; according to local tradition, it was entirely swept away in a twelvemonth, thus furnishing an exact parallel to the legendary destruction of Gaur. The ruin of the place is thus described by an Indian writer in an article on the Cossimbazar Rāj published in the Calcutta Review of 1873.

"The length of the town was three miles, and its breadth was two miles. It was built of bricks, being so thickly studded with pucka houses that it was a common saying that one could make a circuit of it by jumping from one house-top to another.* The population, which consisted chiefly of Hindus, could be estimated at one hundred thousand souls. Contiguous to, or rather adjoining, Cossimbazar were Kālkāpur and Farāshdānga; the former was the headquarters of the factory of the Dutch, and the latter that of the French. Bhātpāra, Bāmangāchi, and Chunākhāli constituted the suburbs. All these places were originally situated on a curve of the river Bhāgīrathi; but, seventy years ago, a straight cut was made forming the chord of the curve, thus changing the course of the river and throwing the towns inland. This engineering operation was followed by the breaking out of an epidemic fever which, in virulence and mortality, is unparalleled by any pestilence save that which destroyed Gaur. In the course of a few years, three-fourths of the population died out; and Cossimbazar, from being at one time a most populous place, is now overgrown with jungle and the abode of wild beasts. During the continuance of the epidemic, the rites of cremation and funeral could not be performed, the dead being carried away in carts for disposal. Thus the great commercial mart of Cossimbazar was laid in ruins. The decimation of the population was closely followed by the dilapidation of the buildings. Most of the houses are now in ruins, the bricks having been removed to supply the materials for buildings elsewhere."

The former channel survives only as a *khāl*, called the Kātigāng, which can be used by small boats in the rains. The main stream formerly flowed past the Residency which was protected from inundation by embankments. This appears from the following account of some floods given in the *Calcutta Gazette* of the 29th September 1785: "We are sorry to learn by letter from Murshidābād that, in consequence of the unusual height of the river (which has been such as was never known in the memory of

---

* A similar popular tradition is that the town was so thickly covered with buildings that the streets never saw the sun.

man), the great river had overflowed its banks and laid the country between the city and Bagwāngola entirely under water, and had, by the channel of Ackbarpore Lake, even penetrated the eastern parts of the city; that from the same unfortunate cause some of the dykes on the Cossimbazār river had likewise given way below the Berhampore Cantonments; and that the water from these two sources, having joined, had overflowed all that part of the country, and had come up to the walls of the Cossimbazar filature."

Existing buildings. Ruins of large buildings and broad mounds of earth are practically all that is left to attest the legendary magnificence of Cossimbazar. It is said that the houses of the rising town of Berhampore were to a great extent constructed with the material obtained from these ruins. There is, however, an old temple of Siva and an old Jain shrine, known as the Nimnāth temple, which is preserved by the Jain merchants of Murshidābād. The palace of Mahārāja Manindra Chandra Nandi, the present representative of the Cossimbazar Rāj (of which an account is given later), is also situated here. It is an imposing building and contains some fine carved stone and pillars, which were taken from the palace of Chait Singh at Benares.

The Residency cemetery. The site of the Residency is three miles north-east of Berhampore and is known as the Residency Hāta Bāgān; it is now, as its name implies, an orchard. On the northern side are the remains of an earthen rampart, and close by is some elevated ground called Phānsitāla, *i.e.*, the place of the gibbet or gallows. To the south, and separated from the Residency by a road, is the old Residency cemetery, which contains several interesting monuments.

Mention may first be made of the monument erected by Warren Hastings to his first wife. According to Colonel Gastrell's Report on Murshidābād (1857), the original inscription ran thus:—

To the Memory of
MRS. WARREN HASTINGS
and her daughter ELIZABETH
She died the 11th July 1759
In the 2 * year of her age.
This monument was erected by her husband
WARREN HASTINGS, ESQ.,
In due regard to her memory.

* So in original; no second figure to mark the unit. *Note by Colonel Gastrell.*

The inscription appears to have become obliterated and now reads as follows:—

In Memory of
MRS. MARY HASTINGS and her daughter ELIZABETH
Who died 11th July 1759 in the 2 year of her age,
This monument was erected by her husband
WARREN HASTINGS
In due regard to her memory.
Subsequently restored by Government of Bengal, 1863.

The "who" in this inscription makes it doubtful whether the reference is to the mother or the daughter: the latter, as we learn from Gleig, survived her birth for only nineteen days. The second figure must have been left out because the exact age was unknown. In the same cemetery there is a monument to a Mr. Dugald Campbell, who died at Rāngāmāti, 6th October, 1782, aged 32. Perhaps he was a connexion of Mrs. Hastings's first husband, Captain Dugald Campbell, who was killed during the capture of Budge-Budge in December 1756.

Another curious inscription reads:—

"Here lieth the body of Mrs. Sarah Mattocks, who departed this life the 4th October, 1788. Aged 27 years. Much lemonted (*sic*) by hir (*sic*) husband Lieutenant-Colonel Mattocks. Was the grand-daughter of the great John Hampden, Esquire, of St. James', Westminster."

"There must," as Mr. Beveridge points out, "be some mistake here, for Hampden was killed at Chalgrove in 1643, and Mrs. Mattocks was not born till nearly 120 years afterwards. It does not appear either why Hampden should be described as of St. James', Westminster."

Yet another interesting epitaph inscription (with inscriptions in Persian and Nāgri below the English one) is on the monument of Mr. Lyon Prager, Diamond Merchant and Inspector of Indigo and Drugs—the plurality of occupations is curious—who died at the age of 47, on the 12th May, 1793, "having fallen a sacrifice to the severe heat of the climate from travelling in a palanquin from Calcutta."

The majority of those who lie in the cemetery died in their youth or were cut off in the prime of life. One only attained a great age—a Charles Cromelin, who died on 25th December 1788, aged 81. It has been suggested that this was Charles Crommelin, a member of a Huguenot family, who had a chequered career. He joined the Company's service in Bombay in 1732 and rose to be Governor of Bombay, 1760-67. After retiring to England, he had great losses, returned to India in 1772 as a free-trader, and was made British Consul at Goa in 1784.

Colonel Gastrell states that some old memorial slabs were "dug out of the bank or mound, apparently part of an old fortification, to the north of the ruins of the Residency. One slab to the memory of Mrs. Charles Adams is inscribed with the date 29th May, 1741." Mr. Beveridge says that this tombstone was removed to Mr. Lyall's compound at Babulbuna near Berhampore, with another bearing a Latin inscription to the memory of Isabella Gray, who died in 1737. George Gray, he says, was probably the Chief of Mālda and afterwards Member of Council at Calcutta, who quarrelled with Clive and left the country in 1766.

Kālkāpur. A little to the west of the Residency cemetery is Kālkāpur, where the Dutch factory stood. Bernier mentions it as in existence in 1666, and says that it employed as many as 700 or 800 men. Teiffenthaler also describes the Dutch buildings as being vast and magnificent. A French man, George Louis Vernet, who was a friend of Warren Hastings, was second in command here in 1756 and showed great kindness to the English after the capture of Cossimbazar and Calcutta by Sirāj-ud-daula. Nothing is now left but the Ducth cemetery, which contains 47 monuments, the oldest being that of Daniel van der Müyl, who died in 1721. The handsomest, which bears no inscription, is a tall structure with two piers of pillars supporting a cupola.

Saidābād. Further to the west, and close to the present channel of the Bhāgīrathi, is Saidābād, where there used to be a French factory and also an Armenian settlement. The French appear to have stayed here at least as late as 1781, for in the Nizāmat records there is a letter of August 1781 from the Governor-General to Mr. Pott, the Resident at Murshidābād, directing, with reference to a letter from M. Dangereux to the Nawāb, that the French at Saidābād be restored to all the rights and privileges which they enjoyed before the war. The great Dupleix is said to have been at one time Resident here. The site of the factory, which is still called Farāsdānga, *i.e.*, the French land, has been much cut away, and part of it is occupied by the pumping station of the Berhampore water-works.

Kunjaghāta to the south-west contains the Rājbāri of a descendant (Debendra Nāth Rai) of Nuncomar (Nanda Kumār), a common-place building, now more or less dismantled, part of which is said to have been the residence of Nuncomar. He probably visited it occasionally or periodically, but cannot have lived there regularly, for his home was at Bhadrapur in Bīrbhūm.

The Armenian settlement dates back to 1665, in which year they obtained a *pharmān* from Aurangzeb authorizing them to form a settlement at Saidābād, which then formed a suburb of Cossimbazar.* Their church, which is about a mile from Kālkāpur, was erected in 1758, possibly under the strength of a charter granted by the East India Company, in which the Company undertook to give a site for a church in any of its settlements in which forty or more Armenians resided. The following account of it is taken from an article entitled *Historical Bengal—An Ancient Church*, by "Artemus," which appeared in the *Journal* (of Calcutta) a few years ago. "Times have changed in Berhampore as well as everywhere else, and the Armenians have given place to others in the local commercial world. The places where they lived are levelled to the ground, and down in Saidābād, where their residences were, one only finds grass and moss-grown ruins. The very roads over which they walked have disappeared, and all that remains of this ancient colony is an occasional walled-in plot of land. To the question 'What place was this?' the guide invariably replies—'A rich merchant lived here. He was ruined, and the house fell.' The crumbling decay of ages, however, has spared to some extent the old church. Time has dealt more gently with it than with the old town, and it stands a grim and time-stained monument of an almost forgotten prosperous community of merchants.

"The sacred building is now only a dilapidated barn. Its walls are bare and crumbling. The inscriptions, mostly in the Armenian tongue, on the upperstones of the flat graves are slowly being obliterated, and the little niches and stoups that once marked the spots where the faithful were wont to bless and sprinkle themselves are almost invisible by the accumulation of the dust and dirt of fifty years of cruel neglect. The font, in the sacristy, where the ancestors of many of Calcutta's prominent Armenian citizens of to-day were admitted into Holy Church, is now a receptacle for rags, whilst on the other side of the building in another vestry, wherein the registers and vessels of the altar were once carefully guarded, was found a specimen of faded millinery probably cast on one side as useless by one of the caretaker's children. The main body of the church is absolutely a dreary waste: a place of desolation, the evidences of a former grandeur on the inner roof and walls but accentuating the impression of that condition.

"But this is not all. For in the east end of the building towers a tall structure that was once the centre of devotion and worship

* Seth's History of the Armenians in India.

of the old-time Armenian community of the district. Aloft, stands a huge picture frame from which the ragged edges of canvas still flutter, and one is told that from here at one time looked down on the worshippers a beautiful picture of Christ. It is satisfactory to know that this beautiful work has been removed to Calcutta and duly preserved. Underneath this great frame-reredos are three rows, one on top of the other, of quaintly painted panels, all in a fair state of preservation, representing incidents in the life of Christ and the ministry of his apostles. From the point of view of artistic merit these are perhaps unimportant, but they have a history contemporary with that of the Church itself, and are or should be of far too great interest to those who love the memories of the time when their ancestors knelt beneath them, to be allowed to be the perching places of the caretaker's poultry which, alas, appears to be their only present use. Little or none of the altar furniture has been left in the Church. In one of the vestries is a tangled mass of lampware and old chains, and on the masonry altar-table were seen two old candlesticks and an ancient wooden book-rest. The verandah surrounding the building, and the tiny compound in which it stands, are covered with the gravestones of Armenians, who lived and flourished in the district between the year 1758, when the church was built, and 1858, when the last burial is believed to have taken place. The last date appears to be the 17th December, 1858, the grave, inscribed in English, being that of "S. M. Vardon, Esquire."

"The Church is now rarely visited save by the curious, and according to the caretaker, himself an Armenian with an imperfect knowledge of English, each year produces two or, at the most, three faithful persons who linger within the once sacred precincts to offer a prayer for the souls of the faithful departed whose last resting-places are within the shadow of the historic old building."

Cossimbazar Rāj.

The Cossimbazar Rāj family trace back their descent to one Kāli Nandi, a resident of Shijla in the Burdwān district, who migrated to Srīpur near Cossimbazar and there set up a small business as a silk dealer. The real founder of the fortunes of the family was his great-grandson Krishna Kānta Nandi, whose connection with Warren Hastings brought him into notoriety under the name of "Canto Babu." He was born in humble circumstances, for his father was merely a small shopkeeper selling silk, betel-nuts and kites; his skill in flying kites, we are solemnly told by the family chronicler, earned for him the name of Khalifa, *i.e.*, "the expert." Kānta Bābu entered the Cossimbazar factory as an apprentice and in due time was brought on the establishment as a clerk, in which capacity he came into contact with Warren

Hastings, who first came to Murshidābād in 1753. Three years later the obscure young clerk had an opportunity of befriending the future Governor-General of India. When the Cossimbazar factory was captured by Ṣirāj-ud-daula, Warren Hastings was sent a prisoner to Murshidābād, but managed to make his escape, with the help, it is said, of Kānta Bābu. The story goes that Kānta Bābu kept him concealed in his house and contrived to have him taken down the river in a boat. In gratitude for his services, Hastings promised to advance his fortunes, and when parting from him gave him a memorandum, which he was to produce as proof of his identity. When Hastings rose to power, a number of men presented themselves before him, all claiming to be Kānta Bābu, but Warren Hastings' questions exposed the personation. At length, Kānta Bābu himself appeared and produced the memorandum, whereupon Hastings gave him an appointment as his Banyan. The explanation of Warren Hastings' favour to Kānta Bābu is quite credible, for he was not the man to forget an old friend or to let a valuable service go unrewarded.

In his position as Banyan, Kānta Bābu succeeded in amassing a large fortune. "In reorganizing the revenue system it was provided by the Governor-General, with the concurrence of his Council, that no farm of lands should exceed the amount of a lakh of rupees per annum; and that no Banyan or other officer of whatever denomination should be allowed to farm lands, or to be security for any farmer. But in contravention of this regulation, Mr. Hastings granted Kānta Bābu farms to the amount of thirteen lakhs of rupees per annum. The illegality and impropriety of this proceeding called forth the severe censure of the Court of Directors, and subsequently formed the subject of Parliamentary enquiry. When Warren Hastings was impeached, the fifteenth charge against him referred to this matter:—'The said Governor-General did permit and suffer his own Banyan or principal black steward, named Kānta Bābu, to hold farms in different *parganas*, or to be security for farms to the amount of thirteen lakhs of rupees per annum; and that after enjoying the whole of those farms for two years, he was permitted by Warren Hastings to relinquish two of them which were unproductive.' On this charge Mr. Hastings was, however, pronounced not guilty. But there is no doubt that Kānta Bābu was directly or indirectly the *ijāradār* of several highly productive zamīndāris, the value of which has now been largely increased.

"When Hastings proceeded to Benares to punish the refractory Rāja Chait Singh, he was accompanied by Kānta Babu.

He there performed an act of chivalry which is worthy of record. When the palace was seized, some of the soldiers and officers, with a view to plunder the Rānis of their jewels and treasure, attempted to force an entry into the *zanāna*. Kānta Bābu remonstrated with them on their unnatural and unmanly conduct, and barred their entrance. But his remonstrances being unheeded, he interceded with Hastings on behalf of the Rānis; and represented to him that noble ladies of the East who were not permitted to cross the precincts of the *zanāna* should not be subjected to the indignity and disgrace of being roughly handled by strangers. On his intercession, Hastings interfered and the Rānis were saved. Kānta Bābu then provided *pālkis* and had the Rānis conveyed from the Rājbāri to a place of comparative safety. Grateful for this act, the Rānis took off jewels from their persons and presented Kānta Bābu with the same. He also obtained from the Rānis, Lakshmi Nārāyan, Sila Ekmukh Rudrashi, Dakshinābartta Sankha, and other idols. These objects of Hindu worship may still be seen at the Cossimbazar Rājbāri. On his return from Benares Mr. Hastings bestowed upon him a *jāgīr* situated at Ghāzipur and Azīmganj, and obtained from the Nawāb Nāzim, the then fountain of honour, the title of Mahārāja Bahādur for his son Loknāth."*

Though Kānta Bābu was only a Teli by caste, Warren Hastings made him president of the Jātimāla Kachahri or Caste Cutcherry, a tribunal which dealt with cases relating to caste matters. When challenged on the subject of his capacity to adjudicate on such matters, Warren Hastings stoutly defended him, asserting that his character was irreproachable and that "as the servant of the Governor, he was considered universally as the first native inhabitant of Calcutta."† The article already quoted contains an interesting reference to the difficulties to which he was exposed by his caste and the manner in which he overcame them. "Kānta Bābu visited Purī to offer his homage and worship to Jagannāth. The arrival of such an immensely wealthy man delighted the hearts of the Pāndas, who expected to reap a rich harvest of rupees from the piety and bounty of the Bābu. But when they heard that he was a Teli, they understood him to be a common Kalu or oilman, whose business it was to manufacture and sell oil. They therefore believed his caste and vocation incapacitated him from making any grant which might be accepted by the Brāhmans. When, therefore, he offered to found an

* *The Kāsimbazar Rāj*, Calcutta Review, 1873.

† G. W. Forrest, *Selections from State Papers (1772-85)*, vol. II, pages 320, 325, 367. *See* also Bengal Census Report of 1911, Part I, pages 453-4.

atke or a fund for feeding the poor, the Pāndas pronounced that he could not be allowed to do so, inasmuch as his gifts were by reason of his low caste not acceptable. Kānta Bābu, to prevent this scandal, wrote to the Pandits of Nadia, Tribeni, and other celebrated Samājes for *vyavasthas* on the subject of his competency to make gifts at Purī. The Pandits thus referred to unanimously gave their verdict in his favour, a verdict founded on the dictum *Tula danda dhāri taulik*, *i.e.*, Telis are not common oilmen, but derive their appellation from the fact of their holding the scales for the weighment of goods, and that the word Teli is the corruption of the word Taulik. As holding the scales and weighing the goods is a vocation common to all merchants and *mahājans*, the Telis came in the same category with other Navasāks or second class Sudras, and, like them, were entitled to the privilege of making gifts. The opinion of the Pandits of Bengal was conclusive and satisfied the Pāndas of Orissa. Accordingly, Kānta Bābu was allowed to found *atkes* and make presents to Brāhmans. The case of Kānta Bābu was remarkable, and is cited by his co-caste men as a precedent. Any opulent Teli now going to visit Jagannāth, when questioned as to his caste, replies that he is of Kānta Bābu's caste."

Kānta Bābu was succeeded in 1778 by his son, Loknāth Rai, who had, as already stated, received the title of Mahārāja Bahādur. The next of the line was the latter's son Harināth, on whom the title of Rāja Bahādur was conferred by the then Viceroy, Lord Amherst. He died in 1832, leaving a minor son named Krishnanāth and a daughter who was married to Nabin Chandra Nandi, the father of the present proprietor of the Rāj. Krishnanāth, on whom the title of Rāja Bahādur was conferred by Lord Auckland in 1841, began to dissipate the family fortunes when he attained his majority, spending no less than 41 lakhs in four years. He committed suicide, by blowing out his brains, in 1844, a day after making his will. By this will he left his property in trust to the East India Company for the establishment of a University at Banjetia to be called the Krishnanāth University, bequeathed three lakhs to a private servant besides several houses and valuable jewellery, and left his widow, Rani Swarnamayi, only an allowance of Rs. 1,500 a month. The Rāni contested the validity of the will, which was set aside on the ground of the testator not having been in full possession of his senses. She held the property till her death in 1897, and devoted the greater part of its income to works of charity and public utility: her benevolence and munificence have, in fact, become proverbial. In recognition of her public spirit, she was made a Mahārāni in 1871 and a member of the Imperial Order of the Crown of India in 1878. On her death the property passed to her mother-in-law Rāni Hara Sundari, the widow of Rāja Harināth, but she executed a deed in favour of her grandson Manindra Chandra Nandi, who is now in possession of the property. He has been made a Mahārāja, and the same title has been conferred on his next heir and successor as a personal distinction subject to the approval of the head of the Bengal Government for the time being.

Dhuliān.—Town in the north of the Jangipur subdivision situated on the Bhāgīrathi. It consists of a group of villages, which were formed into a municipality in 1909. The population within municipal limits, according to the census of 1911, is 8,298. It is one of the most important river marts in the district, being the seat of a large trade in rice and other agricultural produce. It contains a station on the Barharwa-Azīmganj-Kātwa branch of the East Indian Railway, and there is a steamer service to Jiāganj during the rains.

Ghiāsābād.—Village in the Lālbāgh subdivision, situated on the west bank of the Bhāgīrathi about 7 miles north of Azīmganj. The remains discovered here show that it is the site of an old Hindu town. Stones and pillars engraved with Pāli characters, gold coins and broken pottery have been found, but nothing has yet been discovered which throws any light on the history of the place. The old Hindu name of the place was Badrihāt, which the conquering Musalmāns changed to Ghiāsābād There is an old Muhammadan tomb here, which Captain Layard was told was that of a king of Gaur, when he visited the place in 1853.* It has been surmised therefore that the tomb is that of Ghiāsuddin Bahādur, who ruled over Eastern Bengal from 1310 to 1319 and over all Bengal from 1319 to 1323 A.D., but Mr. Beveridge was informed by the guardian of the tomb that the family tradition was that it was built over the remains of a saint.†

Giria.—Village in the Jangipur subdivision, situated on the east bank of the Bhāgīrathi about five miles north-east of Jangipur. It is also the name of a *taraf* or tract of country in *pargana* Shamaskhāli, which includes six villages on the east bank and three on the west bank of the Bhāgīrathi. The name has been given to two battles fought in the neighbourhood, the first between Alī Vardi Khān and Sarfarāz Khān in 1740 and the second between the English and Mīr Kāsim's army in 1763.

---

* Proceedings of the Asiatic Society of Bengal, 1853, p. 577.

† *Old Places in Murshidābād*, Calcutta Review, 1892.

In the earlier battle, Sarfarāz Khān, the third Nawāb of Murshidābād, and the last of the lineal descendants of Murshid Kuli, was defeated and slain by Alī Vardi Khān, who had rebelled and advanced against him from Bihār. An account of this battle, which gave the victor the throne of Bengal, will be found in Chapter II.

In the battle of 1763 the English numbered 750 Europeans and 2,000 sepoys, with a few guns and some native cavalry, commanded by Major Adams of the 84th Regiment; the army of Mīr Kāsim was composed of 12 battalions of sepoys, 15,000 horse and 12 cannon. The engagement was sharply contested for four hours, for the troops of the Nawāb had been carefully trained in European methods by Samru, the notorious German renegade. The enemy, at one time, broke part of the English line, gained possession of two guns, and attacked the 84th Regiment in front and rear. But in the end, the English victory was complete; all the cannon were captured, with 150 boats laden with provisions, and Mīr Kāsim fled towards Monghyr.

Though the two battles have the same name, they were fought on different sides of the river and at some distance apart. The first battle was fought on the east of the Bhāgīrathi, as is clear from the *Riyazu-s-Salātin*, which states that Sarfarāz Khān marched north from Murshidābād passing Diwānsarāi and Khamra, by what is now the Jiāganj-Jangipur road, to the east of the river. The forces of Alī Vardi Khān were, it says, arranged in the form of a circle from Aurangābād at the mouth of the Suti river to the plain of Balkatah. The site, which was near the villages of Momintala and Shibnārāyanpur, has been diluviated.

In this battle an officer of Sarfarāz Khān, named Ghaus Khān, is said to have performed prodigies of valour and fell fighting gallantly. A tomb was erected over his remains at Chāndpur on the east of the Bhāgīrathi, but both village and tomb were washed away about fifty years ago. The tomb was then re-erected on the west side of the river in what is now called Chāndpur, near which there is a new Momintala. Here three mounds are pointed out as the graves of Ghaus Khān and his two sons Kutub and Bābar, who were killed with him. According to the *Sair-ul-Mutākharin*, however, the tomb did not long contain the bodies of Ghaus Khān and his two sons. One Shāh Haidar, a saint and a collateral ancestor of Ghulām Hussain, the author of the *Sair-ul-Mutākharin*, was a great friend of Ghaus Khān and had converted him to the Shia faith. When he heard of his friend's death, he went to Murshidābād and loaded Alī Vardi with reproaches, "which he bore patiently, nor did there come any word from that prince's mouth, but such as savoured of humility and submission." Shāh Haidar then went to Giria and dug up the bodies of Ghaus Khān and his sons and companions, and took them to Bhāgalpur, where he reinterred them.

The second battle of Giria was fought on the west bank of the Bhāgīrathi, near the then mouth of the Bānsloi. Major Adams crossed the Bhāgīrathi near Murshidābād on 27th July and marched up its right bank, while Mīr Kāsim's army abandoned its strong position at Suti and gave battle on the open plain. The battle actually took place in the angle between the right bank of the Bhāgīrathi and the left bank of the Bānsloi. It would be more correct to call it the battle of Suti, as the *Sair-ul-Mutākharin* does.*

Jangipur.—Headquarters of the subdivision of the same name situated on the east bank of the Bhāgīrathi river. It contains a population of 11,408 persons, according to the census of 1911. The name is a corruption of Jahāngīrpur, which is explained by a tradition that the Emperor Jahāngīr founded the place. During the early days of British rule it was an important centre of the silk trade and the site of a commercial residency. In the Nizāmat office records there is a letter, dated 1773, addressed to Mr. Henchman, Collector of Jahāngīrpur, by Mr. Middleton, Resident at the Murshidābād Durbār and Chief of Murshidābād. In 1802, Lord Valentia described Jangipur as "the greatest silk station of the East India Company, with 600 furnaces, and giving employment to 3,000 persons." He added that silk then sold for Rs. 10-4 a seer. In 1835, when the Company's trading monopoly ceased, its filatures were sold to a Mr. Larulletto for Rs. 51,000. The old Residency cemetery was washed away by a flood of the Bhāgīrathi in 1847. A notice in the *Calcutta Gazette* of 4th March 1848 states that seven memorial tablets were removed from the monuments and deposited in the Toll Office, and were available on application by relatives or friends of the deceased.†

The subdivisional courts and offices formerly stood on the east bank of the Bhāgīrathi, and were moved to the west bank in consequence of the encroachments of the river. This quarter of the town is called Raghunāthganj and is within municipal limits. The northern portion of Raghunāthganj is called Bālighāt, and is said to be named after the poet Vālmiki. An ancient banyan tree

---

* *Old Places in Murshidābād*, Calcutta Review, 1892.

† *Bengal Past and Present*, July 1903, p. 358.

is supposed to mark the spot where he used to bathe. Here there is an old mosque with an inscription saying that it was built by Saiyad Kāsim and containing a chronogram, which gives 1075 A.H., or 1664 A.D., as the date. Saiyad Kāsim, who possibly gave his name to Kāsimbazar, is said to be descended from a famous saint, named Saiyad Shāh Martazanand, whose tomb is at Suti: it is mentioned in the *Riyazu-s-Salātin*.

Sir Ashley Eden, Lieutenant-Governor of Bengal from 1877 to 1882, was once stationed at Jangipur and transferred the subdivisional headquarters there from Aurangābād in 1856. Jangipur is still a centre of the silk trade and is the chief toll-station for boats passing along the Bhāgīrathi.

Jangipur Subdivision.—Northern subdivision of the district with an area of 509 square miles. Its population, according to the census of 1911, is 357, 930, the density being 703 per square mile. In shape it resembles an isosceles triangle, bounded on the west by the Sonthal Parganas and Bīrbhūm and on the east by the Padma river, which separates it from Mālda and Rājshāhi; on the south lies the Lalbagh subdivision. The northernmost point is occupied by the Farakkā outpost and the Shamsherganj thana (of which that outpost forms part), south of which is thana Suti. The tract south of Suti is divided into the two thanas of Mīrzapur, to the west, and Raghunāthganj, to the east; south of Raghunāthganj is the Lālgola thana.

The subdivision is divided into two parts by the Bhāgīrathi flowing from north to south. Beginning from the north, the country to the east of that river as far as the town of Jangipur is a long strip of *char* land between the Bhāgīrathi and the Padma. This strip, which represents nearly two-thirds of the whole length of the subdivision, is extremely narrow, its average width being only about 2 miles. It is sparsely populated and thinly wooded, and the houses are only temporary structures. The remainder of the Bāgri, *i.e.*, the country east of the Bhāgīrathi, is about 14 miles in length and 10 miles in width. It is thickly populated and well cultivated. Being a fertile alluvial tract, it bears two crops in the year, and jute is extensively grown. The country to the west of the Bhāgīrathi has also a twofold division throughout its length. The eastern fringe along the Bāghīrathi, which has an average breadth of about 3 miles, is of the same character as the Bāgri. A characteristic feature of this riverain strip is that it abounds in *kul* trees, on which lac is reared; as in the Bāgri, there are numerous mango orchards and bamboo clumps. The western portion extending to the borders of Bīrbhūm and the Sonthal Parganas has a comparatively high and hard undulating surface, on which winter rice is almost exclusively grown. This tract, which has an average breadth of about 7 miles, is called the Rārh.

The chief rivers of the subdivision are the Ganges or Padma and its distributary the Bhāgīrathi. The Ganges has two smaller offshoots, viz., the Gumāni, which takes off at the extreme north of the subdivision near Farakka, and the old channel of the Bhairab, which branches off close to Lālgola. The tributaries of the Bhāgīrathi are the Singa, Bānsloi and Pāgla, all hill streams from the Sonthal Parganas. The united waters of the Bānsloi and Pāgla fall into the Bhāgīrathi near Jangipur. The Singa bifurcates below the former indigo factory at Ankura; the northern branch joins the Bhāgīrathi at Hāzārpur, and the southern at Dhuliān.

The subdivision is liable to inundation during the rains, when boats furnish the main means of communication. As the flood water subsides, the land is sown with *kalāi*, which is extensively cultivated. There are several *bils*, of which the most important are the Chachand and Bānsabāti Bils to the west of the Bhāgīrathi, and the Krishnasail, Porāmāri and Gāngni to the east of that river.

Jiāganj.—Town in the Lālbāgh subdivision, situated on the east bank of the Bhāgīrathi 6 miles north of Murshidābād and opposite Azīmganj station on the East Indian Railway. It forms part of the Azīmganj municipality and is connected with Azīmganj by a ferry across the Bhāgīrathi; during the rains, a steamer service plies to Dhuliān and Calcutta. Though it is no longer such an important emporium as it was, Jiāganj is still a large depôt where rice, jute, silk, etc., are collected for export. It contains some large houses, the property of Jain merchants, many of whom dwell here, though the main colony lives at Azīmganj.

Kālkāpur.—See Cossimbazar.

Kāndi.—Headquarters of the subdivision of the same name, situated near the Mor river, 18 miles south-west of Berhampore.

The town owes much of its importance to its having been the seat of a wealthy and devout family of Uttarrārhi Kayasths, who were originally known as the Kándi Rājas, but having taken up their residence at Pāikpāra in the neighbourhood of Calcutta, are now generally called the Pāikpāra Rājas. The first of the family to settle at Kāndi was Hara Krishna Singh, who was a money-lender and silk merchant. He is said to have been driven to take up his residence at Rāmpur Boalia by the Marātha raids, but this was only a temporary absence, for his son Gaurānga Singh is known to have lived at Kāndi. Here he is said to have built a house with cornices like those on Sirāj-ud-daula's palace. This, it is said, "so exasperated the haughty Nawāb that he immediately ordered the cornices to be pulled down and the builder to be arrested. This mark of vandalism is visible in some parts of the dilapidated house which still exists."*

The real founder of the fortunes of the family was Ganga Govinda Singh, the nephew of Gaurānga Singh, who became the Banyan of Warren Hastings, and in that capacity amassed an immense fortune. Against him Burke thundered in his impeachment of Warren Hastings as "that collected heap of villainy." Warren Hastings, however, spoke of him in the warmest terms of gratitude and, when leaving India, remarked, "The regret which I cannot but feel, in relinquishing the service of my honorable employers, would be much embittered, were it accompanied by the reflection that I have neglected the merits of a man who deserves no less of them than of myself—Ganga Gobinda Singh—who from his earliest youth has been employed in the collection of revenues, and was about 11 years ago selected for his superior talent to fill the office of Diwān to the Calcutta Committee. He has from that time, with a short intermission, been the principal native agent in the collection of the Company's revenues; and I can take upon myself to say that he has performed the duties of his office with fidelity, diligence and ability. To myself, he has given proofs of a constancy and attachment which neither the fears nor expectations excited by the prevalence of direct influence could shake; and at a time, too, when these qualities were so dangerous, that far from finding them amongst the generality of his countrymen, I did not invariably meet with them amongst my own."

Ganga Gobinda Singh was born at Kāndi, and retiring thither in his old age devoted himself to the erection of shrines and images of Krishna. His name has acquired a traditional celebrity for the most magnificent *srāddha*, or funeral obsequies, ever performed in Bengal. They were celebrated in honour of his mother, and are stated to have cost twenty lakhs of rupees. The guests on that occasion included the Rājas and zamīndārs of half the Province, and were presided over by Siva Chandra, son of the revered Brāhman Rāja Krishna Chandra, of Krishnagar. The Brāhmans are said to have been fed with the fresh rice of Jagannāth, brought by relays of posts from Purī to Kāndi.

---

* Kishori Chānd Mitra The *Kāndi Family*, Calcutta Review, 1874.

His grandson, Krishna Chandra Singh, better known by his popular name of Lāla Bābu, who was born in 1775, added largely to the estate, but became an ascetic and took up his residence at Brindāban, where he was distinguished for his liberality and piety. Lāla Bābu's son was Sri Nārāyan, who left no sons. His senior widow adopted Pratāp Chandra Singh, who helped to found the British Indian Association, of which he was Vice-President. He was made a Rāja Bahādur and C. S. I., and founded the Kāndi High School in 1859. He died in 1866, leaving four sons, Giris Chandra (died 1877), Purna Chandra (died 1890), Kānti Chandra (died 1880), and Sarat Chandra, who is still alive. Kāndi owes its dispensary, which is a well equipped institution, to the munificence of Giris Chandra, who bequeathed Rs. 1,25,000 for its construction and maintenance; it was opened in 1888. The junior widow of Sri Nārāyan adopted Iswar Chandra Singh, the younger brother of Pratāp Chandra; he died in 1861 leaving an only son, Indra Chandra, who died in 1894.

The family now live at the Belgāchia Villa at Calcutta, but Kāndi contains the old family residence and the temples they have erected. The shrine of the family god Rādhaballabh Jiu, whose image was placed there by Gaurānga Singh, is described as follows by Bābu Bholānāth Chandra, in his *Travels of a Hindu* (pp. 65-67): "Of all shrines, the shrine at Kāndi is maintained with the greatest liberality. The god here seems to live in the style of the great Moghul. His *masnad* and pillows are of the best velvet and damask richly embroidered. Before him are placed gold and silver salvers, cups, tumblers, *pān-dāns*, and jugs of various size and pattern. He is fed every morning with fifty kinds of curry and ten kinds of pudding. His breakfast over, gold hookahs are brought to him, to smoke the most aromatic tobacco. He then retires for his noonday siesta. In the afternoon he lunches, and at night he sups, upon the choicest and richest viands with new names in the vocabulary of Hindu confectionery. The daily expenses at this shrine are said to be Rs. 500, inclusive of alms and charity to the poor."

Kāndi Subdivision.—South-western subdivision of the district with an area of 435 square miles. Its population, according to the census of 1911, is 301, 493, the density being 589 persons per square mile. It is bounded on the east by the river Bābla, on the south by the Burdwān district, on the west by the district of Bīrbhūm and on the north by the Sadar subdivision. The surface is undulating, but a considerable portion of thana Kāndi is occupied by the depression called the Hijāl, and a large part of thana Bharatpur is a low-lying plain, which becomes water-logged during the rains. The chief rivers are the Dwārka and Mor or Maurākhi; the latter bifurcates, one branch joining the Dwārka at Rangrām, while the other falls into it in the Hijāl.

Kiriteswari or Kiritkona.—Village in the Lālbāgh subdivision, situated to the west of the Bhāgīrathi, three miles west of Murshidābād. The place derives its name from the temple of Kiriteswari, which marks the spot where the crown (*kirit*) of Sati fell when she was dismembered by the discus of Vishnu. It is of some antiquity, being mentioned in the Brahmānda section of the *Bhavishyat Purāna*, which was probably composed in the fifteenth or sixteenth century A.D. It flourished under the rule of the Nawābs, thus disproving the story that Murshid Kuli Khān had all Hindu temples within four miles of Murshidābād pulled down. According to the *Sair-ul-Mutākharin*, Mīr Jafar was persuaded by Nanda Kumār, the Nuncomar of history, to take water in which the sacred emblem of the goddess had been bathed, in the hope that it would be a cure for the malady of which he died. The emblem is a piece of black stone engraved with floral designs. The crown, or frontal bone, itself, which is called *guptapit*, is preserved in a pot covered with red silk and is rarely exposed to view. There are several other temples, one of which bears the date 1765, but all are neglected and in need of repair. According to the *Riyazu-s-Salātin*, Mīr Habīb encamped here when making his raid on Murshidābād with the Marātha horse.

Lālbāgh.—Part of the town of Murshidābād and the headquarters of the subdivision of the same name. When Prince Farrukhsiyar came to Murshidābād from Dacca, after Murshidābād had been made the capital of Bengal, Murshid Kuli Khān assigned him a palace at Lālbāgh, of which no trace now remains. The subdivisional courts and offices are located in a building called the Permit Cutcherry, which was the old customhouse.

Lalbāgh Subdivision.—Subdivision in the centre of the district with an area of 365 square miles. Its population, according to the census of 1911, is 195,128, the density being 535 persons per square mile. It is bounded on the north by the Jangipur subdivision, on the east by the Sadar subdivision and the river Padma, which separates it from the Rājshāhi district, on the south by the Sadar and Kāndi subdivisions and on the west by the Bīrbhūm district. The land to the west of the Bhāgīrathi is called the Rārh and has an undulating surface, on which winter rice is mainly grown. Jute cultivation is almost unknown in this portion except on the river bank and *diāra* land. The eastern portion, which is called the Bāgri, is a flat alluvial tract producing autumn rice and *rabi* crops; the cultivation of jute is also considerable. Unlike the Rārh, which is thinly wooded, it has a luxuriant vegetation. The villages have a heavy jungle round them, and there are numerous mango and other fruit orchards. There is this further difference between the Rārh and the Bāgri, that in the former the Hindus are twice as numerous as the Musalmāns, whereas in the Bāgri the reverse is the case. The Bhāgīrathi enters the subdivision at Gādi. There is a long embankment on its eastern bank, called the Lalitākuri embankment, to protect the country from inundation. The Gobra Nullah once connected the Bhāgīrathi with the Bhairab and other rivers, but its offtake from the Bhāgīrathi has been closed by the embankment, and it is gradually drying up and ceasing to fulfil its former functions as a drainage channel for the country to the east of the Bhāgīrathi.

Maidāpur.—Village in the Sadar subdivision situated three miles east of Berhampore. In the eighteenth century this place, situated on the high road from Calcutta to Murshidābād, was almost a suburb of Murshidābād. Orme speaks of civilians having their country houses here before the battle of Plassey, and about 1768 the Chief of Cossimbazar made it his residence, at least for a time. This is clear from a letter, dated 10th April 1768, from the Council at Calcutta to the Directors, in which Midnapore is a mistake for Maidāpur. It says—

"Mr. Sykes has represented to us the inconvenience he must labour under in transacting the business of the Durbar, from the Council having appropriated Midnapore house to the use of the Chief of Cossimbazar, which place he has for some time past made his principal residence by reason of the unhealthy situation of Motijhil. We could not, with the least degree of delicacy to that Board, take this matter again into consideration; and he was, therefore, told it should be referred to the decision of You, our Honourable employers."*

Lord Teignmouth † (Sir John Shore) was living at Maidāpur in October 1773, in which year it was the official residence of Mr. Samuel Middleton, Resident at the Durbār and Chief of Cossimbazar; the Nizāmat records contain several official letters of his written in 1773 from Maidāpur. It remained the civil headquarters of the district for many years, and the jail and

* Appendix to Verelst's *View of the Rise, Progress and Present State of the English Government in Bengal* (1772), p. 77.

† H. Beveridge, *Old Places in Murshidābād*, Calcutta Review, 1892.

lunatic asylum were located there till 1873-74; the latter buildings are still standing.

A little to the north of Maidāpur is Chunākhāli, an old suburb of Murshidābād, which is famous for the excellence of its mangoes. Near it is Hāthinagar, where the Nawābs seem to have kept their elephants. North of Chunākhāli, on the right-hand side of the road to Murshidābād, is a magnificent avenue of *debdāra* trees (*Polyalthia longifolia*) which leads to Nishāt-bāgh.

Murshidābād.—Town in the Lālbāgh subdivision, situated on the east bank of the river Bhāgīrathi, six miles north of Berhampore.

Though Murshidābād was the capital of Bengal for nearly a century, its history cannot be traced back to any distant date, and there are divergent accounts of its origin. According to Tieffenthaler, it was founded in the time of Akbar, and this seems to be corroborated by the fact that there is a place to the east of the town called Akbarpur. There is, however, no trace of this name in the old records, where it is always known as Makhsusābād, or its variant Makhsudābād. The *Riyazu-s-Salātin* says that the place was called Makhsusābād after a merchant named Makhsus Khān who built a *sarai* there, and its founder may have been a nobleman of that name who is mentioned in the *Ain-i-Akbari*. He was the brother of Said Khān, Governor of Bengal under Akbar (1587-95 A.D.), and served in Bengal and Bihar; a stone mosque at Hājīpur in the Patna district, which was built by a Makhsus Khān, may have been erected by him. There is also a mention of the town, as "Morasudābād founded by a Yavana," *i.e.*, a Musalmān, in the *Brahmānda* section of the *Bhavishyat Purāna*, which was probably composed in the fifteenth or sixteenth century. Yet another account is given by Raymond, the translator of the *Sair-ul-Mutākharin* (*circ.*, 1786), who says it was first called "Colaria" then "Macsoodabad" and finally "Moorshoodabad". Kolaria was a place in the east of the town, where Murshid Kuli Khān had his residence

In the first half of the seventeenth century it began to acquire a reputation for the manufacture of silk fabrics, and in the second half of that century became the seat of a Mughal officer. Tavernier, who visited it in 1666 and called it Madesoubazarki, says that it was a large place and the residence of the Receiver-General (by which he means the Diwān) of the Nawāb Shaista Khān. The English Agents, Streynsham Master and William Hedges, both mention it as the seat of a Governor named

Bolchānd or Bulchānd Ray, who interfered with the English trade under various pretexts and died at "Moxudabad" in 1683, by which time it had become a mint town.*

In 1697, the town was taken and plundered by the Afghān insurgents during the rising commonly known as Subha Singh's rebellion, and in 1700 Murshid Kuli Khān, the Diwān of Bengal, made it the headquarters of the Diwāni in place of Dacca. Three years later Murshid Kuli Khān, who had in the meantime been appointed Deputy Nāzim and really exercised all the powers of Nāzim, called it after himself Murshidābād, and thenceforth it was the acknowledged capital of Bengal. The old name still lingered on, however, and is found (spelt as Muxudabad) in the English records as late as 1760.†

The Nawābs, after the Oriental fashion, built themselves palaces and adorned the capital with other buildings. Throughout their rule Murshidābād was not exposed to the hazards of war except during the war with the Marāthas, when Mīr Habīb made a successful raid on it with a body of Marātha horse. He did not succeed in penetrating the city, but plundered the suburbs, part of which he fired, and carried off a great treasure from Jagat Seth's palace. Murshidābād was fortunate in escaping further attacks, for it was not protected by fortified walls. As it was, the danger of attack by the Marāthas was so real that many of the inhabitants deserted it and fled across the Ganges.

After the battle of Plassey, Murshidābād continued to be the seat of administration for some years. That battle was not regarded at the time as subverting the Muhammadan Government but as a means of substituting a subservient Nawāb for Sirāj-ud-daula, and the work of Government for several years remained in the hands of Muhammadan officials. The first great change was made in 1772 by Warren Hastings, who removed the supreme civil and criminal courts from Murshidābād to Calcutta. After an experience of three years, the tribunal of criminal justice was retransferred to Murshidābād; and it was not till 1790, under Lord Cornwallis, that the entire revenue and judicial staff was established at Calcutta. Before this time, too, the civil headquarters of the district had been fixed at Maidāpur, from which it was transferred to Berhampore. The

* In the Lahore Museum there is a rupee of Aurangzeb with the mint mark of Makhsusābād bearing a date corresponding to 1679 A.D.

† The date of the new name is clearly fixed by the evidence of coins. The name Makhsusābād appears last on a coin of 1704, and Murshidābād appears first on a rupee coined in the year beginning 28th December 1704. See *Notes on Gaur and other old places* by Monmohan Chakravarti, J. A. S. B., July 1904, p. 234.

city of Murshidābād was thus left only as the residence of the Nawāb Nāzim, a descendant of Mīr Jafar, who till 1882 retained certain attributes of sovereignty within his palace and received a pension of 16 lakhs a year. In that year the last Nawāb Nāzim abdicated his position in favour of his son, who succeeded on a reduced pension and without any sovereign rights. The title of the present descendant of the once independent rulers of Bengal, Bihar and Orissa is now simply that of Nawāb Bahādur of Murshidābād.

After the battle of Plassey, Clive wrote: "The city of Murshidābād is as extensive, populous, and rich as the city of London, with this difference, that there are individuals in the first possessing infinitely greater property than in the last city. The inhabitants, if inclined to destroy the Europeans, might have done so with sticks and stones." At that time, the largest dimensions of the city proper are said to have been five miles along the Bhāgīrathi in length, and two and a half miles in breadth on each bank of the river, while the circumference of its extensive suburbs has been put as high as 30 miles. Originally, it is said to have stretched along both sides of the river for 10 miles, and it is noticeable that Orme speaks of Hirājhil on the western bank as being in the *middle* of the city.

Other accounts show that, though large and populous, Murshidābād contained few buildings of any grandeur except the palaces of the Nawābs and was for the most part a city of mean streets. Mrs. Kindersley wrote, on visiting the place in 1766, "Muxudabad, the present capital of the three provinces, is a vile dirty place. The palaces of the Nabob and houses of the great people are built of stone with more expense than taste; those of the common herd are built of straw and bamboo, so low that it is difficult to stand upright in them." Later accounts bear out this description. Hamilton's *East India Gazetteer*, for instance, says—

"The town extends eight miles along both sides of the river, and was never fortified except by an occasional rampart in 1742 during the Mahratta invasion. The buildings are in general bad, and the old palace of the Nabobs, named the Laul Baugh, so insignificant as to be passed without observation; but to the north of that range the Nabob has recently erected a lofty modern European house (named the Aina Mahal), which now forms a conspicuous object viewed from the river. With the exception of the Chowk and the streets leading to it, the city of Murshidābād may be described as a vast assemblage of mud and straw huts, built without the least regard to order, choked up on all sides with trees and vegetation of all sorts, interspersed on the side next the river with a few brick houses, and a considerable number of paltry mosques, being on the whole, with reference to its size and population, probably the meanest capital in Hindustan."

With this may be compared the description given by Colonel Gastrell in the Revenue Survey Report (1857)—

"Numerous brick buildings stand all along the banks of the river, north and south of the palace, which belong to, and are chiefly occupied by, the relatives and adherents of the Nawāb. Many others, some with pretty gardens, are scattered about in the tangled maze of jungle, hovels, holes and tanks which lie to the eastward. Standing on the top of the palace dome, the loftiest place in the district, and looking over the city and its suburbs, little meets the eye but a dense forest of bamboos and trees of all kinds. Hardly a clear spot is to be seen. It is only when one turns to the west that the river and the high land in the north-west of the district present open tracts. A stranger, as he stood and gazed, would never imagine that below was a dense mass of human beings of all classes, crowded together in every description of house and hut. There are no defined limits to Murshidābād as a city, nor is any part known especially by this name. It is given indiscriminately to a collection of temples, mosques, handsome brick houses, gardens, walled enclosures, hovels, huts and tangled jungle, containing the ruins of many edifices that have sprung up and decayed around the many residences of the former and present Nawābs Nāzīm of Murshidābād." This account holds good at the present time, except that the place exhibits even more palpable signs of decline. The earthquake of 1897 destroyed a large number of buildings, which the people have not been able to replace, and the untouched ruins convey a melancholy impression of poverty and decay.

In the beginning of the present century, by which time the decay of the city had already set in, we have several estimates of the population. They cannot be omitted in this place, though for purposes of comparison they are almost useless, as we know neither the area which the city was then supposed to cover nor the modes of enumeration adopted. In 1815, the number of houses was estimated at 30,000, and the total population at 165,000 souls. In 1829, the Magistrate, Mr. Hathorn, took, what is described in the Census Report for 1872 as, "a tolerably accurate census"; and returned the population at 146,176. In 1837, Mr. Adam found the inhabitants to amount to 124,804 persons, which shows a decrease of nearly 15 per cent. in eight years. In 1872, when the first regular census was taken, the population was no more than 46,182; but the old city comprised a much larger area than was included within the municipal boundaries in 1872. It has since still further diminished as shown in the margin; the figures include the population of the suburb of Azīmganj, which formed part of Murshidābād until 1896, when it was made a separate municipality. The population of the area included in the municipal limits of Murshidābād as now constituted was 15,168 in 1901 and fell to 12,669 in 1911.

1872	46,182
1881	39,231
1891	35,576
1901	28,553
1911	24,996

The town contains the administrative headquarters of the Lālbāgh subdivision, but has no industries except a few that were fostered by the luxury of the Mughal Court. Ivory carving is an old speciality of the place: the artificers, now few in number, produce highly-finished work. Other industrial arts are the embroidery of articles with gold and silver lace, the making of musical instruments and *hookahs*, and the manufacture of silk fabrics.

CENTRAL BUILDINGS.

For convenience of reference the buildings and remains at Murshidābād are dealt with in the following account in three groups, viz., central, southern and northern, in the order mentioned.

The palace.

The most conspicuous building in Murshidābād is the palace of the Nawāb Bahādur, which stands on the bank of the Bhāgīrathi. It is an imposing pile, in the Italian style of architecture, and was designed and built under the supervision of General Duncan McLeod of the Bengal Corps of Engineers (father of Sir Donald McLeod); the foundation stone was laid in 1829, and the building was completed in 1837. It is a three-storied building surmounted by a dome. On the ground floor are the *toshākkhāna*, armoury, offices and record-rooms; on the first floor are the Durbār Hall or throne-room, banqueting hall, drawing-room, sitting-rooms and billiard-rooms. The second floor contains a ball-room, library, china-room, bedrooms, etc. The Durbār Hall, banqueting hall and ball-room are particularly fine chambers. The former is crowned by a dome 63 feet high, from which hangs a magnificent candelabrum with 101 branches. The banqueting hall and ball-room are each 189 feet long by 27 feet broad. The palace contains many artistic treasures, rare pictures, costly jewelry, old arms, wonderful copies of the Korān, etc. Many of the most interesting objects have been lent to the Victoria Hall collection at Calcutta.

Nizāmat Kila. The palace itself is called the Bara Kothi or Hazārduāri, *i.e.*, the house with a thousand doors, and the enclosure within which it is situated is known as the Nizāmat Kila. This contains, in addition to the palace, the Imāmbāra, the Medina, a clock tower, three mosques and residential and other quarters. It is entered by several large gates bearing different names, such as Dakshin Darwāza, Chauk and Imāmbāra. The main gates have *naubat-khānas* or musicians' galleries over them, and the entrances are large and high enough for an elephant to pass with a howdah on its back.

"The most striking emblem of royal dignity still maintained at Murshidābād is the imperial music, which may still be heard in the early morning sounding from the great fortified gateway which leads to the palace. This peculiar strain of instrumental music, which was allowed by the Delhi emperors to all *Subahdārs* as a mark of delegated sovereignty, is frequently alluded to by the native chroniclers as the public accompaniment of each important event in the history of the Nawābs. At the present time the musicians have lost their traditional cunning, and the sound is described as 'discordant and jangling'; but what the effect was in the days of the early Nawābs may be learned from the *Sair-ul-Mutākharin*:—'This music consists of *nāgaras* (kettle-drums) of iron, twice as big as those in Europe; *dhols* (ordinary drums); *zurnobs* (hautboys); *kāras* (trumpets); *sils* (cymbals), an instrument lately borrowed by the Europeans from the Turks, but played by the Indians in a more delicate, curious, and scientific manner; *tāshas* (flat kettle-drums) of varying diameter and depth; and lastly, a *karana* or straight speaking-trumpet, which is seven or eight feet in length, and two or three inches in width at the mouth. All these instruments are played together upon the top of the main gateway of a fortress or palace, or upon a structure raised for the purpose on three lofty arches, and therefore called a *tripuliah*. There is produced a very animating music, which at a distance is very pleasing. The long trumpet can be heard a mile away, and might be thought the voice of a Nādir Shāh thundering out his orders to his army.'"*

The Bera. Another old ceremony still observed at Murshidābād, which it will not be out of place to mention here, is the Bera or festival of Khwāja Khizr. This is observed by launching tiny light-ships

* Hunter's *Statistical Account of Bengal*, vol. IX, pp. 68-69. Mr. Mazumdar remarks in *The Masnad of Murshidābād* that "however discordant the music may seem to ears not accustomed, the midnight and the early morning strains are indeed sweet."

on the river, a spectacle which may be seen to great advantage on the Bhāgīrathi. On certain nights in the rainy season thousands of little rafts, each with its lamp burning, are floated down the stream. Their construction is very simple, for a piece of plantain or bamboo bears a sweetmeat or two and the lamp. The festival is celebrated with much magnificence on the last Thursday of the month of Bhādra (September). A raft is constructed of plantain trees and bamboos and covered with earth. On this is erected a small fortress, bearing fireworks on its walls. At a given signal the raft is launched and floated to the further side of the river, when the fireworks are let off, their reflection on the water producing a picturesque effect.

The Imāmbāra on the north of the palace, which was built in 1847, is the largest Imāmbārā in Bengal. It has a frontage of 680 feet, and is divided into three blocks, each with a large quadrangle. The central quadrangle contains the Medina and two curious structures, which are described as follows by Mr. Mazumdar: "In each corner of two of the wings or halls of the quadrangle is a structure, called a *pāhār* or mountain, of bamboos more than 100 years old, covered over with dyed cotton, in the centre of which is a *Burag*, meaning literally the bright one, being a representation of the animal with human face and peacock's tail on which the Prophet ascended to heaven. The tail reaches the ceiling of the first floor and is over fifty feet in height. At the foot of this structure is a reservoir, round which are placed date-trees and camels made of sola and cotton, to remind one of the plains of Arabia. At the back of the *Burag* is a large mirror. Well-polished Indian shields, and china and tin plates, are fitted into the feathers of the tail to represent the eyes of the peacock's feathers. Swords, sabres, daggers and lances, used by Sirāj-ud-daula, are arranged in different designs round them; and thousands of candles, their light reflected in the mirror, make the whole a dazzling scene. With its large proportions, its stately pillars, its spacious marble floors, its innumerable large chandeliers, some of which form part of the presents of the East India Company, and its other magnificent equipments, the Nizāmat Imāmbāra stands unrivalled."*

The Imāmbārā and old Medina.

The present building was erected to replace a more celebrated Imāmbāra, constructed by Sirāj-ud-daula, which was accidentally burnt down during a display of fireworks in 1840. The author of the *Riyāzu-s-Salātin* thus describes its glories: "Of the buildings at Murshidābād, none was noteworthy except the Imāmbāra,

* *The Masnad of Murshidābād*, pp. 123-4.

which was erected by Sirāj-ud-daula. Its praise is beyond description; its equal is not to be found in the whole of Hindustan. Although at present one-tenth of it does not exist, yet a remnant of it is a fair specimen of the original edifice." From this account it appears that by 1788, when the *Riyazu* was written, the building must have fallen into neglect. We also know that "the costly treasures, lavished upon it by Sirāj-ud-daula, were turned into ready money by Mīr Kāsim. This was not, however, to relieve his own necessities—a motive which would have seemed sacrilege to one so religious as Mīr Kāsim,—but to assist the poor of the city, and to despatch a number of indigent Muhammadans on a pilgrimage to Mecca."* All that is left of Sirāj-ud-daula's great Imāmbāra is the Medina, which stands between the palace and the present Imāmbāra. The ground beneath, as is customary with Medinas, was excavated to the depth of a man's stature and filled in with earth brought from Karbela.

Bachāwāli Top.

Close by is a large gun called the Bachāwāli Top, which is believed to have been made between the twelfth and fourteenth century. It has a length of 15 feet and was removed here from a sand bank at Ichāganj, where it formed one of the defences of the city. The name is said to be derived from the fact that, when it was fired, the report was so terrific, that it caused premature delivery among the women for miles round.

The great gun.

About 1½ miles to the east of the palace is the Topkhāna, the site of the artillery park of the Nawābs and the eastern entrance of the city. On the east of this the Gobra Nullah, known locally as the Khatra Jhil, constituted a natural defence. Here is another great gun, resting on and partly imbedded in a *pipal* tree, which has raised it 4 feet from the ground. It is 17½ feet in length, but of somewhat small calibre. Its name is Jahān Kasha, meaning "the world-subduer," as appears from the inscriptions, which further state that it was made, in the reign of Shāh Jahān, and during the Governorship of Islām Khān at Jahāngīrnagar (Dacca), by a blacksmith named Janārdan, in the year corresponding to 1637A.D. Its weight is described as 212 maunds (over 7 tons) and its charge as 28 seers. There are nine Persian inscriptions on brass plates let into the metal, but three are illegible or are covered over by the *pipal* tree. The inscriptions contain eulogies of Islām Khān and of the "dragon-like" gun. It is an object of veneration among the lower classes, who

* *Sārikh-i-Mansuri*, by Saiyid Ali; manuscript translated by Professor Blochmann.

smear it with oil and vermillon and bring offerings of flowers, milk and sweets.

The following account of the circumstances which brought the gun to its present position was given by Major Showers in 1847.* "To the naturalist and the general observer, the Jāhān Kasha is curious from the position in which it is lying. It is grasped by two trunks of a *pipal* tree and supported by them about 18 inches from the ground. Native tradition states that it was brought to the spot on a carriage, and was left there as the wheels sunk into the mud and could not be extricated. The tree must have sprung up under it, and the trunks, as they grew, grasped the gun and continued to support it after the carriage had rotted away and fallen from it. The back trunnion is imbedded in the trunk and cannot be seen; but two stanchions and a ring are visible, which evidently belonged to the carriage. The front trunnion, with the iron work attached, was, until lately, also imbedded in the tree; but within the last six months a part of the trunk has been torn away by a storm, by which it has become exposed to view. The iron work, on which the trunnion rested, corresponds with the dimensions which may be supposed to be necessary to support so large a body on its carriage; and its bulk had, no doubt, so weakened the outer portion of the trunk as to make it yield easily to any force applied to it.

"There is another peculiarity which it may be proper to notice, as exhibiting a second phenomenon in the growth of the tree. There are two trunks which support the gun, but I am inclined to think that they are branches of one tree. The trunk, obstructed in its growth, and pressed down by the weight of the gun, had first spread out under it, then forcing itself up one side and still hugging the gun, it met with a new obstruction, in the trunnion, stanchions, and the heavy iron work attached to them, and, unable to press them aside, yielded to the obstruction and parted and shot up in two large branches."

Khatra Masjid.

A short distance to the north-west of the gun is the Khatra Masjid, a mosque which Murshid Kuli Khân, also called Jafar Khân, built and in which he was buried. The name is derived from the fact that towards the close of his life he determined to make a *khatra*, or market, and to place in the centre of it a mosque and his own tomb. He chose for this purpose the eastern side of the city, and is said to have pulled down a number of Hindu temples in order to get materials. Apparently, the design was not completed; for no remains exist of the Khatra proper, *i.e.*, of

* Proceedings of the Asiatic Society of Bengal, June 1847.

the market-place. The spot is still called Jafar Khān's Khatra, and a small *hāt* is held there twice a week, but it seems never to have become a centre of trade, and is now more or less a jungle. The mosque was a large and stately building, but is now partly in ruins, having been badly damaged in the earthquake of 1897. It is said to have had accommodation for 700 readers of the Korān, and in 1780 was described by the artist Hodges, who has left a coloured view of it in his *Select Views in India*, as "a grand seminary of Musalmān learning, adorned by a mosque which rises high above all the surrounding building." It stands on a high terrace or platform with a frontage of 166 feet, and has two lofty minarets and five domes, of which two collapsed during the earthquake in 1897. Even before this, the mosque and the west of the terrace had sunk by its own weight. An inscription over the doorway gives the date of the building as 1723. Murshid Kuli Khān himself was buried under the stairs at the east end of the terrace. It is said that he ordered this out of humility, so as to be trodden on by all who passed up and down; there may be an allusion to this in the inscription, which runs—"Muhammad, the Arabian, the glory of both worlds. Dust be on the head of him who is not the dust of his portal".

Kadam Sharīf.

About a quarter of a mile to the south of the Khatra Masjid is another mosque, called the Kadam Sharīf or Kadam Rasūl from its containing a much-venerated stone, brought from Gaur, on which is an impression of the feet of Muhammad the Prophet. It was founded in 1782 by the chief eunuch of Mīr Jafar, who, as such, had the title of Nawāb Nāzir, and is maintained by an endowment left by the chief eunuch of Mani Begam.

Sarfarāz Khān's tomb and buildings.

In this neighbourhood in Naktākhāli, known locally as Lengtākhāli or, more commonly, as Nagīnābāgh, in which the palace of Sarfarāz Khān was situated. Here, not far from the railway station, is the grave of Sarfarāz Khān, the only Nawāb who died a soldier's death. He was killed at the battle of Giria, and his faithful *mahaut* brought the body to Murshidābād, where it was buried secretly, and at dead of night, in the grounds of his palace. Close by the tomb is a mosque called the Begam Masjid, which is variously attributed to his wife and mother; an inscription on it bears a date corresponding to 1719 A.D. Of Sarfarāz Khān's palace no trace remains, but at Kumrāpur (three quarters of a mile from the Nawāb Bahādur's palace) there is a mosque called the Phuti Masjid, which was built by him. It is one of the largest mosques in Murshidābād, but appears never to have been completed, some of the domes having been left in an unfinished state. The question naturally occurs whether the building was interrupted by Sarfarāz Khān's sudden death.

The tomb of Shujā-ud-daula or Shujā Khān, Sarfarāz Khān's father and predecessor on the *masnad*, is at a place called Raushnibāgh, *i.e.*, the garden of light, on the west bank of the Bhāgīrathi nearly opposite the palace. At a short distance to the north Shujā Khān laid out a garden, to which he gave the name of Farāhbāgh or garden of joy, and in it built a mosque. The garden has disappeared, and part of the mosque has fallen into the river. To the south-west of Farāhbāgh is the village of Dahapāra, once a suburb of Murshidābād, which the Marāthas sacked and burnt in their raid under Mīr Habīb. Shujā Khān's tomb and buildings.

One and a half mile south-east of the palace of the Nawāb Bahādur is Motijhil, meaning the pearl lake. It is a long horseshoe-shaped lake, the origin of which has been disputed. Rennell, whose authority may be taken as conclusive, says that it is "one of the windings of a former channel of the Cossimbazar river",* *i.e.*, the Bhāgīrathi. A palace, called the Sangidālān, a mosque and other buildings were built here (in the angle between the curves of the lake) in 1743 † by Nawāzish Khān, *alias* Shahāmat Jang, nephew and son-in-law of Alī Vardi Khān. Tieffenthaler describes it as a great and magnificent palace, and the Muhammadan chroniclers, quoted by Stewart in his *History of Bengal*, tell us that it was a stately pile ornamented with pillars of black marble (*i.e.*, basalt) brought from the ruins of Gaur. After the death of Nawāzish Khān, his beautiful wife, Ghasīti Begam, resided here, until she was driven out by Sirāj-ud-daula, who took the palace and seized the treasures in it. An engagement took place here in 1763 between Major Adams and Mīr Kāsim's troops, in which the English stormed the lines held by the latter. SOUTHERN BUILDINGS. Motijhil.

It was in the Motijhil palace that Clive held the first English Punya in May 1766, the young Nawāb (Nazīm-ud-daula) sitting on the *masnad* with Clive, as Diwān, on his right hand. Next year the Punya was again held here with even greater pomp by Mr. Verelst in conjunction with the new Nawāb Saif-ud-daula. The Punya, it may be explained, was a ceremony of great state, at which the annual settlement of the land revenue was made.

---

* Memoir of a Map of Hindostan, p. 345.

† The date is fixed by a petition of the *fakīrs* of Motijhil (preserved in the Nizāmat or Murshidābād Agency letter-book for 1789) setting forth that Shahāmat Jang erected a mosque, *madrasa* and *langarkhānā* or alms-house there in that year. The *langarkhānā* is still kept up by Government.

All the great zamīndārs attended it, and paid homage and presented *nazars* to the Nawāb. *Khilats* were distributed, which were often of great value: in 1767 they amounted to over two lakhs. A similar ceremony, on a small scale, is still held on zamīndārs' estates.

At this time the palace was the official residence of the British Resident at the Durbār, as we learn from a letter of Mrs. Kindersley written from Motijhil in September 1766,* when it was occupied by Mr. Sykes. Her account of it was as follows:—

"Just above Cossimbazar is *Motte Gill* (Mottee-pearl, Gill-lake) or the lake of pearl, one of the prettiest of the Mahomedan Palaces, and now the habitation of the English Resident at the *Durbar*: the spot has its name from a lake of clear water which surrounds it on every side except one small entrance. It was made by a former *Nabob* of Murshidābād. In case of war, this was a place of security for his wives and children to retire to. The buildings are in the style of the country. Along the middle of the ground, at certain distances, are different sets of apartments. Most of the rooms are small and dark, but what I most disapprove of is the useless expense they have been at for walls, for from every set of apartments are extended two long heavy walls, which reach on each side to the water's edge; this is the taste in most of their palaces. The walls do not answer the purpose of our garden walls in England (for they plant no fruit-trees against them), nor any other purpose that I can conceive, but to divide the gardens into smaller parts and by that means lessen the beauty and increase the heat. The most pleasing amongst their buildings are those in the open style, apartments which are not surrounded with a wall, but the roofs supported with double and triple rows of light pillars, which have a very elegant effect. We may easily suppose that the *Nabob*, who expended such great sums of money to build, to plant, and to dig that immense lake, little foresaw that it should ever become a place of residence for an English Chief, to be embellished and altered according to his taste. Much less could he foresee that his successors on the *musnud* should be obliged to court these Chiefs, that they should hold the Subahship only as a gift from the English, and be by them maintained in all the pageantry without any of the power of royalty."

---

* The original is in the British Museum. A copy of it was published by Mr. H. Beveridge in an article entitled *Old Places in Murshidābād*, which appeared in the Calcutta Review of 1892.

In 1768, Motijhil was temporarily abandoned in favour of Maidāpur on account of its unhealthy situation, but was reoccupied later. John Shore, who was subsequently Lord Teignmouth, appears to have resided there in 1771-73 while Resident at the Durbār. In a letter, dated 1st April 1772, he describes himself as living in a garden house of the Nawāb about 4 miles from Murshidābād, and says :—" Here I enjoy cooing doves, whistling blackbirds and a purling stream. I am quite solitary and, except once a week, see no one of Christian complexion." This is poetic license, for the purling stream can only have been the Bhāgīrathi, which in the hot weather is a mere thread of water.

According to the *Riyazu-s-Salātin*, the place was in ruins when that work was written, *i.e.*, as early as 1788. The only remains of Nawāzish Khān's building consist of the mosque and a moss-grown doorless building 65 feet long, 23 feet broad and 12 feet high, which is said to contain treasure. No one, however, dares to break into it, for it is said that some labourers who were employed in opening it died of spitting blood as soon as they started work. There are also a Bāraduāri, said to have been erected by Mīr Jafar in 1758, and the old city gate, both in a ruinous state. Only the plinth of the Sangidālān still exists. In a shed erected in the grounds a tombstone is preserved, which records the death of a child, named Ewan Keating, on 3rd March 1785. Probably he was a son of Mr. Christopher Keating, of Hunter's *Rural Annals*, who was appointed Mint Master at Murshidābād in 1774 and in 1783 was a Judge of the Court of Appeal.

" Apart from historical associations Motijhil is well worth a visit on account of its beauty. The lake curves round a long, broad promontory, and its bright waters and verdant banks form a charming spectacle on a spring morning. When the palace, with its colonnades, stood on the edge of the lake, and the grounds were tended, as tradition says they were, by a hundred gardeners, it must have been a pleasure-house fit for Kubla Khān. An Englishman might, perhaps, prefer the ruddy cliffs and breezy upland of Rāngāmāti, but a Bengali would regard Motijhil as the most beautiful spot in the district, and as a *Bhukailās*, or earthly paradise. The promontory is still known as the Agenti Bāgh, or Agent's Garden, but most of the fruit trees have disappeared."*

Mubārak Manzil or Fendalbāgh.

To the east of Motijhil is Mubārak Manzil, an attractive garden of the Nawāb Bahādur. Here the supreme Criminal and

* H. Beveridge. *Old Places in Murshidābād* Calcutta Review, 1892.

Civil Courts (Nizāmat Adālat and Sadar Diwāni Adālat) and subsequently the Provincial Court of Appeal were located. The buildings were sold in 1831 to Nawāb Humāyun Jāh, who also bought up the adjoining lands, and converted them into a garden, in which he erected a bungalow, now called Lāl Bangāla, *i.e.*, the red bungalow. On the terrace in front of this bungalow stood till recently the *masnad* or throne of the Nawāb Nāzim; it has been removed to Calcutta, where it may be seen in the Victoria Memorial Hall collection. The place is also Fendalbāgh or Findalbāgh, probably after John Fendal, who was a Judge of the Sadar Diwāni Adālat in 1817-19. In 1819 he was Chief Judge, and in the following year he became Member of Council. A building here is still called the Cutcherry, and close by, in a garden called Afzālbāgh, on the bank of the Bānsbāri Bil, is a building, originally a powder magazine, which served as a jail.

Chunākhāli and Nishatbāgh.

In the neighbourhood is Chunākhāli, famous for its mangoes. In some jungle here is the tomb of Masnad Auliya, near which is a stone with an inscription in the Tughra character bearing the date 1490 A.D. " North of Chunākhāli and on the right-hand side of the high road to Murshidābād," writes Mr. Beveridge in *Old Places in Murshidābād* (Calcutta Review, 1892), " we come upon a magnificent avenue of *debdāru* trees (*Polialthia longifolia*). An old Muhammadan, whom I met here, told me that the trees had been planted by Ampiere (?) Sāheb, who preceded Lak (Loch ?) Sāheb, and that the avenue led to the Nishatbāgh and the seat of the Nizāmat, where Nawāb Muzaffar Jang (Muhammad Reza Khān) used to live. Murshidābād is a great place for trees. Nowhere in Bengal have I seen so many fine banyan trees. There are also some fine mahogany trees near the Civil Courts at Berhampore and some good avenues. But this avenue to Nishatbāgh is the noblest of them all. In other places, for instance, on the Kerbala road leading to Cossimbazar, the *debdārus* spread out more, and are short, but here the trees are planted close together and stand up tall and unbending for nearly a mile on each side of the road.

" If we go to the end of this avenue and turn to the right and S.S.E., we shall come, in about half a mile, to Chānd Pāhār, a circular tank with an island in the centre, which supported a Nawāb's bungalow, and if we turn to the left and north-east, we come to Nishatbāgh, or the garden of intoxicating pleasures, but which is now only a small hamlet, occupied by goālās. Nishatbāgh, says the translator of the *Sair-ul-Mutākharin*, is an elegant seat, five miles from Murshidābād, built, furnished and fitted in the English manner. Muhammad Reza Khān *alias* Nawāb Muzaffar Jang, lived here, and carried on his duties as Diwān here, though his family resided in the City, at a palace called Nausakht* (newly-built). It was at Nishatbāgh that he was arrested in 1772, and removed to Calcutta."

Khushbāgh.

About three miles to the west of Motijhil, on the western bank of the Bhāgīrathi (opposite Amāniganj) is the cemetery of Alī Vardi Khān, which bears the name of Khushbāgh or garden of happiness. The cemetery consists of three walled enclosures. The outer of these is entered by a gateway from the east side, in front of which are the ruins of an old *ghāt*, which formerly led down to the Bhāgīrathi, when that river ran under the walls. The wall facing the river is loopholed for musketry, and flanked by octagonal bastions. The grounds inside are laid out as gardens, with hedges bordering the walks. In the outer enclosure there are eighteen tombs, only two of which have any inscription. The middle of the three enclosures is the principal cemetery, and contains the remains of the ablest of the Nawābs, Ali Vardi Khān, and of his grandson Sirāj-ud-Daula, whose mangled body was laid there after having been paraded through the city on an elephant and exposed to the view of his distracted mother Amina Begam. His widow, Begam Lutf-un-nissa, who had accompanied her husband in his flight to Rājmahāl, and had been afterwards banished to Dacca with other ladies of the Court, was subsequently recalled and placed in charge of the cemetery of Khushbāgh. Forster mentions, in 1781, that *mullās* were employed here to offer prayers for the dead, and that the widow of Sirāj-ud-Daula used often to come to the tomb and perform certain ceremonies of mourning. She now lies buried in the mausoleum by the side of her husband.

NORTHERN BUILDINGS. Jafarganj.

The tombs of the later Nawābs from Mīr Jafar to Humayun Jāh, and also of Mani Begam (wife of Mīr Jafar) and other Begams, are in the Nizāmat cemetery at Jafarganj, a mile to the north of the Nawāb Bahādur's palace. The last Nawāb Nāzim, Feredun Jāh (Saiyid Mansur Alī Khān), the grandfather of the present Nawāb Bahādur, who died in 1884, was also buried here—by a strange coincidence, in the only vacant space left in the line of the Nawāb Nāzims' tombs—but the remains were subsequently reinterred at Karbela in accordance with directions given in his will.

Almost opposite the Nizāmat cemetery is the Deori, which was the palace of Mīr Jafar before his elevation to the *masnad*.

---

* This is in the part that used to be called Kolaria.

The audience hall, since turned into an Imāmbāra, and his dwelling-house in the Mahālsarai still exist. Here the last secret audience before the battle of Plassey took place between him and Watts, the Chief of Cossimbazar, who was then living at Murshidābād and came in a *pālki* disguised as a *pardānāsshin* lady. Here, too, Sirāj-ud-daula was murdered by Mīr Jafar's savage son, Mīrān. The murder, according to the most authentic accounts, took place in the compound of the Deori, but the room in which he was put to death has disappeared. Mīrān was killed by lightning on 2nd July 1760, three years to a day after the murder. The palace, which was made over to him by his father, continued to be the residence of his descendants; the present representative of his line is Faiz Alī Khān.

Nāshipur Rājbāri. To the north of Jafarganj is the Nāshipur Rājbāri, the palace of Māhāraja Rānajit Singh of Nāshipur. His ancestor was Devi Singh, who rendered good service to Clive at Plassey, and subsequently became Secretary to the Provincial Council at Murshidābād and Dīwān to the East India Company. He amassed much wealth by taking a farm of estates in Purnea, Rangpur and Dinājpur, but the ryots of Rangpur having risen in rebellion in 1783, was removed from his offices. Devi Singh, who died in 1805, lived in a village near Bokhara railway station. His successor, Rāja Udwant Singh, transferred the family residence first to Ghiāsābād, and then to Nāshipur (in the Lālbāgh subdivision 9 miles north-east of Jiāganj). The Rājbāri was erected by Rāja Kirtichānd Bahādur, who succeeded Udwant Singh in 1850.

Mahimāpur. Mahimāpur, close to the Nāshipur Rājbāri, contains the residence of the famous banker Jagat Seth. Here Watts and Walsh met Mīr Jafar and Rāja Rai Durlabh, three days after the battle of Plassey, and conferred concerning payment of the amounts stipulated for by them before the battle was fought. Clive, Watts, Scrafton, Mīrān and Rai Durlabh were also present here on 29th June 1757, when Clive repudiated the agreement with Omichānd, who left the place a broken man. The house is in ruins, the greater part of it having been swept away by the Bhāgīrathi. The Jain temple has suffered the same fate, but some detached columns and arches, of excellent design and workmanship, may still be seen. A Hindu temple built by Harrakh Chānd in 1801, which is adorned with porcelain tiles, is still extant, but part of it collapsed in the earthquake of 1897. A mound overgrown with vegetation, and a marble cistern are all that remain of the Murshidābād mint, or, according to others, of the bank and council hall. Not far off is a circular temple, with a brass finial, called Satichaura, which marks the site of a *sati*.

On the west bank of the Bhāgīrathi, a short distance below Mahimāpur, stood the palace of Murādbāgh, in which Clive stayed when he came to after the battle of Plassey. "Colonel Clive did not enter the city till the morning of the 29th June, when escorted by a guard of 200 Europeans and 300 sepoys, he took possession of the palace and garden of Murādbāgh, which had been allotted for his residence. Here he was immediately waited upon by Mīrān, the son of Jafar, whom he shortly after accompanied to the palace at Mansurganj."* Murād-bāgh.

Warren Hastings resided at Murādbāgh when Resident at the Murshidābād Durbar (1757-60), and though, as already stated, later Residents lived at Motijhil, Murādbāgh appears to have been used again as a Residency in subsequent years. The report of Warren Hastings' trial contains a letter from Mr. Peter Speke, Resident at the Durbar, dated Murādbāgh, 14th February 1788. Perhaps Murādbāgh was the office and Motijhil the residence at this time, for in Mr. Ritchie's notes on the old records it is mentioned that in 1788 there were sleeping apartments at Motijhil and quarters at Murādbāgh.† The greater part of the palace has been cut away by the river, and a portion only of its foundations remains.

On the same side of the Bhāgīrathi, opposite Jafarganj, were the pleasure grounds of Hirājhil (meaning the diamond lake) and the palace of Mansurganj, which Sirāj-ud-daula erected with materials brought from the ruins of Gaur. Mansur-ganj and Hirā-jhil.

The following story is told of its completion, to explain the name of Mansurganj:—As the building was nearly finished Sirāj-ud-daula invited Alī Vardī to see it. When he came, Sirāj-ud-daula locked him up in a room, and refused to release him unless the zamīndārs there paid a fine for their land. This request the Nawāb was compelled to grant, and also to allow to his petulant grandson the privilege of erecting a granary. This granary the people called Mansurganj, *i.e.*, the Granary of the Victorious, *i.e.*, of Sirāj-ud-daula, who outwitted his grandfather. The *abwāb* or extraordinary taxation, extorted on this occasion, is said to have amounted to five lakhs.

It was from Mansurganj that Sirāj ud-daula set out for Plassey, and here he returned after the battle, before flying to Bhagwāngola and thence up the Ganges. Here, too, Clive

* Stewart's History of Bengal (1813), pp. 533-4.

† H. Beveridge, *Old Places in Murshidābād*, Calcutta Review, 1892.

installed Mīr Jafar on the *masnad*. "He accompanied Mīrān to the palace at Mansurganj; and, upon entering the hall of audience, he there found Mīr Jafar, with a number of officers and the principal inhabitants of the city, expecting his arrival. At one end of the hall was placed the *masnad* of Sirāj-ud-daula, which Mīr Jafar appearing to avoid, Colonel Clive took him by the hand, and leading him to it, seated him thereon. He then presented him with a salver of gold mohurs and congratulated him on his accession to the *masnad* of Bengal, Bihar and Orissa. This example was followed by all the persons present; and the event was announced to the public by the discharge of cannon and the sounds of martial music.*" Mansurganj continued to be MīrJafar's palace until his deposition in 1761.

Here were the famous treasure vaults of Sirāj-ud-daula, which gave rise to Clive's famous saying about his moderation. "Consider the situation in which the victory of Plassey had placed me. A great prince was dependent on my pleasure. An opulent city lay at my mercy. Its richest bankers bid against each other for my smiles. I walked through vaults which were thrown open to me alone, piled on either hand with gold and jewels. Mr. Chairman, at this moment I stand astonished at my own moderation." That this was no idle vaunt is clear from the account given by Raymond, the translator of the *Sair-ul-Mutākharin*. He states that Mr. Walsh, the Commissary of the Army, informed him that he accompanied Colonel Clive. Mr. Watts, the Resident, Mr. Lushington, Rām Chānd the writer, and Naba Krishna the *munshi*, into the vaults of the palace, They found stored up there £176,000 in silver, £230,000 in gold, two chests of gold ingots, four chests of set jewels, and two smaller ones, containing loose stones and gems. It is supposed, however, that this was only the outer treasury, and that the English were deceived by their astute Bengali associates. 'The custom,' says the chronicler, 'was common even with private men of keeping the more precious articles, as well as the bulk of the coined money, within the *zanāna* or women's apartment.' This inner treasury of Sirāj-ud-daula is asserted to have contained eight million pounds sterling. The whole of this enormous sum is said to have been distributed between Mīr. Jafar, Rām Chānd, Naba Krishna, and Amīn Beg Khān. It is not probable that the new Nawāb succeeded in retaining much of his share, but we know enough about the circumstances of the others to render this marvellous story not altogether incredible.

* Stewart's History of Bengal (1813), p. 534.

the eight thanas mentioned above as particularly feverish show an excess of deaths, with the exception of Bhagwāngola, in which the increase was, however, small. The only other thanas similarly situated are Jalangi and Noāda, which have not been classed as specially unhealthy, although the fever rate in the former (36·7) is considerably above the district rate. The health conditions of the district being so well defined, the local opinion as to their distribution accords with what has been said above.

"The recent investigation of Captain Stewart and Lieutenant Proctor touched rapidly the most unhealthy tracts as above defined, and it is in accordance with the conclusions already drawn that the tract comprised in the Manullābazar, Shāhānagar, Daulatbazar, Sujāganj, Gorābazar and Hariharpāra thanas yielded the high average spleen rate of 62·6. . . The presence of Leishman-Donovan infection was not to any extent detected, but this pronouncement should be accepted with caution in view of the decided opinion of Major Nott, I.M.S., who knew the district well, given in the annual sanitary reports for 1904 and 1905, that this disease was unquestionably very prevalent.

"The facts then may be summarised as follows:—(*a*) Some portions of the district are extremely unhealthy, more so than Jessore or Nadia; other portions are comparatively healthy. (*b*) Fever is similarly distributed. (*c*) Local investigation has shown that the fever is malarial, but the presence or absence of Leishman-Donovan infection is an open question. (*d*) The most malarious thanas are Bhagwāngola, Manullābazar, Shāhānagar, Sujāganj, Gorābazar*, Hariaharpāra, Asānpur and perhaps Jalangi. (*e*) The least malarious areas are comprised in the whole of Kāndi subdivision and in the thanas of Shamsherganj, Suti, Raghunāthganj, Mirzāpur and Ṣāgardighi."

A further inquiry, which lasted six months, was made during 1908-09 in five representative thanas, viz., Sujāganj, Daulatbazar, Shāhānagar, Bhagwāngola and Shamserganj, by Major W. H. C. Forster, I.M.S., Professor of Pathology in the Lahore Medical College, who was placed on deputation with the Bengal Government. One of the principal objects in view was to ascertain the extent to which *Kāla Azār* prevailed. The spleen rate (which was ascertained by examining children under 12 years of age) was found to range from 1 per cent. in Shamsherganj to 55 per cent. in Shāhānagar. The thanas in which the highest total mortality was returned also had the highest

* Now included in Sujāganj.

spleen rate as shown in the margin. The spleen rate was also higher in *bil* villages than in villages situated away from the banks of *bils*, being 42·6 in the former and only 25·8 in the latter. As, however, both malaria and *Kāla Azār* give rise to splenomegaly (enlargement of the spleen) and to fever,

Spleen rates.	Total mortality.
1. Shāhānagar.	1. Shāhānagar.
2. Sujāganj.	2. Sujāganj.
3. Bhagwāngola.	3. Daulatbazar.
4. Daulatbazar.	4. Bhagwāngola.
5. Shamsherganj.	5. Shamsherganj.

the value of the splenic index as an indication of malaria was regarded as an open question, and special attention was paid to the endemic index, which consists of ascertaining the percentage of children under 12 years of age who have malaria parasites in their blood. It is, in Major Forster's opinion, "the most valuable test for determining the intensity of malaria in any area. Whilst the splenic index is open to the objection that it includes all forms of splenomegaly, whether malarial or not, the endemic index, as a test for the prevalence of malaria, is not open to any such objection." Observations based on the endemic index and the spleen rates led Major Forster to draw the following conclusions:—

(1) That there is a definite relationship between splenomegaly and the total mortality of the test thanas.

(2) That the total mortality of the test thanas is largely the result of the operation of the causes of splenomegaly.

(3) That, measured by the endemic index, the test thanas are not strikingly malarious.

(4) That there is not the relationship between spleen rate and endemic index which one would expect to find if the spleen rates were entirely due to malaria.

(4) That the spleen rates in the district are not due solely to malaria.

He explained the discrepancy between the spleen rate and endemic index as being due to *Kāla Azār*. As this disease had long been recognised by the Civil Surgeon, Colonel Nott, I.M.S., who could skilfully distinguish clinically between a case of *Kāla Azār* and malaria, Captain Forster worked with him at the Berhampore hospital and verified the diagnosis by splenic puncture. He found that half the villages inspected by him in Sujāganj thana and a quarter in the Bhagwāngola thana were infected, and that the disease seemed to be most prevalent in the area lying between the Bhāgīrathi and Chota Bhairab rivers, the

Rām Chānd, at the time of the battle of Plassey, was a writer on Rs. 60 a month. He died ten years afterwards, worth £720,000 in cash and bills; and he also left 400 large pots, eighty of which contained gold and the rest silver, £180,000 in land, and jewels to the value of £200,000.

With the exception of a few broken walls and foundations, the Bhāgīrathi has swept the whole palace away, and the Hirājhil is no longer a lake. The ruin of the palace was, according to the *Riyazu-s-Salātīn*, complete at the time it was written, *i.e.* by 1788.

Other buildings. The largest mosque in good repair is the Chauk Masjid in the Chauk, or chief market of the city, to the south-east of the Nawāb Bahādur's palace. It was built in 1767 by Mīr Jafar's wife, Mani Begam, on the site of the Chahal Satun or audience hall of Murshid Kuli Khān. The site of Murshid Kuli Khān's palace is in Kolaria to the east of the Nawāb Bahādur's palace. There is a mosque here which was erected in 1731-32 by his wife Naseri Banu Begum, who is buried in a vault under the stairs leading to the terrace. The mosque was rebuilt in the first half of the nineteenth century.

Nāshipur.—*See* article on Murshidābād.

Raghunāthganj.—*See* article on Jangipur.

Rāngāmāti.—Village in the Sadar subdivision situated on the west bank of the Bhāgīrathi, 6 miles south of Berhampore. The land here rises into bluffs, 40 to 50 feet high, which form the only elevated ground in the neighbourhood and are very conspicuous from the river. Old traditions and the remains which have been found here point to its having been the site of an ancient town. Its legendary history has been set forth by Captain Wilford and Captain Layard in articles contributed to the Asiatic Society of Bengal. The former writes in the Transactions of the Society (Vol. IX, p. 89) :—

"Tradition says that the king of Lanka invaded Bengal with a powerful fleet and sailed up the Ganges as far as Rāngāmāti, then called Kusumapuri, and a considerable place, where the king or Mahārāja often resided. The invaders plundered the country and destroyed the city. This happened long before the invasion of Bengal by the Muhammadans in 1204 A.D." Captain Layard, in *The Asiatic Society's Journal*, No. 3, 1853, says:—"Rāngāmāti, anciently named the city of Kansonapurī (*sic*), is said to have been built many hundreds of years ago by a famous Mahārāja of Bengal named Kurun* Sen, who resided chiefly at Gaur. Many

* Karna, according to Hunterian spelling.

interesting spots, connected with legends and traditions of the ancient city, are still pointed out, such as the Demon's Mount and the Rājbārī or palace of Kurun* Sen. The remains of the greater part of the Rājbārī are distinctly traceable on three sides, although now under cultivation; the fourth has disappeared in the river. On the eastern face of the Rājbāri there stood, a few years ago, the ruins of a very old gateway, with two large entrances, called by the people of the neighbouring village of Jadupur the *burj* or tower. It has now entirely disappeared, having crumbled away with the falling bank into the rapid stream below."

The last Hindu Rāja is said to have drowned himself, with all his family, in the Chauti Bil on the approach of the Muhammadan invaders. Mr. Beveridge identifies Rāngāmāti with the capital of the kingdom of Karnasuvarna visited by the Chinese pilgrim Hiuen Tsiang in the seventh century A.D.; but for the reasons explained in Chapter II, it is doubtful whether this theory is sustainable.

It is said that there was a proposal to build the English barracks here, instead of at Berhampore, and that the design was abandoned, because the place was on the wrong side of the river for the control of Murshidābād This need hardly have been an objection in Clive's time, for Murshidābād then lay on both sides of the river, and the Nawāb's palace of Mansurganj was on the west side. Probably the fact of the Calcutta road being on the east side of the river was a more serious objection. At a later period, it was proposed to make the place a sanitarium for the troops and some land was acquired for the purpose near the old Rājbāri. The East India Company had a silk factory here, which was sold in 1835 with 1,500 *bighas* of land attached to it, for Rs. 21,000. It passed into the hands of the Bengal Silk Company, which has recently stopped work and closed the filature; it was advertised for sale in December 1912. In the compound is a monument to one Edward Close, who died in 1790 from the charge of a wild buffalo.

The moat of the Rājbāri may still be seen, though it is dry for the greater part of the year. A mutilated image, of which Captain Layard gave a sketch, is also to be seen under a magnificent old banyan tree, but the Jamuna tank, where it was found, has dried up. The high red bluff on which the silk filature stands, bears on its face remains of pottery and pieces of brick, at points seven or eight feet below the present surface. Well

---

* Karna, according to Hunterian spelling.

rings may be seen still lower down, which, however, may have been always underground. Much of the country round about is covered with broken bricks, and there are many mounds and silted-up tanks, while gold coins and gold rings have been dug up.

"Rāngāmāti," writes Mr. Beveridge in *Old Places in Murshidābād* (Calcutta Review, 1892), "is probably the most picturesque spot in Murshidābād. It stands high and is conspicuous from a great distance, and it combines the scenery of Eastern and Western Bengal. The situation of the factory bungalow is very fine. It is near the edge of the cliffs, and commands a view to the eastward of a vast savannah dotted with trees and cattle, and with the Bhāgīrathi winding through it. To the west we have an undulating woodland which reminds us of England."

Sāgardighi.—Village in the Lālbāgh subdivision, situated 10 miles north-east of Azīmganj, with which it is connected by the Azīmganj branch line of the East India Railway. South of the railway is a large tank, about three-quarters of a mile in length, which is said to have been excavated by a Rāja named Mahipāl. Tradition says that, after Rāja Mahipāl had excavated the tank, the water would not rise. He was told in a dream that if a potter named Sāgar went into the middle of the excavation and struck a blow with a mattock, the water would rise. He sent for Sāgar, who agreed to make the trial, provided the people of the country side were assembled to witness it, and that a canoe was ready for him to escape by. This was agreed to, and Sāgar went into the middle and struck one blow, whereupon the water rushed up with such rapidity as to drown both him and his canoe. The tank is a bare and univiting looking sheet of water, somewhat irregular in shape, and unbeautified by trees or ghāts. The villagers regard it with dread and do not cast nets in it. They do not speak well of its water and prefer that of the Lashkardighi, which is south-west of Sāgardighi and about half its size. They will not even bathe in it, which is not, however, to be wondered at, for it contains crocodiles.

Though Mahipāl dug the tank, his palace was not on its banks, but according to some at some distance to the north-east at a place called Hukarhāt, and according to others, at a village, named Mahipāl after him, a little to the north of the Barala railway station. Mahipāl has been identified with Mahipāla of the Pāla dynasty, who ruled in the eleventh century A. D..

Saidābād.—*See* Cossimbazar.

INDEX.

D

E

F

G

H

I

J

K

L

R

S

T

U

V

W

Z

B. S. Press—23-9-1914—1560J—540—S. C. R.